EPITAPHS

A Dictionary of Grave Epigrams and Memorial Eloquence

Nigel Rees

Carroll & Graf Publishers, Inc.
New York

828.02

Published by arrangement with Bloomsbury Publishing Limited, London

First Carroll & Graf edition August 1994

Carroll & Graf Publishers, Inc.
260 Fifth Avenue
New York, NY 10001

Library of Congress Cataloging-in-Publication Data

Epitaphs : a dictionary of grave epigrams and memorial eloquence /
    [compiled by] Nigel Rees.
        p.   cm.
    ISBN 0-7867-0080-7 : $10.95
    1. Epitaphs. 2. Death—Humor. I. Rees, Nigel, 1944–
PN6291.E64   1994
828'.02—dc20   94-7015
                                                                   CIP

Manufactured in the United States of America

In memory of my father
Stewart Rees
who died 4 December 1989
in his eightieth year.

'And some there be, which have no memorial.'
Ecclesiasticus 44:9

Nor shall death brag thou wandr'st in his shade,
When in eternall lines to time thou grow'st,
    So long as men can breath or eyes can see,
    So long lives this, and this gives life to thee.

William Shakespeare (1564–1616),
Sonnet XVIII

I remember once having made this observation to
Edmund Burke, that it would be no bad definition of
one sort of epitaphs, to call them grave epigrams.
He repeated the words '*grave* epigrams', and gave me
the credit of a pun, which I never intended.

Sir Joshua Reynolds (1723–92),
in a letter dated 31 May 1791

Personally I have no bone to pick with graveyards, I
take the air there willingly, perhaps more willingly
than elsewhere, when take the air I must.

Samel Beckett (1906–89),
'First Love'

INTRODUCTION

An epitaph, in my book, is an inscription upon a grave or memorial that – usually – *says something* about the person beneath or so remembered. Equally, it can be a brief characterization of a life written *as though it could be placed* on a grave or memorial, even if this has not been done or never was the intention.

Epitaphs celebrates both kinds and, unusually if not uniquely for such a collection, strives to provide accurate transcriptions and supporting information. What the book is *not*, is yet another collection of humorous epitaphs, recycled for the fiftieth time, and of dubious authenticity.

What it does is to survey a collection of epitaphs which are interesting or curious in themselves. As in all the best graveyards, those of the famous and the obscure are thrown together willy-nilly, though here they are at least in alphabetical order. Any tendency to include epitaphs solely because they are of famous people and without any other claim on our attention has, with one or two exceptions, been resisted. Mostly the epitaphs are of English-speaking subjects, and of humans. There are, however, one or two of non-human subjects – including a horse and several dogs.

On occasions, I have included the wording off statues not intended as memorials in the normal sense. I have also included some spoken remarks (see DE GAULLE). Both these cases have epitaph-like material.

I am drawn in particular to epitaphs which describe at news-bulletin length what a person did and which throw in idiosyncratic detail (see especially Bridgett APPLEWHAITE and Lady O'LOONEY). I am also entertained by the extent to which some epitaphs assume in the reader a knowledge of the deceased's achievements (Jane AUSTEN, the Revd Sydney SMITH), as compared with those which do not – and which, rather like advertisements, actively *sell* the product (as with Wilkie COLLINS and Thomas HOOD). Then I am especially entertained by those of obscurer people whose relatives felt it behoved them to spell out in detail some specific achievement (like Bennet WOODCROFT, inventor of a pitch screw propeller, and A.J. COOPER, who predicted the Chilean earthquake of 1918). Those who die in rail, air or automobile accidents (William HUSKISSON, John PORT, Sir Charles ROSE, Maurice C. SELBACH) are often subjected to similarly detailed, and not entirely welcome, accounts.

Coming to this graveyard from many years toiling in the quotations vineyard, I have also been drawn to inscriptions – often on the graves of the obscure – which make use of texts, biblical and other, taken from elsewhere. I have tried to find sources for these, or at least to comment on the earliest appearance of the commonest. What a relief it is, however, to escape from the thousandth example of 'At the going down of the sun . . .', 'Greater love hath no .nan . . . he gave his life that others might live', 'In the midst of life we are in death' (see SHEE), and find a pleasing, allusive use of a less worn text. I am thinking of 'Quiet consummation have' – from Shakespeare's 'Fear no more the heat o' th' sun' – on a recent memorial in Highgate Cemetery (West). Renownèd that grave certainly deserves to be.

Has the art of epitaph-writing died out? No, it has not. The comparatively recent lapidary inscriptions on Gordon HAMILTON-FAIRLEY, Lord THOMSON and Dame Sybil THORNDIKE surely prove that it is still possible to produce the arresting phrase or the one that can bring a lump to the throat. But, yes, epitaphs of the last two centuries are mostly cautious to the point of speechlessness compared to the florid, rambling and hugely-entertaining effusions of the sixteenth and seventeenth centuries. Victorian epitaphs are mostly pompous or dull. In our own century, caution on the part of those in authority over graveyards has largely stamped out individuality of composition. The deceased's name and dates, plus a well-worn biblical text are, for the most part, all that one can expect. The brevity, especially, is a cause for regret, though I do maintain a slinking regard for those austere non-epitaphs often accorded to military commanders. 'WELLINGTON', 'NELSON', 'SLIM', 'WAVELL', 'TEDDER' is all that it will say on their graves and memorials, as if the surname was enough to make us stop and shudder, and so it may be. Then, of course, the simple fact is that most people nowadays are cremated (67% in the UK, according to one source) and not all of these are accorded a burial of ashes, a commemorative tablet, or a mention in some book of remembrance. This dictionary is dedicated to my father who was cremated and who has no memorial except in the minds of those who remember him. My brother and I took this somewhat modern view of death – possibly out of a desire not to take up space on this crowded earth with another dead body – though we fully understand that others might and do prefer a more tangible token of the departed. I know that I am coming dangerously near to suggesting that it would be a help if only the widely-known and interesting should be accorded graves and epitaphs, but I know that that is not a practicable suggestion.

This book is an attempt to revive the centuries-old custom of collecting epitaphs, but with rather more attempt at accuracy of transcription and location and context. There is an honourable tradition of epitaph collections – the London Library has shelves full of them – from Stow (1598), Camden (1610) and Weever (1631) to the rather less honourable rash of little books full of 'comic and curious' epitaphs published in recent years. These last seem mainly to recycle earlier books (and multiply their mistakes). The most curious thing about *comic* epitaphs, however, is that they should have existed at all, but exist they undoubtedly did (see, for example, that on Stephen RUMBOLD), though it is often impossible to find the originals these days.

That, of course, is one of the problems with gravestones and memorials. If they are in the open air, they are now subject to acid rain and other forms of wear and tear, and it is rare for them to survive from before, say, 1800, in a legible form. Even indoors (it is a smidgen discomforting to discover), Shakespeare's memorable epitaph at Stratford was so decayed a century after his death that it had to be re-cut.

As dictionaries go, this is a very subjective selection from the untold millions of epitaphs that have ever been composed. But it seems worth calling it a dictionary because of the information it contains. The epitaphs are listed under the surname of the subject. Where this is not known, or where the text is in common use, they are filed under 'Unknown'. The index at the close of the book is based on names, locations, theme words and theme ideas.

Where only part of the total wording on a grave or memorial is given, omissions are indicated by dots, thus . . . An asterisk * indicates that the text given has been checked by me against the original grave or memorial, or against a photograph. What strikes me, looking at old epitaph books, is how careless so many of the transcriptions are. An effort has also been made to reproduce the lay-out and capitalization of the original epitaphs, where possible, though not the various sizes and styles of lettering. Where I am sure of the original spelling, I have retained it, while mostly turning 'ye' into 'the', 'yt' into 'that', and so on. Where a 'U' has been cut as a 'V', this has not usually been retained. I make no claims for accurate reproduction of the original punctuation which may now be quite impossible to decipher.

It has, for me, been an immensely enjoyable experience, 'grubbing in churchyards' as John Aubrey put it, but if I might make a plea, it would be that those who look after graveyards could do visitors an immense service by signposting the way to significant graves. But even directions are not everything. The ultimate in completely useless signposting occurs on the cemetery island of San Michele in Venice. The prominent signposts to the graves of Stravinsky, Diaghilev and Ezra Pound do not actually help you find the graves (and, no, these do not have epitaphs on them even if you do eventually stumble on them by chance). It was only on returning to London that I was able to ascertain that Ezra Pound's grave simply bears his name and dates, for I was unable to locate it on the island.

In Britain, some of the larger cemeteries (I am thinking of the two at Highgate here) may be getting themselves organized at long last, increasingly through 'Friends of' groups, and taking the lead in producing maps and guidebooks, but there is still a long way to go. Searching in Kensal Green's magnificent jumble can be like looking for a needle in a haystack, though the thrill of discovery and the pleasures of serendipity in some way make up for this. When it comes to searching for the graves of one's own ancestors, as I have done in the north-west of England, the rewards are even greater – though, as with those of the famous, a curious rule seems to apply that you have to pay three visits to a graveyard before you find exactly what you are looking for.

So what this book presents is unquestionably a disarray of epitaphs – or perhaps even a 'nice derangement', as Mrs Malaprop said – but I hope an enjoyable one. William Wordsworth in one of his two essays on epitaphs recalls the story (old even in his day, I imagine) of the person who, tired of reading so many fulsome epitaphs on 'faithful wives, tender husbands, dutiful children and good men of all classes', exclaimed, 'Where are all the *bad* people buried?' Charles Lamb, as a boy in the 1780s, is credited with having remarked to his sister, on observing the fulsome epitaphs in a churchyard: 'Mary, where are all the naughty people buried?' Well, whoever first made that remark, Wordsworth argues that there is a lot to be said for having, 'in an unkind world, one enclosure where the voice of Detraction is not heard . . . and there is no jarring tone in the peaceful concert of amity and gratitude.'

I agree; but by introducing a liberal sprinkling of 'suggested' memorials, usually of a more caustic kind, it is to be hoped that any tone of unalloyed, sanctimonious and pompous praise in *Epitaphs* has been avoided.

I have been aided by many helpful informants, among them: Kathleen Adams, the George Eliot Fellowship; Dr Eric Anderson; John H. Antell; Fr Ian Brady, editor, *The Chesterton Review*; Anne Gaw, the Burns Federation; Dr James Gibson, the Thomas Hardy Society; Ian Gillies; the late Dr Robert Gittings; Celia Haddon; Donald Hickling; Charles Lewsen; Lynn S. Maury, the Ivor Novello Memorial Society; Joan McCluskey, the D.H. Lawrence Society; Jan Morris; the late Vernon Noble; Diana Raymond (Mrs Ernest Raymond); Anthony W. Shipps, formerly of Indiana University Library; Rosamund Strode, the Holst Foundation; Martin Walker; Barbara Wild; John Wilkins, editor, *The Tablet*; Ursula Vaughan Williams (Mrs Ralph Vaughan Williams); and all those named as having drawn individual entries to my attention. My thanks to all of them.

NIGEL REES
London, 1993

ABBREVIATIONS

The following list explains the bibliographic abbreviations used throughout
the book to indicate sources where appropriate.

Andrews	William Andrews, *Curious Epitaphs*, 1883 (1899 ed.)
Aubrey	Oliver Lawson Dick (ed.), *Aubrey's Brief Lives*, 1949
Bailey	Brian Bailey, *Churchyards of England and Wales*, 1987
Bakewell	Bakewell, Joan and Drummond, John, *A Fine and Private Place*, 1977
Bartlett	*Bartlett's Familiar Quotations*, 1968/1980 eds.
Beable	W.H. Beable, *Epitaphs: Graveyard Humour & Eulogy*, 1925
Benham	W. Gurney Benham, *Cassell's Book of Quotations*, 1907/ Sir Gurney Benham, *Benham's Book of Quotations*, 1948
Booth	Rev. John Booth, *Metrical Epitaphs Ancient and Modern*, 1868
Brewer	*Brewer's Dictionary of Phrase and Fable*, 1989 ed.
Briscoe	J. Potter Briscoe, *Gleanings from God's Acre Being A Collection of Epitaphs*, 1883 (1901 ed.)
Brown	Raymond Lamont Brown, *A New Book of Epitaphs*, 1973
Collection	Anon., *A Collection of Epitaphs and Monumental Inscriptions* (2 vols.), 1806
Diprose	John Diprose, *Diprose's Book of Epitaphs: Humourous, Eccentric, Ancient & Remarkable*, 1879
DNB	*The Dictionary of National Biography*
Fairley	W. Fairley, *Epitaphiana: or the Curiosities of Churchyard Literature*, 1875
Frobisher	*Frobisher's New Select Collection of Epitaphs; Humorous, Whimsical, Moral & Satyrical*, ?1790
Grigson	Geoffrey Grigson, *The Faber Book of Epigrams and Epitaphs*, 1977
Haining	Peter Haining, *Graveyard Wit*, 1973
Harrap	Conrad Bailey, *Harrap's Guide to Famous London Graves*, 1975
Hyman	Robin Hyman, *A Dictionary of Famous Quotations*, 1967 ed.
Klinger	Samuel Klinger, *Graveyard Laughter*, 1979
Mackae	David Mackae, *A Pennyworth of Queer Epitaphs*, ?1910
Meller	Hugh Meller, *London Cemeteries*, 1981
Morrell	J.B. Morrell, *The Biography of the Common Man of the City of York*, 1948
Norwich	John Julius Norwich, *Christmas Crackers*, 1980; *More Christmas Crackers*, 1990
OED2	*The Oxford English Dictionary* (2nd ed.), 1989
Reder	Philip Reder, *Epitaphs*, 1969
Russell	G.W.E. Russell, *Collections and Recollections*, 1898
Stewart	Aubrey Stewart, *English Epigrams and Epitaphs*, 1897
Tegg	William Tegg, *Epitaphs, Witty, Grotesque, Elegant &c.*, 1876
Wright	Geoffrey N. Wright, *Discovering Epitaphs*, 1972

ADDISON

~

**NE'ER TO THESE CHAMBERS, WHERE THE MIGHTY REST,
SINCE THEIR FOUNDATION, CAME A NOBLER GUEST;
NOR E'ER WAS TO THE BOWERS OF BLISS CONVEYED
A FAIRER SPIRIT, OR MORE WELCOME SHADE!
OH, GONE FOR EVER! TAKE THIS LONG ADIEU,
AND SLEEP IN PEACE NEXT THY LORD MONTAGUE.**

This is the epitaph on the *grave of Joseph Addison (1672–1719), essayist and politician, in the North Aisle of Henry VII's chapel in Westminster Abbey. The floor slab, topped by a bold 'ADDISON', lies a few inches from the foot of the monument to Charles Montague, 1st Earl of Halifax (*d* 1715), parliamentary orator, founder of the Bank of England, and Addison's close friend. The epitaph is by another friend, the poet Thomas Tickell, and is taken from his Elegy, printed in the first volume of Addison's works (1721) which Tickell edited.

I do not know when this gravestone was affixed, but it appears to have been restored by 'Egerton, Earl of Ellesmere PC 1849', though this lettering and some other has been worn away by people's feet and is difficult to read. It may have acknowledged Tickell's authorship.

Nathaniel Hawthorne commented, in *Our Old Home* (1863): 'Addison is buried among the men of rank . . . not on the plea of his literary fame, but because he was connected with nobility by marriage and had been a Secretary of State. His gravestone is inscribed with a resounding verse from Tickell's lines to his memory, the only lines by which Tickell is himself now remembered, and which (as I discovered a little while ago) he mainly flinched from an obscure versifier of somewhat earlier date.'

Addison *is* commemorated in the Abbey on account of. his literary achievement – by a statue, with Latin inscription, in Poets' Corner, though this was not erected until 1809. The double tribute is particularly appropriate because Addison wrote the finest of meditations on the practice with which this book is chiefly concerned. No. 26 of his *Spectator* essays concerns Westminster Abbey specifically:

> When I look upon the tombs of the great, every
> emotion of envy dies in me; when I read the
> epitaphs of the beautiful, every inordinate desire
> goes out; when I meet with the grief of parents,

upon a tombstone, my ˙ heart melts with compassion; when I see the tomb of the parents themselves, I consider the vanity of grieving for those, whom they must quickly follow. When I see kings lying by those who deposed them; when I consider rival wits placed side by side; or the holy men, that divided the world with their contests and disputes; I reflect, with sorrow and astonishment, on the little competitions, factions, and debates of mankind. When I read the several dates of the tombs, of some that died yesterday, and some six hundred years ago, I consider that great day, when we shall all of us be contemporaries, and make our appearance together.

ALFRED
~

The mildest, justest, and most beneficent of Kings,
Who drove out the Danes, scour'd the Seas, promoted
   Learning,
Established Juries, crush'd Corruption.
Guarded Liberty,
And was the Founder of the English Constitution.

Memorial to Alfred the Great (849–899), King of Wessex, in the Temple of British Worthies at Stowe, Buckinghamshire, and recorded thus by Frobisher (?1790). King Alfred's actual burial place is not known, though he may lie in the grounds of St Bartholomew's Church, Winchester.

ANDREW

~

JAMES ANDREWE
Anagram
Reede I was man

Epitaph beneath a wall *memorial in St Dunstan's Chapel of what is now Leicester Cathedral. Andrew, who died in 1638, is also shown in a small sculpture, among the books of which he was obviously very fond. For the anagram to work, 'James' has to be read as 'Iames'. In addition, there is a substantial Latin text about the man.

ANTELL

~

IN MEMORY OF
JOHN ANTELL
Who was Born . . . . 18 . . .
Died 1878

HE WAS A MAN OF CONSIDERABLE
LOCAL REPUTATION AS A SELF-MADE
SCHOLAR, HAVING ACQUIRED A VARIED
KNOWLEDGE OF LANGUAGES, LITERATURE
AND SCIENCE BY UNAIDED STUDY, &
IN THE FACE OF MANY UNTOWARD
CIRCUMSTANCES.

This proposed epitaph was written and designed by Thomas HARDY, the novelist and poet, for his uncle by marriage. A cobbler by trade, Antell was, as may be appreciated from the epitaph, in part the original of 'Jude Fawley' in Hardy's *Jude the Obscure*. According to Robert Gittings, *Young Thomas Hardy* (1975) and *The Older Hardy* (1978), the self-taught Antell acquired enough Latin, Greek and Hebrew to open a little school in Puddletown. He also had a weakness for drink. Alas, Hardy's epitaph was not used on John Antell's actual gravestone which stands under a yew tree towards the east end of St Mary's Church, Puddletown. This merely records that he was 'born August 12th 1816' and 'died December 21st 1878'. His father – also John Antell – is buried under a similarly straightforward stone in the same churchyard ('died March 16 1849, aged 76 years'). However, yet another John Antell (1848–1935), son of the 'Jude' model, is buried in the extension to the churchyard under an interesting stone, reflecting his own artistic achievements – he was a poet, sketcher and musician. According to the present John H. Antell of Dorchester (1991), Hardy had a hand in the design of this tombstone.

APPLEWHAITE

~

M S

Between the Remains of her Brother EDWARD,
And of her Husband ARTHUR
Here lies the Body of BRIDGETT APPLEWHAITE
Once BRIDGETT NELSON.
After the Fatigues of a Married Life,
Born by her with Incredible Patience,
For four years and three Quarters, bating three Weeks;
And after the Enjoiment of the Glorious Freedom
Of an Early and Unblemisht Widowhood,
For four Years and Upwards,
She Resolved to run the Risk of a Second Marriage-Bed
But DEATH forbad the Banns –
And having with an Apoplectick Dart,
(The same Instrument, with which he had Formerly
Dispatch't her Mother,)
Touch't the most Vital part of her Brain;
She must have fallen Directly to the Ground,
(as one Thunder-strook,)
If she had not been Catch't and Supported
by her Intended Husband.
Of which Invisible Bruise,
After a Struggle for above Sixty Hours
With that Grand Enemy to Life,
(But the Certain and Mercifull Friend to Helpless Old Age,)
In Terrible Convulsions Plaintive Groans, or Stupefying

18

Sleep,
Without Recovery of her Speech, or Senses,
She Dyed, on the 12th Day of Sept: in ye Year
(of our Lord 1737
(and
(of her own Age 44.

Behold! I Come, as a Theif. Rev. 16th Ch. 15th V.

But Oh! Thou source of Pious Cares
Strict Iudge without Regard
Grant, tho' we Go hence Unawares,
We Go not Unprepar'd.

AMEN

On a *ledger stone in the chancel, immediately before the altar steps, of the church of St Andrew, Bramfield, Suffolk. The epitaph is less bad-tempered, however, than that of Bridgett Applewhaite's husband, Arthur, whose gravestone is immediately to the right of hers. It appears that Arthur died intestate to spite her (she having inherited her father's property) and quite a proportion of that easy widowhood was taken up with lawsuits to recover her patrimony from Arthur's brother. This is expressed in an *inscription, possibly contrived by Bridgett herself, which reads, in part: 'Here lies the Body of ARTHUR APPLEWHAITE . . .[who died, aged 39, in 1733] . . . He Married BRIDGETT the Eldest Daughter, and at length, Sole Heiress of LAMBERT NELSON late of this Parish Gent, By Whom he had no Issue. And to whom (Having by his Father's Instigation made no will) He left no legacy, But a Chancery-Suit with his Eldest Brother For her own Paternal Estates In this Town, and Blyford.'

The 'M S' at the top of the slab is one of a number of common abbreviations for Latin phrases used on gravestones – it is short for *Memoriae Sacrum*, meaning 'sacred to the memory of'.

19

ARTHUR

~

His jacet Arthurus, rex quondam rexque futurus.

'Here lies Arthur, the once and future king' – that is what Sir Thomas Malory in *Le Morte d'Arthur* (*c* 1450) says was written on the tombstone of the legendary King Arthur. On the other hand, if a King Arthur did exist (in the sixth century AD, if at all), there is a notice in the ruins of Glastonbury Abbey, Somerset, which claims to mark the site of his tomb.

It states: 'In the year 1191, the bodies of King Arthur and Queen Guinevere were said to have been found on the south side of the Lady Chapel. On 19th April 1278, their remains were removed in the presence of King Edward I and Queen Eleanor to a black marble tomb on this site. This tomb survived until the dissolution of the abbey in 1539.'

ASHMAN

~

O, THAT HE HAD ONE MORE SONG TO SING.

On the tombstone of the songwriter Howard Ashman in Baltimore, Maryland. Ashman, who wrote the lyrics for the Disney films *Beauty and the Beast* and *The Little Mermaid*, died of AIDS complications in 1991. At the Academy Awards ceremony of April 1992, Ashman's Oscar for the song 'Beauty and the Beast' was accepted by his longtime companion, who quoted the inscription.

ASQUITH
~

"Unmoved,
Unshaken, unseduced, unterrified,
His Loyalty he kept, his Love, his Zeal;
Nor number, nor example with him wrought
To swerve from truth, or change his constant mind."

Part of the memorial *tablet on a pillar in the North Transept of Westminster Abbey to Herbert Henry Asquith, 1st Earl of Oxford and Asquith (1852–1928), British Liberal Prime Minister (1908–16). The lines, from Milton's *Paradise Lost* (Bk V, l.898), were chosen 'after much thought by his family' – according to Asquith's biographer, Roy Jenkins – and are preceded by the words, 'Parliament placed this stone here . . .'

Asquith is buried in the churchyard of All Saints', Sutton Courtney, Oxfordshire, a short distance from his country home, The Wharf. His grave bears a factual inscription and nowadays is at an appropriately tipsy angle – appropriate, that is, for a politician whose nicknames included 'Squiff' and 'P.J.' (for 'Perrier-Jouët', of which he was particularly fond) and whose proclivity was alluded to in the song 'Another Little Drink Wouldn't Do Us Any Harm'.

ATWOOD
~

Mary, Sarah and Eliza Atwood . . . who were poisoned by
eating funguous vegetables mistaken for champignons
on the 11th day of October 1808 and died at the ages
of 14, 7 and 5 years within a few hours of each other
in excruciating circumstances. The Father,
Mother and now, alas, an only child, partakers of
the same meal, have survived with debilitated
constitutions and to lament so dreadful a calumny.
This monument is erected to perpetuate the fatal
events as an awful caution to others, let it be too
a solemn a warning that in our most grateful
enjoyments even in our necessary food may lurk
deadly poison . . .

From Mitcham Cemetery, Church Road, Mitcham and quoted in Meller (1981).

21

AUDEN
∼

In The Prison Of His Days
Teach The Free Man How To Praise.

On the memorial *slab to W.H. Auden (1907–73) in Poets' Corner, Westminster Abbey. The quotation is taken from Auden's elegy on YEATS and the memorial was unveiled on 2 October 1974. Auden is buried at Kirchstetten, Lower Austria.

AUSTEN
∼

In Memory of
JANE AUSTEN
youngest daughter of the late
Revd GEORGE AUSTEN,
formerly Rector of Steventon in this County,
she departed this Life on the 18th of July, 1817,
aged 41, after a long illness supported with
the patience and the hopes of a Christian.

The benevolence of her heart,
the sweetness of her temper, and
the extraordinary endowments of her mind
obtained the regard of all who knew her, and
the warmest love of her intimate connections.

Their grief is in proportion to their affection,
they know their loss to be irreparable,
but in their deepest affliction they are consoled
by a firm though humble hope that her charity,
devotion, faith and purity, rendered
her soul and acceptable in the sight of her
REDEEMER.

From the *slab on the grave in the North Aisle of the nave of Winchester Cathedral. Jane Austen (1775–1817), the novelist, died at Winchester, having completed *Emma* the previous year; *Northanger Abbey* and *Persuasion* were published posthumously in 1818. The inscription makes no direct mention of her works, but there is a brass *plaque on the wall beside her grave which does. It states: 'Jane Austen known to many by her writings, endeared to her family by the buried charms of her Character, and ennobled by Christian Faith and Piety, was born at . . .' The plaque also quotes Proverbs 31:26: 'She openeth her mouth with wisdom; and in her tongue is the law of kindness.'

BARFORD

~

THIS WORLD TO HER WAS BUT A TRAGED PLAY,
SHE CAME AND SAW'T, DISLIKT, AND PASS'D AWAY.

On Susanna Barford who died aged ten. This epitaph was recorded by
Aubrey before 1697, but its whereabouts remain untraced.

BAYLIE

~

Asleep beneath this humble Stone,
Lies honest, harmless, simple John:
Who free from Guilt & Care & Strife,
Here clos'd his inoffensive Life.
His worth was great, his failings few,
He practis'd all the good he knew.
And did no harm, his only Sin
Was that he lov'd a drop of Gin;
And when his favourite was not near
Contented took his horn of Beer:
Tho' weak his head, to make amendes
Heav'n gave him health, content & Friends.
This little Village Nurs'd and Bred him,
'Twas there he Liv'd, Caress'd by all,
The favourite of the Servant's Hall,
With them he eat his daily Bread:
They lov'd him Living, mourn him Dead.
And now have kindly Join'd to Raise
This little Tombstone to his praise,
Nor should the learned and the wise
Such humble merit e'er Despise;
Who knows but John may find a place
Where wit must never show its face.
Farewell John. Grant Heaven that we
Harmless may live and die like thee.

JOHN BAYLIE, DIED APRIL 2ND 1777
AGED 45 YEARS.

A 'Quaint *Epitaph at Stratfield Saye' (later the site of the 1st Duke of
Wellington's residence), reproduced on a postcard (1982).

BEACH

~

**TO THE MEMORY OF
MARY BEACH
WHO DIED NOV.5.1725 AGED 78**

**ALEX.POPE, WHOM SHE NURSED IN
HIS INFANCY AND CONSTANTLY AT-
TENDED FOR THIRTY EIGHT YEARS
IN
GRATITUDE TO A FAITHFUL OLD SERVANT,
ERECTED THIS STONE.**

Memorial *tablet on the outside north-east corner of St Mary the Virgin Church, Twickenham, where she is buried. As with Winston CHURCHILL's Mrs EVEREST, this is another stone erected to a beloved nurse by a famous child. Here, however, the name of the donor, Alexander POPE, appears to be in even larger type, and her role in *his* life more important, than the subject of the tablet.

BEECHAM

~

**NOTHING CAN COVER
HIS HIGH FAME BUT
HEAVEN. NO PYRAMIDS
SET OFF HIS MEMORIES
BUT THE ETERNAL
SUBSTANCE OF HIS
GREATNESS.**

Epitaph on the *grave of Sir Thomas Beecham, CH (1879–1961), the orchestral conductor. He was originally buried in Brookwood Cemetery, near Woking, but was re-interred at the parish cemetery of Limpsfield, Surrey, in April 1991. Thus he came to lie a few feet from Frederick Delius, the composer whose work he championed (and at whose funeral he spoke and conducted in 1934).

The inscription is taken from John Fletcher's play *The False One* (*c* 1620). Beecham arranged music for several productions of Fletcher's plays and gave the Oxford Romanes Lecture on the playwright in 1956. According to *Beecham Stories* (compiled by Harold Atkins and Archie Newman, 1978), after producing Fletcher's *The Faithful Shepherdess*, Beecham received a letter from the Inland Revenue asking for the playwright's address for the purposes of taxation, as they had been unable to discover his whereabouts. 'I was able to reply that to the best of my knowledge his present residence was the South Aisle of Southwark Cathedral,' said Beecham.

BELLOC
~

WHEN I AM DEAD, I HOPE IT MAY BE SAID:
'HIS SINS WERE SCARLET, BUT HIS BOOKS WERE READ'.

Hilaire Belloc (1870–1953) wrote this epitaph for himself in 'On his Books' (1923). He is actually buried in a family grave at the Church of Our Lady of Consolation, West Grinstead, Sussex, but without this inscription. A few yards away, a *plaque on the tower commemorates him, noting that he had been a member of the congregation for 48 years. The tower and spire were completed in 1964, 'in grateful recognition of his zealous and unwavering profession of our Holy Faith which he defended in his writings and noble verse.' Then follow his lines from 'The Ballade of Our Lady of Czestocjowa': *'This is the Faith that I have held and hold/and This is That in which I mean to die.'*

BETTINGTON
~

IN DEEP RESPECT FOR THE MEMORY OF
LIEUT. C.A. BETTINGTON & SECOND
LIEUT.E. HOTCHKISS
OF THE ROYAL FLYING CORPS, WHO MET THEIR DEATHS
IN THE WRECK OF A MONOPLANE, 100 YARDS NORTH
OF THIS SPOT

ON TUESDAY SEPT.10.1912.

SYMPATHISERS IN OXFORD AND WOLVERCOTE TO
THE NUMBER
OF 2225 HAVE ERECTED THIS STONE AS A TRIBUTE
TO THE
BRAVERY OF THESE TWO BRITISH OFFICERS WHO
LOST THEIR
LIVES IN THE FULFILMENT OF THEIR DUTY.

This memorial *stone – which also bears a picture of a Bristol-Coanda monoplane – may be found by Port Meadow bridge, Wolvercote, near Oxford. The number of 'sympathisers' is remarkable for an air crash in peace time – perhaps it was the first such accident that most of them had encountered? (The first British aviator to be killed in a flight had been the Hon. Charles Stewart Rolls, in 1910.)

BILL
~

HERE LIES BILL. HE DONE HIS DAMNEDEST.

On a mule, in the US, and quoted by Naomi Lewis on *Quote* . . . *Unquote*, BBC Radio, 1 December 1981, though untraced. Compare what President Harry S Truman said in Winslow, Arizona on 15 June 1948: 'You know, the greatest epitaph in the country is here in Arizona. It's in Tombstone and says, "Here lies Jack Williams. He done his damnedest." I think that is the greatest epitaph a man could have. Whenever a man does the best he can, then that is all he can do; and that is what your President has been trying to do for the last three years for this country.'
In 1964, Truman more precisely located the epitaph in Boot Hill Cemetery, Tombstone, and said that it went on, 'What more could a person do?' He added, of himself, 'Well, that's all I could do. I did my damnedest and that's all there is to it.'

BLACKNALL
~

When once they liv'd on earth one bed did hold
Their bodies which one minuite turn'd to mould.
Being dead, one grave is trusted with that prize
Until the trump doth sound and all must rise.
Here death's stroke even did not part this pair,
But by this stroke they more united were . . .

Part of a poem commemorating John Blacknall and his wife Jane, on their monument in the church of St Nicholas, Abingdon. The couple died on the same day, 21 August 1625, probably of the plague. The monument – mentioned in *Three Men in a Boat* as being to 'Blackwall' – was not erected until 1684, i.e. after the Civil War and the Commonwealth.

BLEWIT
~

MARTHA BLEWIT,
of the Swan Inn at Bathorn-End
in this Parish,
buried May 7th, 1681:
was the Wife of nine Husbands successively,
but the ninth outlived her.
The Text to her Funeral Sermon was
"Last of all the Woman died also."

ROBERT HOGAN
of this Parish
was the Husband of Seven Wives successively,
he married Ann Livermore his seventh Wife
January 1st 1739.

A joint celebration of a much-married pair, on a *tablet in Birdbrook church, Haverhill, Essex, though presumably they were never married to each other. This version of the text is from Haining (1973). The biblical quotation (which is only of slight relevance) is from St Matthew 22:27, concerning the woman who was married to seven brothers.

BLIGH

~

On the *tomb of Captain Bligh in the grounds of St Mary's Church, Lambeth. He earned the nickname 'Bread Fruit Bligh' on account of his discovery of that crop when accompanying Captain Cook on his voyage of 1772-74. Understandably, the inscription makes no mention of what Bligh is most notorious for: being the cause of the 1789 mutiny on his ship, HMS *Bounty*, though it is argued that he was not quite the tyrant as portrayed, for example, by Charles Laughton in the 1935 film of the incident. Lest modern novels and films be blamed for portraying Bligh as a tyrant, be it noted that the *DNB* was noting his 'irascible temper and overbearing conduct' as the cause of the mutiny in 1886.

BLOOMFIELD

~

Here lies
Captain Ernest Bloomfield
Accidentally shot by his Orderly
March 2nd 1789
'Well done, thou good and faithful servant'.

Beable (1925) has not only this, but also a version involving 'Major James Brush . . . 1831 (Woolwich Churchyard)'. Beable also finds the similar, 'Erected to the Memory of/John Phillips/Accidentally Shot/As a mark of affection by his brother'. Earlier, Mackae (?1910) had found the same epitaph in India. One suspects it is no more than a joke and never actually appeared on a grave.

The *Faber Book of Anecdotes* has it that James Whitcomb Riley (1849–1916), the American poet, said of a cook who had worked for a family many years, and who fell asleep over her stove and was burned to death, 'Well done, good and faithful servant'.

The phrase 'good and faithful servant' derives from Matthew 25:21 and Luke 19:17.

BOATSWAIN
~

Near this Spot
are deposited the Remains of one
who possessed Beauty without Vanity,
Strength without Insolence,
Courage without Ferocity,
and all the Virtues of Man without his Vices.
This praise, which would be unmeaning Flattery,
if inscribed over human Ashes,
is but a just Tribute to the Memory of
BOATSWAIN, a *DOG*
who was born in *Newfoundland*, May 1803,
and died at *Newstead*, Nov. 18, 1808.

On the *memorial to Lord BYRON's beloved Newfoundland dog, buried in the gardens of Newstead Abbey, Nottinghamshire. The wording, once attributed to Byron himself, is now thought to have been written by John Cam HOBHOUSE, his close friend. The poet at one time intended to be buried in the same vault as the dog.

Byron's own poem dated 30 November 1808 is appended beneath the inscription and runs, in part:

When some proud Son of Man returns to Earth,
Unknown to Glory, but upheld by Birth,
The sculptor's art exhausts the pomp of woe,
And storied urns record who rests below:

When all is done, upon the Tomb is seen,
Not what he was, but what he should have been
. . . Ye! who perchance behold this simple urn,
Pass on – it honours none you wish to mourn:
To mark a friend's remains these stones arise;
I never knew but one – and here he lies.

BOGESS
~

A house she hath, 'tis made of such good fashion,
The tenant ne'er shall pay for reparation.
Nor will the landlord ever raise her rent
Or turn her out of doors for nonpayment;
From chimney tax this cell is free.
To such a house who would not tenant be?

'For Rebecca Bogess, Folkestone, died 22 August 1688' – recalled by
Bartlett (1968).

BOND
~

Under this stone interr'd doth lie
The mirrour of true Charitie
To God, his Friends, & Country dear,
The poores Supporter farr & near.
His days hee spent in peace & Quiet
He never gave himself to riot
A Vertue strong in those his days
When it was scorn'd and Vice had praise.
He lived long and did survive
Fully the Years of Seventy Five
And at ye last expir'd his date
April the 8th in (16) 68.

From the monument to 'Christopher Bond, Gent.' in The Cathedral of
the Forest, Newland, Gloucestershire. Transcribed by David Wishart at
the Hayloft Press, Birmingham.

BOND
~

Here lie the bodies
Of THOMAS BOND and MARY his Wife.
She was temperate, chaste, charitable,
BUT
She was proud, peevish, and passionate.
She was an affectionate wife, and a tender mother;
BUT
Her husband and child, whom she loved,
Seldom saw her countenance without a disgusting frown,
Whilst she received visitors, whom she despised,
With an endearing smile.
Her behaviour was discreet towards strangers,
BUT
Imprudent in her family.
Abroad, her conduct was influenced by good breeding
BUT
At home by ill temper.
She was a professed enemy to flattery,
And was seldom known to praise or commend;
BUT
The talents in which she principally excelled
Were difference of opinion, and
Discovering flaws and imperfections.
She was an admirable economist,
And, without prodigality,
Dispensed plenty to every person in her family;
BUT
Would sacrifice their eyes to a farthing candle.
She sometimes made her husband happy
With her good qualities;
BUT
Much more frequently miserable
With her many failings;
Insomuch, that in thirty years' cohabitation,
He often lamented
That maugre all her virtues
He had not, in the whole, enjoyed
Two years of matrimonial comfort.
AT LENGTH
Finding she had lost the affection of her husband,
As well as the regard of her neighbours,

Family disputes having been divulged by servants,
She died of vexation, July 20, 1768 aged 48.
Her worn-out husband survived her
Four months and two days,
And departed this life, Nov 28, 1768, aged 54.

WILLIAM BOND, Brother to the deceased,
erected this stone
as a weekly monitor to the surviving
wives of this parish,
that they may avoid the infamy
of having their memories handed down to posterity,
with a patch-work character.

Collection (1806) has this as coming from 'Horsley-Down Church, Cumberland'; Russell (1898) has it 'in a churchyard in Northumberland' and as reprinted in the *Annual Register*. Brown (1973) and Haining (1973) both have it in 'Horsley Church, Cumberland'; 'To be found in the churchyard of Horsleydown, Cumberland' – Nancy McPhee, *The Second Book of Insults* (1981). I can find no 'Horsley-down' in that part of the world, though there are two Horsleys in Northumberland.

More convincingly, Bakewell (1977) (who gives the above transcription) says it is from St John, Horsleydown, Bermondsey, London. Indeed, there used to be such a church (in Tower Bridge Road) but it was gutted by bombing in the Second World War, and now has a modern building on the old foundations. A few gravestones are visible, though not, alas, this splendid one.

BOVARY
~

Sta viator: amabilem conjugem calcas.

Put on the grave of Emma Bovary in Gustave Flaubert's novel *Madame Bovary* (1857). It is chosen by Homais, the dull chemist, after Emma, a doctor's wife, has taken her own life after committing adultery. The conventional Latin inscription means, 'Hold your step, wayfarer, for you tread on a beloved wife.'

BOWRA

~

... Send us to Hell or Heaven or where you will,
Promise us only, you'll be with us still:
Heaven, without you, would be too dull to bear,
And Hell will not be Hell if you are there.

Part of the poem 'C.M.B.', on Sir Maurice Bowra (1898–1971), by John Sparrow. First published in the *Times Literary Supplement* on 23 June 1972, it was reprinted, in this altered form, in *Grave Epigrams and Other Verses* (1981). Bowra was a noted Oxford personality and Warden of Wadham. Sparrow was part of his circle, the Warden of All Souls, and a connoisseur of inscriptions and epitaphs. Bowra's actual grave in St Cross churchyard bears his name in suitably bold letters but no epitaph.

BRADBURY

~

HERE LIE INTERRED THE DREADFULLY
BRUISED AND LACERATED BODIES OF
WILLIAM BRADBURY AND THOMAS HIS SON
BOTH OF GREENFIELD WHO WERE TOGETHER
SAVAGELY MURDERED IN AN UNUSUALLY
HORRID MANNER ON MONDAY NIGHT, APRIL 2 1832 ...

Such interest did their tragic end excite
That, ere they were removed from human sight,
Thousands on thousands daily came to see
The bloody scene of the catastrophe ...

Andrews (1899) has this from Saddleworth church graveyard, Yorkshire. Norwich (1980) adds that the letters are 'carved nearly an inch deep'.

BRITTEN
~

See HOLST.

BROOKE
~

RUPERT BROOKE 1887–1915

IF I SHOULD DIE, THINK ONLY THIS OF ME:
THAT THERE'S SOME CORNER OF A FOREIGN FIELD
THAT IS FOR EVER ENGLAND. THERE SHALL BE
IN THAT RICH EARTH A RICHER DUST CONCEALED;
A DUST WHOM ENGLAND BORE, SHAPED, MADE AWARE,
GAVE, ONCE, HER FLOWERS TO LOVE, HER WAYS TO
ROAM,
A BODY OF ENGLAND'S, BREATHING ENGLISH AIR,
WASHED BY THE RIVERS, BLEST BY SUNS OF HOME.
AND THINK, THIS HEART, ALL EVIL SHED AWAY,
A PULSE IN THE ETERNAL MIND, NO LESS
GIVES SOMEWHERE BACK THE THOUGHTS BY ENGLAND
GIVEN;
HER SIGHTS AND SOUNDS; DREAMS HAPPY AS HER DAY;
AND LAUGHTER, LEARNT OF FRIENDS; AND
GENTLENESS,
IN HEARTS AT PEACE, UNDER AN ENGLISH HEAVEN.

Marble *plaque on the Greek island of Skyros where the poet is buried. The memorial, bearing his most famous sonnet, was unveiled in 1983 (*The Times* of 18 August had a report) and may have replaced an earlier plaque bearing a quotation from the same poem. Published in 1914, 'The Soldier' makes a perfect epitaph for Brooke, who died at Lemnos on 23 April 1915 of acute blood poisoning. He was then a sub-lieutenant in the Royal Naval Division and was on his way by boat to fight in the Dardanelles. According to Edward Marsh's *Memoir*, at Brooke's burial, a pencil inscription in Greek was put on a large white cross at the head of his grave, stating: 'Here lies the servant of God, Sub-Lieutenant in the English Navy, who died for the deliverance of Constantinople from the Turks.'

BROOMFIELD

~

The chief concern of her life for the last
twenty-five years was to order and provide
for her funeral. Her greatest pleasure
was to think and talk about it. She lived
many years on a pension of 9d per week,
and yet she saved £5, which at her own
request was laid out on her funeral.

On the *grave of Mary Broomfield, who died aged 80 in 1755, at
Macclesfield in Cheshire. Text from Bakewell (1977).

BROWN

~

OR GLORY

NEAR HERE IS THE GRAVE OF
TRUMPETER JOHN BROWN 1815–1898
WHO SOUNDED THE TRUMPET FOR
THE 17TH LANCERS AT THE CHARGE
OF THE LIGHT BRIGADE BALACLAVA
25TH OCTOBER 1854.

Stone *tablet lying flat in the grass of St Michael on Greenhill
churchyard, Lichfield. 'Or Glory' on a Death's Head [skull and
crossbones] is the official motto of the 17th Lancers ('The Death or
Glory Boys') and was selected by the first Colonel of the regiment in
honour of General Wolfe.

Oddly, what is called 'the Balaklava Bugle' is now displayed in the
museum of the 17th/21st Lancers at Belvoir Castle, where it is said to
have been *carried* by Trumpeter William Brittain who died of the
wounds he received during the incident. Is it possible that Brittain carried
the trumpet and Brown sounded it? Or is there a dispute as to which
man actually sounded the charge?

BROWN
~

**STRANGER! APPROACH THIS SPOT WITH GRAVITY!
JOHN BROWN IS FILLING HIS LAST CAVITY.**

'On a Dentist' – Hyman (1967). Haining (1973) has a similar rhyme more precisely from 'St George's Church, Edinburgh'.

BROWN
~

**THIS STONE
IS ERECTED IN AFFECTIONATE REMEMBRANCE OF
JOHN BROWN,
the devoted and faithful personal attendant and
beloved friend of Queen Victoria . . . 'That friend on
whose fidelity you count, that friend given you by
circumstances over which you have no control, was
God's own gift.'**

'In the churchyard of Crathie' – Russell (1898). The inscription was chosen by Queen VICTORIA for the headstone of the tomb of John Brown (1826-83), her Balmoral gillie (retainer) for 34 years. The Queen also had a hand in composing his obituary in *The Times* (29 March 1883), which succeeded in obscuring the precise nature of an attachment which was viewed with suspicion by her family and the world at large. He died at Windsor.

BROWNING
~

**ELIZABETH
BARRETT BROWNING**

**WAS BORN AT
COXHOE, NORTHUMBERLAND
ON 6TH MARCH 1806**

AND DIED IN FLORENCE
ON 29TH JUNE 1861.
SHE LIVED AT HOPE END
FROM 1809 UNTIL 1832,
NEVER TO RETURN.

GREEN THE LAND IS WHERE MY DAILY
STEPS IN JOCUND CHILDHOOD PLAYED,
DIMPLED CLOSE WITH HILL AND VALLEY,
DAPPLED VERY CLOSE WITH SHADE;
SUMMER-SNOW OF APPLE-BLOSSOMS RUNNING
UP FROM GLADE TO GLADE.

Not an epitaph exactly, but as good as one, this *inscription was carved on a stone and placed during 1991 on the enchanting site of Hope End house, near Ledbury, Herefordshire, where the poetess spent her formative years and first began writing poetry. The verse is from 'The Lost Bower' (1844-50).

Elizabeth Barrett Browning was buried in Florence. A plaque on the Casa Guidi, the house the Brownings lived in in the centre of that city, now bears the epitaphic: '*Qui scrisse e morì Elizabeth Barrett Browning, che in cuore di donna conciliara scienze di dotto e spirito di poeta e fece del suo verso aureo anello fra Italia e Inghilterra. Pose questa memoria Firenze grata, 1861*' – ('Here wrote and died Elizabeth Barrett Browning, who in a woman's heart brought together the knowledge of a scholar and the spirit of a poet and made of her verses a golden link between Italy and England. Placed in grateful Florentian remembrance, 1861.')

BROWNLOW
~

In
gratitude to GOD
and in ever loving memory of
DOROTHY CARLOTTA
1907–1966
deeply loved wife of
PEREGRINE LORD BROWNLOW.
She sleeps in peace in the deep blue Jamaican Sea

A BIRD with a broken wing
A CHILD with a crippled limb
A MAN with a wounded body
A GIRL with an aching heart

They were her especial children
whom she loved and of such is
the Kingdom of Heaven.

Memorial *tablet on the wall of the Brownlow family chapel at Belton church, near Belton House, Grantham (see also CUST). Lady Brownlow was born in the United States and had been married to the 2nd Earl Beatty. She subsequently became the second wife of the 6th Baron (*d* 1978), a close friend of King Edward VIII, Lord-in-Waiting during the brief reign, and the King's supporter during the Abdication crisis. Lady Brownlow's death took place in London and the wording of the memorial would suggest that her ashes were scattered on the sea in the West Indies.

On 23 May 1966, an advertisement appeared on the Court page of *The Times* containing a tribute written by Sacheverell Sitwell which, it explained, had been 'rejected by the Editor of *The Times* and is now published by the order and at the expense of Lord Brownlow'. It described the departed's 'exceptional gifts', her beauty and talents ('almost of the female "clown"'), and her Jamaican home where 'she was on the same terms with the coloured maidservants and with the quarrelsome but hibiscus-loving humming birds on their hovering, darting flight along the open galleries.'

BUNN
~

Here lies John Bunn
Who was killed by a gun.
His name wasn't Bun, but his real name was Wood,
But Wood wouldn't rhyme with gun,
So I thought Bunn should.

Fairley (1875) and Beable (1925) both have this, the latter noting 'a distinctly American flavour'. Tegg (1876) has the similar: 'Underneath this ancient pew/Lie the remains of Jonathan Blue;/His name was Black, but that wouldn't do.'

Compare Jessica JONES.

BURBAGE
~

EXIT BURBAGE.

On the leading Elizabethan actor, Richard Burbage (?1567-1619), who was a colleague of William Shakespeare. Burbage probably died of the plague and was buried at St Leonard's, Shoreditch, as was his father, James, who built the first London theatre in 1576. What Richard's actual epitaph (if any) was, is not known (the present church is of more recent vintage), though several poetic epitaphs on him survive. The above, suggested 'briefest epitaph on any man', first appeared in William Camden's 'Remains' (1674 edition). *Collection* (1806) calls him 'Burbridge'.

BURNHAM
~

EDWARD 1ST BARON BURNHAM K.C.V.O.
OF HALL BARN
IN THE COUNTY OF BUCKINGHAM AND OF
The Daily Telegraph
FLEET STREET IN THE CITY OF LONDON
BORN 28TH DECEMBER 1833
DIED 9TH JANUARY 1916.

On the *grave of the newspaper proprietor, outside the West Door of St Mary and All Saints' Church, Beaconsfield, Buckinghamshire. The name of the newspaper is carved in the script as used on the paper's masthead. Nearby is the *grave of his son, 'Harry Lawson Webster Lawson [1st] Viscount Burnham' (1862–1933):

... HE DEVOTED 50 YEARS OF HIS
LIFE TO PUBLIC SERVICE IN MANY SPHERES & COUNTRIES,
AND STROVE
CONSTANTLY TO PROMOTE HARMONY &
UNDERSTANDING AMONG
THE PEOPLES OF THE WORLD.
IN HIS DIRECTION OF THE DAILY TELEGRAPH HE
ACCEPTED
THE HIGH RESPONSIBILITY WHICH THE POWER OF
PUBLICITY
ENTAILED AND EVER MAINTAINED THE HIGHEST
TRADITIONS
OF THE BRITISH PRESS ...

This Burnham gave his name to the scales of teachers' salaries which grew out of the committee of inquiry he chaired.

BURNS
~

"THE POETIC GENIUS OF MY COUNTRY FOUND ME AT THE PLOUGH AND THREW HER INSPIRING MANTLE OVER ME. SHE BADE ME SING THE LOVES, THE JOYS, THE RURAL SCENES AND RURAL PLEASURES OF MY NATIVE SOIL, IN MY NATIVE TONGUE. I TUNED MY WILD, ARTLESS NOTES AS SHE INSPIRED."

Robert Burns (1759–96) is buried in a mausoleum at Dumfries. A large, seated statue of him with this *text below is to be found in Victoria Embankment Gardens in London (a city he never visited). The quotation comes from his address 'to the Noblemen and Gentlemen of the Caledonian Hunt' prefacing the 1787 'Edinburgh' edition of his poems. The Caledonian Hunt was an association of noblemen and country gentlemen who shared a keen interest in field sports, races, balls and social assemblies. The original text reads: 'The Poetic Genius of my

Country found me, as the prophetic bard Elijah did Elisha – at the *plough* – and threw her inspiring mantle over me. She bade me sing the loves, the joys, the rural scenes and rural pleasures of my natal Soil, in my native tongue. I tuned my wild, artless notes, as she inspired. She whispered me to come to this ancient metropolis of Caledonia, and lay my Songs under your honoured protection. I now obey her dictates . . . I do not approach you, my Lords and Gentlemen, in the usual style of dedication, to thank you for past favours; that path is so hackneyed by prostituted Learning, that honest Rusticity is ashamed of it. Nor do I present this Address with the venal soul of a servile Author, looking for a continuation of those favours: I was bred to the Plough, and am independent . . .'

Burns is also commemorated by a bust in Poets' Corner, Westminster Abbey. When one of these stately monuments to his memory was erected, his mother is said to have commented: 'Ah, Robbie, ye asked them for bread and they hae gi'en ye a stane.' [Compare the epitaph on BUTLER.]

BURTON
~

"FAREWELL, DEAR FRIEND, DEAD HERO! THE GREAT LIFE
IS ENDED, THE GREAT PERILS, THE GREAT JOYS:
AND HE TO WHOM ADVENTURES WERE AS TOYS,
WHO SEEMED TO BEAR A CHARM 'GAINST SPEAR OR KNIFE
OR BULLET, NOW LIES SILENT FROM ALL STRIFE
OUT YONDER WHERE THE AUSTRIAN EAGLES POISE
ON ISTRIAN HILLS. BUT ENGLAND, AT THE NOISE
OF THAT DREAD FALL, WEEPS WITH THE HERO'S WIFE.
OH, LAST AND NOBLEST OF THE ERRANT KNIGHTS,
THE ENGLISH SOLDIER AND THE ARAB SHIEK!
OH, SINGER OF THE EAST, WHO LOVED SO WELL
THE DEATHLESS WONDER OF THE "ARABIAN NIGHTS",
WHO TOUCHED CAMOEN'S LUTE AND STILL WOULD SEEK
EVER NEW DEEDS UNTIL THE END! FAREWELL!"

Sir Richard Burton (1821–90), the explorer, soldier and writer, is buried in an extraordinary *tomb in the cemetery of St Mary Magdalen's (RC) Church, North Worple Way, Mortlake, London SW14. It is in the shape of a Bedouin tent and the Forest of Dean stone is carved to look like canvas. Burton's wife, Isabel (*d* 1896), who shares the tomb, had been refused a burial for him in Westminster Abbey, presumably because rumours concerning his private life were known to the authorities, and so she came up with this instead.

The entrance to the tent was originally practical and Lady Burton is said to have conducted séances there, but it was blocked up after vandals damaged the tomb in 1951. Now on the 'entrance', apart from a plaque giving details and dates of husband and wife, there is the somewhat uneasy poem (as above) by Justin Huntly McCarthy, a journalist who had helped Lady Burton produced a watered-down edition of Sir Richard's translation of the *Arabian Nights*. ('Istrian hills' alludes to Trieste where Burton died working as British Consul; 'shiek' for 'sheik' and 'Camoen's' for 'Camoëns's' are as carved. Burton translated much of Camoëns, the Portuguese poet.)

All in all, the tomb marks something of a takeover by Lady Burton. Her husband was not a Roman Catholic as she was, nor indeed a practising Christian at all. She also destroyed his journals and other writings of which she did not approve. A curious feature of the monument as it was renovated is that, if you ascend an iron staircase at the back, you can see into the tomb through a clear pane that replaced the original stained glass. The two coffins are visible.

BUTLER

~

Sacred to the memory of
SAMUEL BUTLER,

Who was born at Strensham, in Worcestershire, 1612, and died at London 1680; a man of uncommon, wit, and probity: as admirable for the product of his genius, as unhappy in the rewards of them. His satire, exposing the hypocrisy and wickedness of the rebels, is such an inimitable piece, that as he was the first, he may be said to be the last writer in this peculiar manner. That he, who, when living, wanted almost everything, might not, after death, any longer want to so much as a tomb, JOHN BARBER, citizen of London, erected this monument 1721.

Translated from the Latin *inscription below the bust of Samuel Butler in Poets' Corner, Westminster Abbey. Butler – author of *Hudibras* (in part a satire on the Civil War) – had died in poverty and John Barber, a printer, arranged the monument for the reasons stated when he was Lord Mayor of London, forty-one years after Butler's death. Alexander POPE, never one to miss an opportunity to be snide, commented: 'But whence this Barber? that a name so mean/Should joined with Butler's on a tomb be seen.'

Earlier, Butler had been buried in St Paul's, Covent Garden, without stone or inscription, and in due course a medallion portrait (based on that in the Abbey) was placed in the portico (though no trace remains today), together with these lines by 'Mr O'Brien':

> A few plain men, to pomp and pride unknown,
> O'er a poor bard have rais'd this humble stand,
> Whose wants alone his genius could surpass,
> Victim of zeal! the matchless HUDIBRAS . . .

This in turn grave rise to an epigram by 'Mr S Wesley':

> Whilst BUTLER (needy wretch!) was yet alive,
> No gen'rous patron would dinner give;
> See him, when starv'd to death, and turn'd to dust,
> Presented with a monumental bust!
> The poet's fate is here in emblem shown,
> He asked for bread, and he received a stone.

BYNG
~

To the perpetual Disgrace
of Public Justice,
The Honourable JOHN BYNG,
Admiral of the Blue,
Fell a Martyr to
Political Persecution,
On March 14, in the Year 1757;
When Bravery and Loyalty
Were insufficient Securities
For the Life and Honour
Of a Naval Officer.

*Inscription in Southill Church, Bedfordshire. Admiral Byng (1704–57) was executed at Portsmouth after failing to relieve Minorca, giving rise to Voltaire's comment in *Candide* (1759) that in England it was 'thought well to kill an admiral from time to time to encourage the others'.

BYRON
~

... He died at Missolonghi, in Western Greece, on the
19th April, 1824,
Engaged in the glorious attempt to
restore that country to her ancient
freedom and renown.
His sister, the Honourable
Augusta Maria Leigh,
placed this tablet to his memory.

Part of the *tablet over the vault containing the remains of the poet George Gordon, 6th Baron Byron (1788–1824) in St Mary Magdalen Church, Hucknall Torkard, Nottinghamshire. Augusta Leigh was the half-sister who probably bore him a daughter in 1814. At Byron's death, his body was refused by the Deans of Westminster Abbey and St Paul's Cathedral. Now, however, in Poets' Corner, Westminster Abbey, Byron is remembered by a slab bearing his lines from *Childe Harold* (Canto 4, St. 137): 'But there is that within me which shall tire/Torture and time, and breathe when I expire.' As the Abbey's *Official Guide* (1988) puts it: 'For many years the open profligacy of his life proved an obstacle to his commemoration in the Abbey, but his poetic genius and mastery of the art of letter-writing at length prevailed' (under the auspices of the Poetry Society in 1969).

CADMAN
~

Let this small Monument record the name
Of CADMAN, and to future times proclaim
How by'n attempt to fly from this high spire
Across the Sabrine stream he did acquire
His fatal end. 'Twas not for want of skill
Or courage to perform the task he fell:
No, no, a faulty Cord being drawn too tight
Hurried his Soul on high to take her flight
Which bid the Body here beneath good Night:
Febry 2nd 1739 aged 28.

From a memorial *tablet to Robert Cadman on the exterior wall of the tower of St Mary's Church, St Mary's Street, Shrewsbury.

CALVERT
~

In memory of Edwin Calvert, son of Richard Calvert, of Skipton, known by the title of 'Commander in Chief'. He was the smallest and most perfect human being in the world, being under 36 inches in height, and weighing 25 lb . . He died much lamented and deeply regretted by all who knew him, August 7th 1859, aged 17 years.

The Skipton (Yorkshire) Town Council *Yearbook* (drawn to my attention by Richard Lowe in 1987) states that this 'remarkable record' is to be found at the east end of Christ Church burial ground in the town.

CAMERON
~

And when he goes to heaven
To Saint Peter he will tell:
Another Marine reporting, sir,
I've served my time in hell!

Epitaph on the grave of Pfc. Cameron of the US Marine Corps. Guadalcanal (1942), quoting from 'The Marines' Hymn' which dates from 1847 – Bartlett (1980).

CAMPBELL

~

Thomas Campbell LLD, author of *The Pleasures of Hope*, died June 15, 1844, aged 67.

The inscription on the coffin of the Scottish poet (1777–1844) is ironic in the light of what is reported by William Keddie in his *Cyclopedia of Literary and Scientific Anecdote &c.* (1859): 'Campbell once explained to a friend why he did not like to be associated with his famous work, *The Pleasures of Hope*. "When I was young," he said, "I was always greeted among my friends as Mr Campbell, author of *The Pleasures of Hope*. When I married, I was married as the author of *The Pleasures of Hope*; and when I became a father, my son was the son of the author of *The Pleasures of Hope*".'

He is buried in Poets' Corner, Westminster Abbey, and there is a statue of him, bearing lines from his 'Last Man' but fortunately no mention of *The Pleasures of Hope*.

It was probably Campbell rather than BYRON who said 'Now Barabbas was a publisher'. He once toasted Napoleon at a literary dinner with the words: 'We must not forget that he once shot a bookseller.' It was Campbell, also, who said, ''Tis distance lends enchantment to the view' (in *The Pleasures of Hope*, of course).

CARTHEW

~

Here lies the body of Joan Carthew, Born at St. Columb, buried at St. Kew. Children she had five, Three are dead, and two alive. Those that are dead chusing rather To die with their Mother Than live with their Father.

This much-recalled epitaph may be found in *Collection* (1806). 'Unfortunately cannot now be found, but was inscribed on an 18th Century headstone' – according to the guidebook (1982) of the church at St Ewe, near St Austell, Cornwall. Bakewell (1977) gives the version as above as though from St Agnes, which is on the north coast of Cornwall, near Redruth. However, St Agnes *is* nearer to St Columb, if that is relevant.

CASTLEREAGH
~

Posterity will ne'er survey
A nobler grave than this:
Here lie the bones of Castlereagh:
Stop, traveller, and piss.

BYRON wrote this epitaph on Viscount Castlereagh (1769–1822) apparently the year *before* the Foreign Secretary's death by suicide. Castlereagh is buried in Westminster Abbey and is commemorated by a standing figure on a pedestal. He holds a scroll inscribed 'Peace of Paris' (which he concluded in 1814). He attracted the poet's enmity either because Byron supported Napoleon or on account of Castlereagh's role in the Peterloo massacre of 1819 (which inspired SHELLEY's lines, 'I met murder on the way/He had a mask like Castlereagh . . .'). In any case, the statesman was singularly unpopular: it is said that a great cheer went up when his coffin was carried into Westminster Abbey.

CAVELL
~

HUMANITY

EDITH CAVELL
BRUSSELS
DAWN
OCTOBER 12TH
1915

PATRIOTISM IS NOT ENOUGH
I MUST HAVE NO HATRED OR
BITTERNESS FOR ANYONE.

Edith Cavell (1865–1915) was a British Red Cross nurse who, though regarded as a kind of martyr, unquestionably broke the rules of war by using her position to help Allied prisoners escape from German-occupied territory She was condemned to death by a German court-martial for 'conducting soldiers to the enemy' and was shot. Her last 'message to the world': 'This I would say, standing as I do in view of God and eternity: I realize that patriotism is not enough; I must have no hatred and bitterness towards anyone.' These were not in the form of 'last words' spoken before the firing squad but were said the previous day to a British chaplain, the Revd Stirling Gahan, who visited her in prison.

Bernard Shaw complained in his Preface to *Saint Joan* (published 1924): 'Her countrymen, seeing [in her death] a good opportunity for lecturing the enemy on his intolerance, put up a statue to her, but took particular care not to inscribe on the pedestal [these words], for which omission, and the lie it implies, they will need Edith's intercession when they are themselves brought to judgement.' This may have been true at the time Shaw wrote it, but subsequently the words (as above) *were* carved on the *statue by Sir George Frampton (1920) that stands opposite the National Portrait Gallery in London. Above the Cavell statue is a sculpture of Humanity Protecting the Small States (represented by a woman and child), with the words 'FOR KING AND COUNTRY'. This and the wording as given above is all on the front face of the monument. On the tops of the three other faces are the words 'SACRIFICE FORTITUDE DEVOTION', and at the rear of the memorial the text 'FAITHFUL UNTO DEATH' is also to be found (see J.W. STANDING).

It was at that the unveiling of this ugly monument – and not very great likeness – that the artist James Pryde exclaimed, 'My God, they've shot the wrong person!'

Cavell's grave is outside the south-east transept wall of Norwich Cathedral, to which her remains were brought in 1919 having been disinterred from where she had been shot in Belgium. The Norwich grave bears simple inscriptions: 'Who gave her life for England'; 'Her name liveth for evermore'; though *not* 'Patriotism is not enough...'

CAXTON

~

Thy prayer was 'Light – more Light – while Time shall last!'
Thou sawest a glory growing on the night,
But not the shadows which that light would cast,
Till shadows vanish in the Light of Light.

Tennyson's epitaph on William Caxton, 'the Father of Printing', alludes
to Caxton's motto *'Fiat lux'*. It is to be found on a wall *tablet still in
place beneath the East Door window of St Margaret's Church,
Westminster. Unfortunately, the window raised by the 'printers of
London, AD 1882' was destroyed in the Second World War and was not
replaced. Also by the East Door is an 1820 *tablet commemorating
Caxton, 'who first introduced into Great Britain the art of printing'.

Indeed, Caxton established the first English printing press in 1477 near
St Margaret's. When he died in 1491, he was buried either in the earlier
church on this site or in the churchyard. The whereabouts of his grave
are not known.

CECIL

~

DOROTHY CECIL UNMARRIED
AS YET.

From an undated newspaper cutting (possibly from the early 1900s):
'"C.W." writes: "While lately strolling through an old Surrey church
containing altar-tombs, escutcheons and memorials of the House of
Exeter, [this] epitaph on a large marble slab, suspended high in the
mortuary chapel, arrested my attention. It is printed in uncials, and I
reproduce the arrangement in facsimile".'

CHAMBERLAYNE

~

Sacred to posterity.

In a vault, near this place, lies the body of
ANNE, the only daughter of
EDWARD CHAMBERLAYNE, LL.D.
Born in London, January 20, 1667,
Who,
For a considerable time, declined the matrimonial state,
And scheming many things
Superior to her sex and age,
On the 30th of June, 1690,
And under the command of her brother,
With the arms and in the dress of a man,
She approv'd herself a true VIRAGO,
By fighting undaunted in a fire ship against the French,
Upwards of six hours.
She might have given us a race of heroes,
Had not premature fate interposed.
She returned safe from that naval engagement,
And was married, in some months after, to
JOHN SPRAGGE, Esq.
With whom she lived half a year extremely happy,
But being delivered of a daughter, she died
A few days after,
October 30, 1692.

This monument, to his most dear and affectionate wife, was
erected by her most disconsolate husband.

Collection (1806) has this from 'St Luke's, Chelsea'. The present church
built in the 1820s does not appear to contain any remnant of this
inscription, even among the many old stones arranged round St Luke's
Gardens.

CHANNON

~

Heureux qui comme Ulysse a fait un beau voyage.

('Happy he who, like Ulysses, has made a great journey.') On the headstone of the grave of Sir Henry Channon (1897-1958), the American-born socialite, Conservative MP, and diarist. He is buried at Kelvedon in Essex. Robert Rhodes James, editor of *Chips: The Diaries of Sir Henry Channon* (1967), refers to 'the words [from a sonnet] of Du Bellay which had been his special favourite'.

CHARLES II

~

Here lies a great and mighty king
Whose promise none relies on;
He never said a foolish thing,
Nor ever did a wise one.

A familiar jesting epitaph on Charles II, written by John Wilmot, 2nd Earl of Rochester (1647-80). Other versions include, 'Here lies our sovereign Lord the King . . .' and 'Here lies our mutton-eating king' (where 'mutton' = prostitute). Charles II's reply is said to have been: 'This is very true: for my words are my own, and my actions are my ministers.'

Charles II, who lived 1630–85, is buried in the royal vault below the South Aisle of Henry VII's Chapel, Westminster Abbey, and the covering stone – in common with those of most monarchs – has no epitaph.

CHARLOTTE

~

Here lies the bones of Copperstone Charlotte
Born a virgin, died a harlot.
For sixteen years she kep' her virginity
A damn'd long time in this vicinity.

Brown (1973) has this 'from the US'. Compare: 'Here lie the bones of Elizabeth Charlotte,/That was born a virgin and died a harlot./She was aye a virgin till seventeen –/An extraordinary thing for Aberdeen' – quoted in Donald and Catherine Carswell, *The Scots Week-End* (1936).

CHARTRES

~

HERE continueth to rot
The Body of FRANCIS CHARTRES,
Who with an INFLEXIBLE CONSTANCY,
and INIMITABLE UNIFORMITY of Life,
PERSISTED,
In spite of AGE and INFIRMITIES,
In the Practice of EVERY HUMAN VICE;
His insatiable AVARICE exempted him from the first,
His matchless IMPUDENCE from the second.
Nor was he more singular
in the undeviating *Pravity* of his *Manners,*
Than successful
In *Accumulating* WEALTH,
For, without TRADE or PROFESSION,
Without TRUST of PUBLIC MONEY,
And without BRIBE-WORTHY Service,
He acquired, or more properly created,
A MINISTERIAL ESTATE.
He was the only Person of his Time,
Who could CHEAT without the Mask of HONESTY,
Retain his Primeval MEANNESS
When possess'd of TEN THOUSAND a Year,
And having daily deserved the GIBBET for what he *did,*
Was at last condemn'd to it for what he *could* not *do.*
Oh Indignant Reader!
Think not his Life useless to Mankind!
PROVIDENCE conniv'd at his execrable Designs,
To give to After-ages
A conspicuous PROOF and EXAMPLE,
Of how small Estimation is EXORBITANT WEALTH
in the Sight of GOD,
By his bestowing it on the most UNWORTHY of ALL MORTALS.

In Alexander POPE's 'Epistle to Bathurst' (1744), the poet mentions Chartres in his discussion 'Of the Use of Riches' and prints John Arbuthnot's suggested epitaph, as above. In addition, Pope calls Chartres a 'man infamous for all manner of vices . . . He took to lending of money at exorbitant interest and on great penalties . . . in a word, by a constant attention to the vices, wants, and follies of mankind, he acquired an immense fortune. His house was a perpetual bawdy-house. Hewas twice condemn'd for rapes, and pardoned; but the last time not without imprisonment in Newgate, and large confiscations. He died in Scotland in 1731, aged 62. The populace at his funeral rais'd a great riot, almost tore the body out of the coffin, and cast dead dogs, & c. into the grave along with it.'

CHESTERTON
~

Here lies nipped in this narrow cyst
The literary contortionist
Who prove[d] and never turn[ed] a hair
That Darwin's theories were a snare . . .

'Epitaph for G.K. Chesterton' – part of an unfinished verse by Thomas HARDY, found among the poet's papers at his death and first published in the *Complete Poems* (ed. Dr James Gibson, 1976). E.V. Lucas also composed a mock epitaph:

Poor G.K.C., his day is past –
Now God will know the truth at last.

Chesterton (1874–1936) is buried in the Roman Catholic Cemetery at Beaconsfield, Buckinghamshire, beneath a stone incorporating a carving by Eric GILL and the text, 'PRAY FOR THE SOUL OF GILBERT KEITH CHESTERTON . . . *TERMINO NOBIS DONET IN PATRIA'*. The Latin words are taken from the final stanza of the Matins hymn for the Feast of Corpus Christi. The entire office was written by St Thomas Aquinas, and Chesterton was said to have known large parts of it by heart. As Father Ian Brady, editor of *The Chesterton Review*, points out, the words would also have been familiar to him because they formed part of the hymn sung at the popular short devotional service of Benediction (until the introduction of the vernacular, about the time of Vatican 2), the hymn which began with the words, 'O *salutaris hostia*', and concluded with this prayer to the Holy Trinity:

Uni trinoque Domino
sit sempiterna gloria,
qui vitam sine termino
nobis donet in patria.

('Everlasting glory be to the Lord, Three in One, who gives us life without end in heaven.') In Maisie Ward's *Return to Chesterton*, there is a letter from one of Chesterton's Beaconsfield friends in which Chesterton is quoted as saying that he regarded the phrase '*in patria*' as a perfect definition of heaven. 'Our native land,' he said, 'it tells you everything.' Fr Brady adds that perhaps the fact that Chesterton died on the Sunday within the Octave of Corpus Christi also influenced the choice of these words for his monument.

Interestingly, the words were also an especial favourite of Chesterton's friend and colleague, Hilaire BELLOC. It is said that Belloc was unable to hear the closing lines of the hymn without being moved to tears.

CHETTLE
~

This keeps alive the worthy fame of Margaret
Chettle, maiden lady, who educated the youth of her
sex for forty years at Ripon in useful learning and
adorned them with her virtues. Free from the gloss
of wealth or ostentation, heaven graced her humble
walk in life with majesty of mind and look, and acts
of pure benevolence, for though her scanty means
sprung only from her own industry she made them flow
with silent sweetness to help the work of charity.
Died 1813, aged 81.
Merit claimed this tribute to her memory from her
surviving friend, John Coates, solicitor of this
town.

'On a tablet in Ripon Cathedral' – drawn to my attention by Mrs E.S. Nutt of Chesterfield (1982).

CHILDE-PEMBERTON

~

'IS IT WELL THE CHILD? IT IS WELL.'

On the grave of Major Charles Childe-Pemberton, near the hamlet of Acton Homes, Natal, South Africa. Childe-Pemberton came from Shropshire and was killed in middle age during the Boer War, fighting with the South African Light Horse. A racing man, his nickname was 'Monsieur L'Enfant', or 'The Child'. He had a presentiment of his death and requested that the abbreviated version of 2 Kings 4:26, as above, be put on his grave. James Morris in *Farewell the Trumpets* (1978) confirmed that this had been done, though the grave has been moved to a military cemetery in Acton Homes.

CHURCHILL

~

REMEMBER WINSTON CHURCHILL.
IN ACCORDANCE WITH THE WISHES OF
THE QUEEN AND PARLIAMENT
THE DEAN & CHAPTER PLACED THIS STONE
ON THE TWENTY-FIFTH ANNIVERSARY OF
THE BATTLE OF BRITAIN 15 SEPTEMBER 1965.

Ledger-slab *memorial in the Nave and near the West Door of Westminster Abbey. Churchill's *gravestone in the churchyard of St Martin's at Bladon, Oxfordshire, where he is buried near to his father, mother and brother, simply states:

WINSTON
LEONARD
SPENCER
CHURCHILL
1874
1965

CLARE
~

John Clare. 1793–1864
Poet
"Fields were the
essence of the
song."

On the memorial *tablet set into a wall of Poets' Corner, Westminster Abbey. The 'Northamptonshire Peasant Poet' is also remembered on a Gothic memorial in Helpston, Cambridgeshire, where he was born and where he is buried in the churchyard of St Botolph. He died in an asylum for the insane.

The quotation is from Clare's 'Progress of Rhyme':

> Fields were the essence of the song
> & fields & woods are still as mine
> Real teachers that are all divine
> So if my song be weak or tame
> Tis I not they who bear the blame.

CLEMENS
~

Warm summer sun, shine kindly here;
Warm southern wind, blow softly here;
Green sod above, lie light, lie light –
Good-night, dear heart, good-night, good-night.

On Olivia Susan Clemens who died 18 August 1890, aged 24, written by her father, Mark Twain. Adopted from an epitaph written by Robert Richardson in c 1885.

'May the earth lie light upon thee' was an epitaph common on Roman tombs (compare Sir John VANBRUGH).

CLIFFORD
~

IN THIS TOMB LIES ROSAMOND, THE ROSE OF
THE WORLD, THE FAIR, BUT NOT THE PURE.

Epitaph on The Fair Rosamond, mistress of King Henry II, who is said to have been poisoned out of jealousy by his Queen Eleanor in c 1177. The king kept Rosamond in a labyrinthine house in Woodstock, so that only he could find her, but Eleanor succeeded in locating her rival using the thread method.

Rosamond was buried at Godstow Nunnery, near Oxford. The tomb became a shrine, until a scandalized bishop forbade the nuns to pay homage to the memory of a courtesan. The nunnery was destroyed in 1646 by General Fairfax, commander of Cromwell's New Model Army, and the only record we have of the tomb is in the writings of one Ranulf Higden, a monk of Chester (c 1350). He says Rosamond was the daughter of Walter, Lord Clifford, and gives her epitaph in the original Latin:

> *Hic jacet in tumba Rosa mundi, non Rosa munda;*
> *Non redolet, sed olet, quae redolere solet*

E.C. Bentley, in our own century, translated this pointedly as:

> Here Rose the graced, not Rose the chaste, reposes;
> The smell that rises is no smell of roses.

CLIVE
~

Sacred to the Memory of
Mrs CATHERINE CLIVE
Who died December the 7th 1785
aet 75 Years

Clive's blameless life this tablet shall proclaim,
Her moral virtues and her well-earn'd fame,
In comic scenes the stage she early trod
"Nor sought the critic's praise, nor fear'd his rod."

In real life was equal praise her due,
Open to pity, and to friendship true,
In wit still pleasing, as in converse free,
From aught that could afflict humanity:
Her generous heart to all her friends was known
And e'en the stranger's sorrows were her own.
Content with fame, e'er affluence she wav'd,
To share with others what by toil she sav'd;
And nobly bounteous from her slender store
She bade two dear relations not be poor.
Such deeds on life's short scences true glory shed,
And heav'nly plaudits hail the virtuous dead.

*Tablet on the outside north-east corner of St Mary the Virgin, Twickenham. Kitty Clive (1711-85) was a noted eighteenth-century actress. In his *Life of Johnson*, Boswell quotes Bennet Langton: 'He [Johnson] had a very high opinion of Mrs Clive's comick powers, and conversed more with her than any of [the other actresses in the green room of Drury Lane Theatre]. He said, "Clive, Sir, is a good thing to sit by; she always understands what you say." And she said of him, "I love to sit by Dr Johnson; he always entertains me".' Johnson also said of her: 'Mrs Clive in the sprightliness of humour, I have never seen equalled. What Clive did best, she did better than Garrick; but could not do half so many things well; she was a better romp than any I ever saw in nature.'

According to the *DNB*, 'she made her way to eminence by sheer force of a vigorous genius, in spite of a want of refinement,' and, despite what might be expected of an actress, 'her character . . . to the last was unblemished'. In her retirement, Horace Walpole found her a house at Strawberry Hill, Twickenham, as he 'obviously found in her rough, outspoken humour a delightful contrast to the insipidities of the fine ladies of his circle'.

The epitaph includes phrases concerning Kitty Clive which had earlier appeared in Charles Churchill's *The Rosciad* (1761):

> Easy, as if at home, the stage she trod,
> Nor sought the critic's praise, nor fear'd his rod.
> (lines 689–690)

Churchill died in 1764, so the epitaph must indeed be by another hand.

COBBETT
~

Beneath this Stone lie the Remains of
William Cobbett,
Son of George and Anne Cobbett. Born in the Parish of Farnham
9th March 1762. Enlisted into the 54th Regiment of Foot in 1784
of which he became Sergeant Major in 1785
And obtained his discharge in 1791.
In 1794 he became a Political Writer. In 1832 was returned to
Parliament for the Borough of Oldham and represented it till
his death which took place at Normandy Farm in the adjoining
Parish of Ash on the 13th of June 1835.

This *epitaph is included because of its curious refusal to acknowledge
what was truly outstanding about its subject, who was a Radical, a
campaigner and a great champion of the poor. It is to be found just
outside the North Door of St Andrew's Parish Church, Farnham, Surrey.
Cobbett was born in Farnham though he lived mostly elsewhere. A
memorial *plaque with profile carving, inside the church tower, also says
nothing of his achievements and puts the name of the donor of the
plaque on a par with the subject's ('IN MEMORY OF/WILLIAM
COBBETT/THIS TABLET IS PLACED IN THE CHURCH/OF HIS
NATIVE PARISH/BY HIS COLLEAGUE IN PARLIAMENT/JOHN
FIELDEN'). Amends are made in Gostrey Meadow near the river where a
column with bust calls Cobbett 'champion of Democracy, master of
English Prose and enemy of cant in public affairs'.

COLLINS
~

IN MEMORY OF
WILKIE COLLINS

AUTHOR OF "THE WOMAN IN WHITE"
AND OTHER WORKS OF FICTION.

On the *grave of Collins (1824-89) in Kensal Green Cemetery, London. Whereas some inscriptions on novelists seem reluctant to admit they ever wrote anything (Jane AUSTEN, George ELIOT), this one has no such qualms. The 'other works of fiction' number about twenty and included *The Moonstone* (1876). On the other hand, there is no mention of Collins's mistress who is said to be buried with him.

COLLINS
~

YE! WHO THE MERITS OF THE DEAD REVERE,
WHO HOLD MISFORTUNE SACRED, GENIUS DEAR,
REGARD THIS TOMB! WHERE COLLINS, HAPLESS CAME
SOLICITS KINDNESS, WITH A DOUBLE CLAIM.
THO' NATURE GAVE HIM, AND THO' SCIENCE TAUGHT,
THE FIRE OF FANCY, AND THE REACH OF THOUGHT,
SEVERELY DOOM'D TO PENURY'S EXTREME,
HE PASS'D IN MADD'NING PAIN LIFE'S FEVERISH DREAM;
WHILE RAYS OF GENIUS ONLY SERV'D TO SHEW
THE THICK'NING HORROR, AND EXALT HIS WOE.
YE WALLS THAT ECHOED TO HIS FRANTIC MOAN,
GUARD THE DUE RECORD OF THIS GRATEFUL STONE!
STRANGERS TO HIM, ENAMOUR'D OF HIS LAYS,
THIS FOND MEMORIAL OF HIS TALENTS RAISE;
FOR THIS THE ASHES OF A BARD REQUIRE,
WHO TOUCH'D THE TENDEREST NOTES OF PITY'S LYRE:
WHO IOIN'D PURE FAITH TO STRONG POETIC POWERS,
SOUGHT ON ONE BOOK HIS TROUBLED MIND TO REST,
AND RIGHTLY DEEM'D THE BOOK OF GOD THE BEST.

On the *memorial to the poet William Collins (1721–59) in Chichester Cathedral. He is buried elsewhere and is best remembered for his 'Ode to Evening' and 'How Sleep the Brave'. The lines above by William Hayley, another Chichester man (see also under Thomas RUSSELL), are inscribed on a marble monument (by Flaxman, 1795) which shows Collins reading the New Testament in that 'Book of God'. The poet had financial troubles towards the end of his life and became mentally ill.

CONRAD

~

SLEEP AFTER TOYLE, PORT AFTER STORMIE SEAS,
EASE AFTER WARRE, DEATH AFTER LIFE, DOES GREATLY PLEASE.

On the tombstone of the Polish-born novelist Joseph Conrad (1857–1924) in the cemetery of St Thomas's Roman Catholic Church, Canterbury. The inscription omits any mention of his novels. The quotation had been used by Conrad as the epigraph to his last complete work, *The Rover*, and is from Spenser, *The Faerie Queen* (Bk 1, c.IX.xl). The text is a popular one. It was also put, for example, on the bronze statue of Admiral Robert Blake (1599–1657) at Bridgewater, Somerset.

COOPER

~

IN LOVING REMEMBRANCE
OF
ALFRED JOPLING COOPER
(COMMODORE OF THE P.S.N. CO.)
WHO PASSED AWAY NOV:16TH 1923:
ON THE EVE OF HIS 76TH BIRTHDAY.

HE DISCOVERED THE SOLECTRIC THEORY WHICH
ENABLES US TO UNDERSTAND THE FORCES WHICH
ARE ACTING TO CAUSE NATURAL PHENOMENA,
EARTHQUAKES, VIOLENT STORMS, TORNADOES, ETC.

THE NEGATIVE CIRCLE OF INTENSE SOLECTRIC FORCE
HAS A RADIUS ON EARTH'S SURFACE OF 57½°:
THE POSITIVE CIRCLE HAS A RADIUS OF 88°.

HE PREDICTED THE VALPARAISO EARTHQUAKE
OF AUG:16:1906, AND HE ALSO PREDICTED IN THE
VALPARAISO "MERCURIO" OF OCT:10: AS CONFIRMED
IN PAGE 7 OF "THE TIMES" OF DEC:7:1918, THE
DAY AND HOUR OF THE CHILIAN EARTHQUAKE
OF DEC:4:1918, HENCE 8 WEEKS BEFORE ITS
OCCURRENCE.

A gloriously detailed epitaph on a *grave in the Roman Catholic Cemetery, Beaconsfield, Buckinghamshire.

COOPER
~

This perishable stone marks the grave of
DUFF COOPER
whose name is imperishable in the memory of
England and of those who loved him.
Attached to this world but free of its trammels
he loved the light and did not fear
the coming of the dark.

Written by his wife, Lady Diana Cooper, this epitaph is to be found on the tombstone in her family's mausoleum at Belvoir Castle, Leicestershire (she was a daughter of the 8th Duke of Rutland). No mention is made that the statesman, diplomat and writer (1890–1954) had been created 1st Viscount Norwich. Nor is that mentioned on the memorial tablet in the South Choir Aisle of Westminster Abbey.

COOPER
~

The left leg & part of the thigh
of Henry Hughes Cooper was
cut off & interr'd here
June 18th 1759.

'From a tombstone on the left of the church at Strata Florida, mid-Wales . . . He had encountered a stage coach in his village nearby of Pontrhydfendigaid, and after a suitable funeral the rest of him went to America' – drawn to my attention by Ms M. Pakenham-Walsh of Ystrad Meurig, Dyfed (1981).

COPENHAGEN

**HERE LIES
COPENHAGEN
THE CHARGER RIDDEN BY
THE DUKE OF WELLINGTON
THE ENTIRE DAY, AT THE
BATTLE OF WATERLOO**

BORN 1808 DIED 1836

**GOD'S HUMBLER INSTRUMENT, THOUGH MEANER CLAY,
SHOULD SHARE THE GLORY OF THAT GLORIOUS DAY.**

On the horse's *grave in the Ice House Paddock at Stratfield Saye House (Wellington's country home), where the chestnut stallion had spent a long retirement and was buried with full military honours.

CORBETT
~

Here rests a Woman Good without pretence,
Blest with plain Reason, & with sober Sence;
No Conquests she, but or'e her Self, desir'd,
No Arts essay'd, but not to be admir'd.
Passion & Pride were to her Soul unknown,
Convinc'd that Virtue only is our own.
So Unaffected, so compos'd a Mind;
So firm, yet soft; so strong, yet so refin'd,
Heav'n, as it's purest Gold, by Tortures try'd;
The Saint sustain'd it, but the Woman dy'd.

Alexander POPE's epitaph 'On Mrs. Corbet Who died of a Cancer in her Breast', published 1730, can still be found, exactly as above, on a *plaque on the north wall of St Margaret's Church, Westminster. Mrs Elizabeth Corbett died at Paris on 1 March 1724 'after a long and Painfull Sickness'.

Dr Johnson, in his essay on Pope's epitaphs, extolled it highly and pronounced it the best of the collection. Wordsworth in his essay 'Upon Epitaphs' grants that it *may* be the best of Pope's epitaphs, but then takes pains to demolish it: 'The Author forgets that it is a living creature that must interest us and not an intellectual existence.'

COURTENAY

~

What wee gave, wee have;
What wee spent, wee had;
What wee left, wee lost.

Epitaph on Edward Courtenay, Earl of Devon (*d* 1419) and his wife, at Tiverton. Compare 'That we spent, we had:/That we gave, we have:/That we left, we lost' – Epitaph of the Earl of Devonshire as quoted by SPENSER in 'The Shepherd's Calendar', ('May', l. 70). In a 'digression on the Earls of Devon' in *The Decline and Fall of the Roman Empire* (Chap. LXI, 1788), Edward Gibbon ascribes the epitaph to the Earl known as 'Edward the Blind' – 'After a grateful commemoration of the fifty-five years of union and happiness which he enjoyed with Mabel his wife, the good earl thus speaks from the tomb' – and adds, 'By some it is assigned to a Rivers Earl of Devon but the English denotes the XVth rather than the XIIIth century.'

Brewer compares Martial:

> *Extra fortunam est quidquid donatur amicis*
> *Quas dederis, solas semper habebis opes*

– and says there are similar epitaphs in many churches, e.g. St George's, Doncaster, which has: 'How now, who is here?/I, Robin of Doncastere/And Margaret, my feere./That I spent, that I had;/That I gave, that I have;/That I left, that I lost.'

Benham (1907) comments similarly: 'Epitaphs in almost identical words are found in many churches.' On a wayside monument on the A10 in Norfolk to L.H. Pratt of Ryston Hall and C.D. Prangley of Bexwell, two friends killed on the same day a year apart in the First World War, are the words: 'All that we had we gave.'

COWARD

~

'A TALENT TO AMUSE'.

Part of the *inscription on the memorial to Sir Noël Coward (1899–1973), the actor and writer, in the South Choir Aisle of Westminster Abbey. From the lyrics of his song 'If Love Were All' from the show *Bitter Sweet* (1932): 'I believe that since my life began/The most I've had is just/A talent to amuse . . .' The memorial was unveiled on 28 March 1984. Coward is buried where he died, in Jamaica.

CRADOCK

~

**HERE lie deposited
the Remains of
JOSEPH CRADOCK
Who was Born
the 17th of Novr 1689:
and Died
the 20th of April 1759**

**Enough, that Virtue fill'd the space between,
Prov'd, by the ends of being, to have been.**

Epitaph credited to Alexander POPE on a *memorial in St Dunstan's Chapel of what is now Leicester Cathedral. *Pope's Poetical Works* (1966) does not include the couplet. Cradock was a Leicestershire squire, musician and writer.

CRAGGS

~

**Statesman, yet Friend to Truth, of soul sincere,
In Action faithful, and in Honour clear.
Who broke no Promise, serv'd no private end,
Who gain'd no Title, and who lost no Friend,**

Ennobled by Himselfe, by All approv'd,
Prais'd, wept, and honour'd, by the Muse he lov'd.

Part of the *monument to James Craggs in Westminster Abbey, words written by Alexander POPE. Craggs (1686–1721) was a Privy Councillor and Secretary of State before the age of thirty-two but died three years later. In Pope's 'Epistle V To Addison' the above lines are reproduced except for the last, which appears as, 'And prais'd, unenvy'd, by the Muse he lov'd'.

CRAIK
~

A TRIBUTE TO WORK OF NOBLE AIM AND TO A VIRTUOUS LIFE

DINAH MARIA MULOCK – MRS CRAIK . . .

SHE WROTE JOHN HALIFAX GENTLEMAN

"Each in his place is fulfilling his day, and passing away, just as that Sun is passing. Only we know not whither he passes; while whither we go we know, and the Way we know, the same yesterday, today and for ever."

This epitaph is to be found on the marble neo-Renaissance memorial *tablet to the authoress 'Mrs Craik' (1826–87), in the South Transept of Tewkesbury Abbey. The most celebrated of her many novels is set in and around that town. Born in Stoke-on-Trent, Dinah Mulock married the publisher G.L. Craik, died in Bromley, Kent, and is buried in Keston churchyard. The *DNB*, while noting her successes, concludes, 'She was not a genius'.

The quotation comes from the final chapter of her most famous work, *John Halifax, Gentleman* (1857). Shortly before Halifax dies, Phineas Fletcher, the narrator, tells how new tenants of the old family house are going to turn it into an inn. Halifax says, 'What a shame! I wish I could prevent it. And yet, perhaps not . . . Ought we not rather to recognize and submit to the universal law of change? how each in his place is fulfilling his day, and passing away . . .'

CROSFIELD

~

Beneath this stone Tom Crosfield lies,
Who cares not now who laughs or cries.
He laughed when sober, and when mellow
Was a harum-scarum, heedless fellow.
He gave to none designed offence,
So Honi soit qui mal y pense.

Benham (1948) has this from 'Hendon Churchyard, London (His own epitaph) (19th century)'.

CRUIKSHANK

~

In Loving Memory
OF
GEORGE CRUIKSHANK
ARTIST
DESIGNER, ETCHER, PAINTER
BORN SEPT 27TH 1792
DIED FEB 1ST 1878
AT 263 HAMPSTEAD RD, LONDON
AGED 86

FOR 30 YEARS A TOTAL ABSTAINER
AND ARDENT PIONEER AND CHAMPION
BY PENCIL, WORD AND PEN,
OF UNIVERSAL ABSTINENCE
FROM INTOXICATING DRINKS . . .

THIS MONUMENT IS ERECTED
BY HIS AFFECTIONATE WIDOW
ELIZA CRUIKSHANK.

Memorial *tablet in Kensal Green Cemetery. Cruikshank only lay here for a few months before his remains were moved to the crypt of St

Paul's Cathedral, but his widow evidently felt it necessary to erect this stone which gives more space to his work as an abstainer than to his achievement as an artist. In his youth Cruikshank had been addicted to gin. In 1847 he had great success with a series of drawings called *The Bottle* which showed the degradation of a family through drink. He then became a total abstainer himself.

A bust and other ornaments have been removed from the memorial. The widow herself is apparently buried at this spot. Note the helpful address. Mrs Cruikshank also wrote and signed the *epitaph in St Paul's. It is on the wall near the floor slab covering his grave, refrains from mentioning his temperance work, and concludes:

> In Memory of his Genius and his Art
> His matchless Industry and worthy work
> For all his fellow-men. This Monument
> Is humbly placed within this sacred Fane
> By her who loved him best, his widowed wife.

CURZON
~

> Mary Victoria
> Lady Curzon of Kedleston
> **Born May 27 1870. Died July 18 1906**
> Perfect in love and loveliness
> Beauty was the least of her rare gifts
> God had endowed with like Graces
> Her mind and soul
> From illness all but unto death
> Restored, only to die.
> She was mourned in three continents,
> And by her dearest will be
> For ever unforgotten.

On a memorial shield within All Saints' church, Kedleston, Derbyshire, where she is buried and was later joined by her husband, George Nathaniel Curzon, 1st Marquess Curzon of Kedleston, the statesman and Viceroy of India. Mary was his first wife, a Chicago-born debutante who became Vicereine of India (hence the 'three continents'). Curzon wrote the words himself. After *his* death, his second wife went down into the vault to look at his coffin and came across a card, in his handwriting, on a ledge, saying: 'Reserved for the second Lady Curzon'.

The epitaph on Curzon's own tomb in the same church includes the words:

> In diverse offices and in many lands
> as explorer, writer, administrator and ruler of men,
> he sought to serve his country
> and add honour to an ancient name.

CUST
~

OF ALL SORTS ENCHANTINGLY BELOVED.

. . . HIGH HEART HIGH SPEECH HIGH DEEDS

Wording on the *tomb of 'Henry Iohn Cokayne Cust' in Belton Church, Leicestershire, which also bears a Greek inscription and the Latin motto *OMNI DITIOR AESTIMATIONE* ('richly endowed beyond all estimation'). Harry Cust (*b* 1861) was heir to the childless 3rd Earl Brownlow but predeceased him in 1917, without leaving any legitimate children. He was an MP, edited the *Pall Mall Gazette* and wrote poetry – the words 'High heart, high speech, high deeds 'mid honouring eyes' occur in his poem '*Non Nobis*' which is in the *Oxford Book of English Verse*.

Cust chiefly occupied himself, however, as a lover and seducer of everyone from housemaids to duchesses. Estimates of the children he sired outside wedlock range from half-a-dozen to twenty-seven and may have included Lady Diana Cooper because of his long liaison with Violet, Duchess of Rutland. Cust's widow Nina ('who designed, fashioned and now shares his tomb', according to a notice at one side) chose the possibly relevant words for his tomb and also had the name 'Cokayne', interestingly, put in place of the correct spelling 'Cockayne'.

My attention was drawn to this tomb by Angela Lambert's article in the *Independent* (20 July 1991) which also relates the scurrilous rumour that Cust may have been an ancestor, through one of her grandmothers, of Grantham's most famous daughter, Margaret Thatcher.

DAI
~

Deep in this grave lies lazy Dai
Waiting the last great trump on high.
If he's as fond of his grave as he's fond of his bed
He'll be the last man up when that roll call's said.

'From Nevern – translated from the Welsh' – quoted by Wynford
Vaughan-Thomas (1982).

DALE
~

Know posterity that on the 8th April in the year of grace
1737, the rambling remains of the aforesaid John Dale, in
the 86th year of his pilgrimage, laid upon his two wives.

This thing in life might raise some jealousy.
Here all three lie together lovingly,
But from embraces here no pleasure flows.
Alike are all their human joys and woes.

Here Sarah's chiding John no longer hears,
And old John's ramblings, Sarah no more fears.
A period's come to all their toylsome lives,
The good man's quiet, – still are both his wives.

Drawn to my attention in 1982 by O.C. Spencer, Burnham, Bucks.:
'From Bakewell churchyard [Derbyshire] . . . I have taken this from the
family scrap-book, the original [note] about a hundred and fifty years
old.'

DAWSON

~

Near this marble
Lies the Body of *Samuel Dawson*, Esquire, late Merchant,
Son and Grandson of two worthy Gentlemen who were (in
their turns) Ld. Mayors of this Ancient City, which
Honour He himself modestly declined
In every relation of Life worthy of Imitation.
A Father, Husband equally Prudent and Indulgent
A kind Master, an upright Magistrate
(in an extensive commission of the Peace)
An Englishman truly Honest
A subject truly loyal upon the best principles;
A Serious, Charitable, Devout Christian
who never by an unseasonable Gravity or Affectation was
irksome to the Freedom of Conversation, nor from too
Studious a desire to please would enter into any Indecent
Levities of Discourse, or Follies not becoming a
Gentleman.
He sought not a Hasty encrease of Riches by undue
means nor deemed it to be His
true interest, knowing by
a proper Estimation how to be just
to others, and to benefit Himself.
He continued thro' Life to encrease a fortune and
to make his Correspondents (in business) His friends.
His surviving widow, conscious of the many Virtues
of a Husband (to whom she was most Dear)
Caused this Monument to be Erected as a
Testimony of His merit, and Her lasting sense of it.
He died June the 24th, 1731

From a tablet in the church of St Martin-cum-Gregory, York – recorded
by Morrell (1948).

DAY-LEWIS

~

See LEWIS.

DEAN

~

B.27005 SAPPER
R.A.DEAN
CORPS OF
ROYAL CANADIAN ENGINEERS
22ND OCTOBER 1942 AGE 42

GONE BUT NOT FORGOTTEN.

On a *grave in Brookwood Military Cemetery, Surrey. I have selected this gravestone because of the simple line chosen, presumably by relatives, at the foot. It is one of the hundreds of graves maintained by the Commonwealth War Graves Commission – all of which have identical stones, placed symmetrically, producing an overwhelming impression by their number and order. Each grave has a cross upon it, some appropriate decoration (in this case the Canadian maple leaf), and – if so desired by relatives – a brief personal inscription or quotation.

'Gone But Not Forgotten' is a sentiment frequently displayed on tombstones, memorial notices and such, and used as the title of a Victorian print showing children at a grave. The earliest example of its use I have found (in a far from exhaustive search) is on the grave of William Thomas Till (*d* 1892, aged 28 years) in the churchyard of St Michael on Greenhill, Lichfield. Ludovic Kennedy in his autobiography *On My Way to the Club* (1989) suggests that it is an epitaph much found in the English graveyard at Poona, India.

DE GAULLE

~

NOW SHE IS LIKE THE OTHERS.

Jean Lacouture in his biography (1965) of Charles de Gaulle recorded the remark the future French President made at the graveside of his mentally-retarded daughter, Anne, who died shortly before her twentieth birthday in 1948: '*Maintenant, elle est comme les autres.*' At her birth, Yvonne de Gaulle had written to a friend: 'Charles and I would give everything, everything, health, fortune, promotion, career, if only Anne were a little girl like the others.' Hence, the particular nature of the later, poignant remark.

DIAS

~

Here lies the body of *Martha Dias*,
Who was always uneasy, and not over pious.
She liv'd to the age of threescore and ten,
And gave that to the worms she refus'd to the men.

Collection (1806) has this from 'Shrewsbury church-yard'.

DIGBY

~

Under this Tomb the Matchless Digby lyes,
Digby the Great, the Valiant, and the Wise;
This Age's Wonder, for his Noble Parts,
Skill'd in six Tongues, and learn'd in all the Arts;
Born on the day he Died, th'Eleven OF JUNE,
And that day bravely fought at SCANDEROON.
It's Rare, that one and the same day should be
His Day Of Birth, of Death, of Victory!

On Sir Kenelm Digby (1603–65), author, naval commander and
diplomatist, an epitaph composed by 'R. Farrar'. It is mentioned in
Aubrey and said to have been found in Christ Church, Newgate Street,
London, to which he had been a great benefactor but of which only the
steeple now survives. However, the *DNB* notes that Richard Ferrar
merely wrote 'verses on his death' and that, by his will, Digby 'directed
that he should be buried at the side of his wife in Christ Church,
Newgate, and that no mention on him should be made on the tomb.' He
was the elder of two sons of Sir Everard Digby who was executed for his
part in the Gunpowder Plot. After various court appointments, Kenelm
became a privateer and successfully captured French and Dutch ships.
Scanderoon near Zante/Zakinthos in the Ionian Sea was the scene of
Kenelm Digby's victory over French and Venetian ships on 10/11 June
1628.

DISRAELI

~

From the *monument on the north side of the chancel of St Michael and All Angels' church, Hughenden, Buckinghamshire. 'It was penned, I believe, by an illustrious hand' – G.W.E. Russell, *Collections and Recollections* (1898). Indeed, Queen VICTORIA's gesture is unique in that it is the only example of a memorial in a parish church raised by a reigning sovereign to one of her subjects. Disraeli, who served Victoria as Prime Minister, was born in 1804 and died in 1881. He is buried in the Disraeli family tomb below the east window in the churchyard. There the inscription gives more prominence to his wife, Mary-Anne, who predeceased him.

There is a memorial statue of Disraeli in Westminster Abbey.

DODGSON

~

Part of the *gravestone of the author of *Alice's Adventures in Wonderland* (1965), to be found in Guildford Cemetery, Surrey. The texts are from the Lord's Prayer and John 12:26. In Poets' Corner, Westminster Abbey, Dodgson/Carroll is remembered by a *stone (unveiled 17 December 1982) bearing the line, 'Is all our Life, then, but a dream?' from the introductory poem to his *Sylvie and Bruno*. Compare the concluding line of the end-poem to *Through the Looking Glass*: 'Life, what is it but a dream?'

DONNE
~

Reader, I am to let thee know,
Donne's body only lies below;
For could the grave his soul comprise,
Earth would be richer than the skies.

Epitaph on the grave of John Donne in St Paul's Cathedral, London, according to Wright (1972). However, I have only been able to find the sober, Latin text which accompanies the extraordinary effigy there of Donne wearing his shroud. This was the only monument at St Paul's to survive intact the Great Fire of London in 1666. The poet was Dean of St Paul's and died in 1631.

DOWNE
~

A real unpretending and almost unconscious good sense and
a firm desire to act right on all occasions to the best
of her judgment were her most distinguished
characteristics, hereditary personal grace of both form
and face which even in age had not disappeared completes
her picture. For her character and other particulars see
the Gentleman's Magazine for May, 1812.

Part of the tablet in York Minster to Viscountess Downe who died in 1812. According to Morrell (1948), these words are preceded by an account of her ancestry and family connections.

As for the last sentence, compare, from Mackae (?1910): 'Here lie several of the Stows,/Particulars the last day will disclose'; and, from Reder (1969), in Tetbury church, Gloucestershire: 'Here lie several of the Saunderses of this Parish./Further particulars the last day will disclose./ Amen.' The eighteenth-century epitaph on Anne Thursby, wife of John Harvey Thursby, on the south wall of Abington parish church, Northampton, includes: 'What Sort of Woman She Was/The Last Day Will Determine.'

DOYLE
~

**STEEL TRUE
BLADE STRAIGHT
ARTHUR CONAN DOYLE
KNIGHT
PATRIOT, PHYSICIAN & MAN OF LETTERS
22 MAY 1859 – 7 JULY 1930
AND HIS BELOVED, HIS WIFE
JEAN CONAN DOYLE
REUNITED 27 JUNE 1940**

On the *grave of the creator of Sherlock Holmes in All Saints' Churchyard, Minstead, Hampshire. The quotation, rather curiously, comes from Robert Louis STEVENSON's poem 'My Wife' in *Songs of Travel* (1896): 'Steel-true and blade-straight/The great artificer/Made my mate.' Presumably, the widow chose the epitaph.

DUCROW
~

**WITHIN THIS TOMB
ERECTED BY GENIUS FOR THE RECEPTION
OF ITS OWN REMAINS ARE DEPOSITED THOSE OF
ANDREW DUCROW**

MANY YEARS LESSEE OF THE ROYAL AMPHITHEATRE,
LONDON,
WHOSE DEATH DEPRIVED THE ARTS AND SCIENCES
OF AN EMINENT PROFESSOR AND LIBERAL PATRON,
HIS FAMILY OF AN AFFECTIONATE HUSBAND AND FATHER,
THE WORLD OF AN UPRIGHT MAN . . .

AND TO COMMEMORATE SUCH VIRTUES
HIS AFFLICTED WIDOW HAS ERECTED
THIS TRIBUTE.

Ducrow (1798–1842) has been called 'one of the greatest trick-horse riders and pantomime actors of his day' and his equestrian performances are celebrated in the *DNB*. A ringmaster's hat and gloves are carved at the base of the elaborate Egyptian-style *tomb to be found in Kensal Green Cemetery, London. One learns that, appropriately, vast crowds attended his funeral. One wonders, though, who wrote the elaborate text? Was it the widow – or did the showman himself compose it before he died?

DU MAURIER
~

A LITTLE TRUST THAT WHEN WE DIE
WE REAP OUR SOWING, AND SO – GOODBYE.

George Du Maurier (1834-96), novelist and *Punch* illustrator, was the author of *Trilby* whence these lines come. According to Benham they are inscribed on his memorial tablet in the churchyard of St John's, Church Row, Hampstead.

DU VALL
~

Here lies Du Vall: Reader, if male thou art,
Look to thy Purse; if Female to thy heart.
Much havoc has he made of both; for all
Men he made stand, and women he made fall.

The second conqueror of the Norman race,
Knights to his arms did yield, and Ladies to his face,
Old Tyburn's glory; England's illustrious thief,
Du Vall, the Ladies' joy; Du Vall, the Ladies' grief.

Verse said to have been used for the inscription on the tombstone of the
French-born highwayman, Claude du Vall (1643–70) in St Paul's Church,
Covent Garden, London. The grave is thought to be located in the centre
aisle under a stone with the first two lines as epitaph, though nothing is
now visible.

Du Vall was handsome, had a legendary way with women, and was
hanged at Tyburn. His admirers gave him a magnificent funeral and this
tombstone, which is recorded in *Collection* (1806).

DYER
~

My dearest dust, could not thy hasty day
Afford thy drowsy patience leave to stay
One hour longer: so that we might either
Sit up, or go to bed together?
But since thy finished labor hath possest
Thy weary limbs with early rest,
Enjoy it sweetly: and thy widow bride
Shall soon repose her by thy slumbering side.
Whose business, now, is only to prepare
My nightly dress, and call to prayer:
Mine eyes wax heavy and the day grows old.
The dew falls thick, my blood grows cold.
Draw, draw the closed curtains: and make room:
My dear, my dearest dust; I come, I come.

On the alabaster monument of Sir William Dyer (*d* 1641) in the church
of St Denis at Colmworth, Bedfordshire, and written by his widow
Catherine. This text is from *Collection* (1806).

EDWARDS

~

JOHN EDWARDS WHO PERISHED IN A FIRE 1904.
NONE COULD HOLD A CANDLE TO HIM.

An epitaph from the burial ground near the present Anglican Cathedral in Liverpool. Recalled by Beryl Bainbridge on *Quote . . . Unquote*, BBC Radio, 29 June 1988. She said that another in the same place, on a certain 'G. Wild', bore the words, 'Not worth remembering'.

ELGINBRODDE

~

Here lie I, Martin Elginbrodde:
Have mercy o' my soul, Lord God,
As I wad do, were I Lord God
And ye were Martin Elginbrodde.

'Aberdeen Churchyard. From George Macdonald, *David Elginbrod*, 1862, ch. 13' (Bartlett, 1968); *Collection* (1806) recorded it, probably wrongly, as: 'Here lies old JOHN HILDIBROAD,/Have mercy upon him GOOD GOD;/As he would do, if he was GOD,/And thou wert old JOHN HILDIBROAD'; Grigson (1977) has, 'Said to come from a tombstone in St Giles's churchyard, Edinburgh'.

ELIOT

~

"OF THOSE IMMORTAL DEAD WHO LIVE AGAIN
IN MINDS MADE BETTER BY THEIR PRESENCE"

HERE LIES THE BODY
OF
'GEORGE ELIOT'
MARY ANN CROSS.

On the obelisk-shaped *monument over the grave of the novelist (née Evans) (1819–1880) in Highgate Cemetery (East), London. Although her books are not mentioned, at least her pen-name is. The quotation is from one of her poems, 'Oh May I Join the Choir Invisible' which was sung by the graveside at her funeral.

To the rear of George Eliot's grave, and almost touching it, is that of George Henry Lewes who lived with her until his death in 1878. Shortly before she died, still lamenting the loss of Lewes, she married J.W. Cross, who presumably permitted the close proximity of the graves of the former lovers.

The novelist is also commemorated on a floor *slab in Poets' Corner, Westminster Abbey, which bears the quotation: 'The first condition of human goodness is something to love; the second something to reverence.' This is a quotation from Chapter 10 of her *Scenes of Clerical Life*. 'It is a quotation of which we are particularly fond,' says the Secretary of the George Eliot Fellowship, which was responsible for the worldwide appeal for funds to place the memorial stone in 1980, 'and it describes, we feel, George Eliot's own philosophy.'

ELIOT

~

Remember Thomas Stearns Eliot, poet

. . . In my beginning is my end. In my end is my beginning.

Part of the memorial tablet to the American-born poet T.S. Eliot (1888–1965) in St Michael's Church, East Coker, Somerset, where he is buried. His ancestors had gone to America from there in the seventeenth century and the quotation is taken from 'East Coker' in Eliot's *Four Quartets*. He is also commemorated by a stone in Poets' Corner, Westminster Abbey (unveiled 4 January 1967), which bears the quotation: 'The communication/Of the dead is tongued with fire beyond/the language of the living' (from 'Little Gidding' in *Four Quartets*).

ELPHINSTONE
~

Here lieth Martin Elphinstone
Who with his sword did cut in sunder
The daughter of Sir Harry Crispe
who did his daughter marry.

She was fat and fulsome,
But men will sometimes
Eat bacon with their beans
And love the fat as well as lean.

Said to come from Alnwick, Northumberland – and difficult to understand. Text from Wright (1972).

ENGLISH CRICKET
~

IN AFFECTIONATE REMEMBRANCE
of
ENGLISH CRICKET
Which died at the Oval,
on
29th August, 1882.
Deeply lamented by a large circle
of sorrowing friends and acquaintances.
R.I.P.
N.B. – The body will be cremated, and the
ashes taken to Australia.

The 'trophy' played for in Test cricket matches between England and Australia is known as 'the Ashes'. Whichever side wins is said to have 'retained' or 'regained the Ashes'. In fact, whichever side wins, the trophy always resides in the pavilion at Lord's cricket ground in London. However, it was allowed to be taken to Australia during the bicentennial celebrations in 1988. The name dates back to 1882 when an Australian team won for the first time in England – by seven runs in an exciting game. A group of supporters of the English team inserted the above mock death notice in the *Sporting Times*. The following winter, when England defeated Australia and retrieved its honour, a group of ladies in Melbourne burned straw and placed the ashes in a small urn and then presented it – saying that it contained the ashes of the stumps and bails – to the English captain who duly carried it back to Lord's.

EVELYN
~

Here lies the Body
of JOHN EVELYN Esq.
of this place second son
of RICHARD EVELYN Esq.
who having served ye Publick
in several employments, of which that
of Com'issioner of ye Privy Seal in ye
Reign of K. James ye 2d was most
Honourable: & perpetuated his fame
by far more lasting Monuments than
those of Stone, or Brass, his Learned
& usefull works fell asleep ye 27th day
of February 1705/6 being ye 86th Year
of his age in a full hope of glorious
resurrection thro' faith in Jesus Christ.
Living in an age of extraordinary
events, and revolutions he learn't
(as himself asserted) this truth
which pursuant to his intention
is here declared
That all is vanity wch is not honest,
& that there's no solid Wisdom
but in real Piety . . .

Part of the *inscription written on the top of the diarist John Evelyn's coffin-shaped tomb in the Evelyn Chapel of St John's Church, Wotton, Surrey. The inscription captures quite well the personality of a man of whom his fellow-diarist, Samuel Pepys, said: 'In fine a most excellent person he is and must be allowed a little for a little coinceitedness; but he may well be so, being a man so much above others'; and of whom Virgina Woolf wrote: 'He was, we cannot help suspecting, something of a bore, a little censorious, a little patronizing, a little too sure of his own merits, and a little obtuse to those of other people.'

EVEREST
~

Erected in Memory
of
ELIZABETH ANNE EVEREST
who died 3rd July 1895
Aged 62
by
WINSTON SPENCER CHURCHILL
JACK SPENCER CHURCHILL.

From the City of London Cemetery, Manor Park, London E12. This is a touching example of the otherwise questionable habit of the donor of a gravestone putting his name as prominently as that of the buried. 'Everest' was Winston Churchill's boyhood nanny, to whom he was devoted. In *My Early Life* (1930), he wrote of her death: 'She had lived such an innocent and loving life of service to others and held such a simple faith, that she had no fears at all, and did not seem to mind very much. She had been my dearest and most intimate friend during the whole of the twenty years I had lived.' He also quotes Edward Gibbon's tribute to *his* nurse from the *Autobiography*: 'If there be any, as I trust there are some, who rejoice that I live, to that dear and excellent woman their gratitude is due.' Churchill adds, 'I thought of Mrs Everest; and it shall be her epitaph.'

According to Randolph Churchill's biography of his father (Vol.1), 'For many years afterwards he paid an annual sum to the local florist for the upkeep of the grave.'

EYRE

~

This marble is sacred to the memory of Chas. Eyre, a youth of great promise; who an only son, was deservedly beloved by his parents: to wit Geo. & Marguerite (Eyre). A too early fate snatched him out of this life when not born quite 10 Yrs. He was one of the students in the college of Boulogne-sur-Mer, in France, where he eminently distinguished himself in his studies, & endeared himself to his fellow collegeans.

He died the 8th of the month of Jan. AD 1869, oppressed by a deadly fever. His relicks, not his soul, are buried in the vault of Chas. Eyre his ancestor, outside this Church. Charlie is not dead: the darling is now gone to school, where he will learn forever goodness. Jesus himself is his father, brother & best guide. Christ rules the blessed in heaven by love alone, in that tranquil region the ever dear one lives: the guardian angel holds his tender hands.
Death has not taken him: he whom we say is snatched away by gloomy fate, still lives, ever freed from pollution's stain.
A friend, Rd. Wilson D.D. of Cambridge composed this inscription.
The principal of the college has declared, that Charlie has left at the college the remembrance of a beautiful intelligence & Excellent heart. The principal wished & Advised that the memory of a youth so excellent & ingenuous & his intelligence should be especially kept in remembrance. The weeping heavily distracted father has taken care that this monument should be erected.

Charlie was born 24th Jan. 1859; died of typhus fever; & he learned to speak French in 7 months, fluently; he possessed a noble mind, and loved truthfulness: indeed, his father ever abominating guile, taught him sincerity. He intended, God willing, when he had finished his education in France, that he should consecutively enter

85

universities in Germany & Italy: & then, if he
pleased, should take a degree in an English
university: but alas his father's hopes have been
suddenly blasted: this affliction is as appalling, as
any ever recorded. By universal law, death is
decreed: but the time may be strayed by the
intercessory prayer of parents; but here that was
wanting.

On three panels of the large chest *tomb of Charlie Eyre (who died on 8 January 1869, aged 9), by the south wall of the churchyard of St Mary's, Ewelme, Oxfordshire. The original is entirely in capital letters. A version in Latin and French can be found inside the church on a tablet of the north wall of the nave. The Revd Peter Renshaw, in *A Guide to the Memorials and Brasses of Ewelme Church* (1987), adds this footnote reminiscent of Victorian melodrama to the rambling epitaph: 'George Eyre, single and lonely, [had] advertised in the newspapers for a wife. A young French girl, Marguerite, wrote at once accepting the offer. However, when she arrived at Ewelme she felt she had been deceived: by the man himself and by the circumstances in which he lived. Moreover, Eyre proved to be unreasonably and cruelly jealous, keeping her locked in her room for days on end sustained only by bread and water (so runs the village legend). They had one son, Charlie, who died of Typhus fever . . . Shortly afterwards, [Marguerite] in a fit of melancholy ended her own life by taking poison. Her place of burial is not known but it was suspected at the time that Eyre had dug a grave for her corpse in his own garden. As this disagreeable old man grew more eccentric he was more disliked. It is said that the youth of the village used to serenade him outside his house at night "with rough music".'

Near to the indoors version of the epitaph is a tablet to this father: 'George Eyre, solicitor, who died 1885 aged 81.' He appears to have been buried in the same grave as his son. The epitaph to Charlie was recut in 1934.

FAIRBANKS

~

GOOD-NIGHT, SWEET PRINCE,
AND FLIGHTS OF ANGELS SING THEE TO THY REST.

On the grave of Douglas Fairbanks (1883–1939), the actor of swashbuckling film roles, chiefly in the silent cinema. The lines are Horatio's about the Prince from Shakespeare's *Hamlet* (V.ii.364). 'Inscribed on the white marble sarcophagus at the head of a 125-foot lagoon in Hollywood Cemetery' – Barnaby Conrad, *Famous Last Words* (1961).

FIDO

~

To the memory of
SIGNOR FIDO,
An Italian of good extraction,
Who came into England,
Not to *bite* us, like most of his countrymen,
But to gain an honest livelihood.
He *hunted* not after fame,
Yet acquired it.
Regardless of the praise of his friends,
But most sensible of their love.
Tho' he liv'd among the great,
He neither learnt nor flattered any vice.
He was no bigot,
Tho' he doubted of none of the thirty-nine articles:
And if to follow nature,
And to respect the laws of society
Be philosophy,
He was a perfect philosopher,
A faithful friend,
An agreeable companion,
A loving husband,
And, tho' an Italian,
Was distinguished by a numerous offspring,
All which he liv'd to see take good *courses*.
In his old age he retir'd
To the house of a clergyman in the country,
Where he finish'd his *earthly race*.

And died an honour and an example to the
whole species.
Reader,
This stone is guiltless of flattery;
For he, to whom it was incrib'd,
Was not a man,
But a ——————— GREYHOUND.

Collection (1806) has this from 'Stow Gardens' – does this mean the
gardens of Stowe, Buckinghamshire?

FIELDS
~

ON THE WHOLE I'D RATHER BE IN PHILADELPHIA.

What W.C. Fields (1880–1946), the American comedian, actually
submitted as a suggested epitaph, when asked to do so by *Vanity Fair*
magazine in 1925, was: 'Here lies W.C. Fields. I would rather be living in
Philadelphia.' There had apparently been an earlier expression, 'Sooner
dead than in Philadelphia'. To Fields is also attributed the snubbing
remark, 'I went to Philadelphia and found it was closed.' There is no
reference to the city on his actual tombstone which simply bears his
name and dates. Two years after his death he lay in an unmarked grave
at Forest Lawn (Hollywood), 'the pretentious burial park that he
frequently derided', according to a biographer.

FITZHARRIS
~

SACRED TO THE MEMORY OF HARRIET SUSAN,
VISCOUNTESS FITZHARRIS,
DAUGHTER OF FRANCIS BATEMAN DASHWOOD ESQ. OF
WELL VALE IN THE COUNTY OF LINCOLN,

AND WIFE OF JAMES EDWARD VISCOUNT FITZHARRIS,
    OF HERON COURT IN THIS PARISH,
WHICH SHE DEPARTED THIS LIFE ON MONDAY NIGHT
    SEPTEMBER 4TH 1815,
IN THE THIRTY SECOND YEAR OF HER AGE.

GIFTED BY NATURE WITH UNCOMMON BEAUTY OF
    PERSON AND COUNTENANCE,
POSSESSING MANNERS EQUALLY DIGNIFIED AND
    ENGAGING,
SHE NEVER ALLOWED HERSELF TO BE INFLUENCED BY
    THE FLATTERIES AND ALLUREMENTS
OF THE WORLD, BUT ENJOYED WITH RATIONAL
    CHEERFULNESS THOSE HOURS WHICH SHE
COULD SPARE FROM THE PERFORMANCE OF HER
    DOMESTIC DUTIES.
THE CARE AND EDUCATION OF HER CHILDREN WERE
    HER DARLING OBJECTS,
ON THEM SHE EQUALLY BESTOWED THE VIGILANT
    FONDNESS OF A MOTHER, AND THE
SUCCESSFUL EFFORTS OF A WELL CULTIVATED MIND:
WHILE ALL WHO SHARED HER LOVE, AND ATTACHMENT
    EXPERIENCED IN THE VARIOUS
RELATIONS OF A WIFE, A DAUGHTER, A SISTER, AND A
    FRIEND, UNCEASING PROOFS
OF THE AMIABLE AND ENDEARING QUALITIES OF HER
    DISPOSITION.
SO DEEPLY IMPRESSED WITH THE FEELINGS AND
    CONFIDENCE OF A TRUE CHRISTIAN
WAS THIS PIOUS AND EXCELLENT WOMAN:
SO FULLY PREPARED WAS SHE AT ALL TIMES FOR
    ANOTHER WORLD, THAT THE SUDDEN AND
UNEXPECTED APPROACH OF DEATH COULD NOT
    DISTURB THE SWEET SERENITY OF HER MIND,
NOR DID ONE REPINING WORD ESCAPE HER THRO'
    FOURTEEN DAYS OF ACUTE SUFFERING,
BUT AWAITING HER END WITH THE UTMOST
    COMPOSURE AND RESIGNATION, SHE CALMLY GAVE
    UP
HER SOUL INTO THE HANDS OF HER CREATOR,
    QUITTING ALL SHE LOVED WITH THE WORDS,
"I HAVE HAD MY FULL SHARE OF HAPPINESS IN THIS
    WORLD."

HER REMAINS LIE INTERRED IN THE CATHEDRAL
   CHURCH OF SALISBURY,
BUT HER AFFLICTED HUSBAND HAS RAISED THIS
   MARBLE TO HER MEMORY, PERSUADED THAT
WHERE SHE WAS BEST KNOWN THERE WOULD HER
   MANY VIRTUES LONGEST LIVE
IN THE RECOLLECTION OF HER FRIENDS AND
   NEIGHBOURS.

On the *memorial in the Priory Church, Christchurch, Hampshire. A
sculpture (by John Flaxman) of the seated Viscountess, holding a baby
and a book, and with two children standing close to her knees, is to be
found above this long inscription. She married the Viscount in 1806. He
was MP for Helston and subsequently Governor of the Isle of Wight,
succeeding his father and becoming the 2nd Earl Malmesbury. Their
various children – some of whom held public office – are listed on
another panel.

FLEMING

~

He travelled widely in far places:
Wrote, and was widely read.
Soldiered, saw some of danger's faces,
Came home to Nettlebed.

The squire lies here, his journeys ended –
Dust, and a name on a stone –
Content, amid the lands he tended
To keep this rendezvous alone.

Verse written for his *gravestone by Peter Fleming, the travel writer, who
died 18 August 1971, aged 65. Signed with the initials 'RPF', it is to be
found in the churchyard of St Bartholomew, Nettlebed, Oxfordshire,
next to the *grave of his widow, Dame Celia Johnson (1908–82) – 'A *fine*
actress & beloved mother'.

FLETCHER

~

Reader!
If thou hast a heart fam'd for
Tenderness and Pity, Contemplate this Spot.
In which are deposited the Remains
of a Young Lady, whose artless Beauty,
innocence of Mind and gentle Manners,
once obtained her the Love and
Esteem of all who knew her, But when
Nerves were too delicately spun to
bear the rude Shakes and Jostlings
which we meet with in this transitory
World, Nature gave way; She sunk
and died a Martyr to Excessive Sensibility.
Mrs SARAH FLETCHER
Wife of Captain FLETCHER,
departed this Life at the Village
of Clifton, on the 7 of June 1799.
In the 29 Year of her Age.
May her Soul meet that Peace in
Heaven which this Earth denied her.

One of the most delightful epitaphs of all — to be found on a floor *slab in Dorchester Abbey, Oxfordshire. The 'Clifton' presumably refers to the nearby village of Clifton Hampden.

FOOTE

~

HERE LIES ONE FOOTE, WHOSE DEATH MAY THOUSANDS SAVE,
FOR DEATH HAS NOW ONE FOOT WITHIN THE GRAVE.

A punning epitaph on Samuel Foote (1720–77), actor and dramatist, famous for his mimicry and for making Samuel Johnson laugh against his will. He was, however, buried in Westminster Abbey cloister by torchlight and in an unmarked grave. This epitaph is recorded in *Collection* (1806). Another, playing upon his role as mimic, was: 'Foote from his earthly stage, alas! is hurled;/Death took him off, who took off all the world.'

To have one foot in the grave means to be near death. The earliest citation in the *OED2* is from Burton's *Anatomy of Melancholy* (1621). Swift uses the phrase in connection with the immortal Struldbruggs of Laputa (1721). However, long before this, in 1509, Barclay was writing in *Ship of Fools*, 'Thy grave is open, thy one fote in the pyt', and Bartlett provides a translation of Plutarch's *Morals: Of the Training of Children* which goes, 'An old doting fool, with one foot already in the grave.'

FORD
~

AT LAST I GET TOP BILLING.

Wallace Ford (1897–1966) was a British actor who went to Hollywood in the early 1930s. After a number of 'semi-leads', Ford was condemned to a succession of supporting roles in Hollywood films and decided that his gravestone epitaph should read, 'At last – I get top billing.' This inscription was duly put on his grave. Then along came a graffiti artist and chalked above it, 'Clark Gable and Myrna Loy supported by...' Probably apocryphal, and I have no idea what is actually written on his grave.

FORMBY
~

IN LOVING REMEMBRANCE
OF
GEORGE FORMBY
(COMEDIAN)
DIED 8TH FEBRUARY 1921
AGED 45 YEARS
"After Life's Fitful Fever –
He Sleeps Well."

ALSO GEORGE FORMBY O.B.E.
SON OF THE ABOVE
WHO DIED 6TH MARCH 1961,
AGED 56 YEARS.
"A Tradition Nobly Upheld."

ALSO ELIZA ANN, DEVOTED WIFE OF GEORGE (SNR)
WHO DIED 31ST JULY 1981
AGED 102 YEARS.

On the splendid *grave of father and son entertainers, both called George Formby, in the main cemetery at Warrington. The father is the principal occupant of the grave and is represented by a medallion-type portrait flanked by theatrical curtains of stone. The first quotation, from Shakespeare, *Macbeth* (III.ii.23) – what Macbeth says of the murdered King Duncan – has a certain relevance to the life of George Formby Snr. He was a music-hall comedian who invented the Wigan Pier joke and one of his catchphrases was 'Coughin' well tonight' – often tragically true. He had a convulsive cough, the result of a tubercular condition which eventually killed him. His son was the more famous of the two and became hugely popular from the 1930s onwards for his grinning gormlessness (in several cheap film comedies) and for his slightly rude songs sung to ukelele accompaniment. George Jnr's wife, Beryl, who managed him and had a fearsome reputation for keeping him in his place, predeceased him in 1960 and is, perhaps pointedly, not buried in the tomb. His mother, who is, was clearly formidable, too, if only in her own great age at death.

At the foot of the grave is a stone bearing the words:

> Your songs are ended
> But the melodies linger on.
> Mother and Louie.

(The signatories are Eliza and her daughter, George Jnr's sister, Mrs Louisa De Hailes.) This is an adaptation of Irving Berlin's 1927 song title 'The Song Is Ended (But the Melody Lingers On)' and is presumably addressed to George Jnr rather than his father (who was not noted for his songs, although he did recite).

FRANKLIN
~

The body
of Benjamin Franklin, printer,
(Like the cover of an old book,
Its contents worn out,
And stript of its lettering and gilding)
Lies here, food for worms!
Yet the work itself shall not be lost,
For it will, as he believed, appear once more
In a new
And more beautiful edition,
Corrected and amended
By its Author!

An epitaph for himself suggested by the American scientist, diplomat and writer (1706-90), and written *c* 1728. Andrews (1899) compares it to other similarly punning printers' epitaphs. Benham quotes the Revd Joseph Capen (19th century), 'Lines on Mr John Foster': 'Yet at the resurrection we shall see/A fair edition, and of matchless worth,/Free from erratas, new in heaven set forth.' Benham also suggests that the idea was borrowed from the Revd Benjamin Woodbridge, chaplain to Charles II, who wrote these 'Lines of John Cotton' (1652): 'O what a monument of glorious worth,/When in a new edition he comes forth,/Without erratas, may we think he'll be/In leaves and covers of eternity!'

In fact, Franklin lies with his wife under a simple inscription in Christ Church, Philadelphia: 'Benjamin and Deborah Franklin 1790'.

FRANKLIN
~

O YE FROST AND COLD, O YE ICE AND SNOW
BLESS YE THE LORD PRAISE HIM AND MAGNIFY HIM FOR
   EVER.

NOT HERE! THE WHITE NORTH HAS THY BONES; AND
   THOU, HEROIC SAILOR-SOUL,
ART PASSING ON THINE HAPPIER VOYAGE NOW
   TOWARD NO EARTHLY POLE.

Part of the *inscription on the monument to the Arctic explorer Sir John Franklin (1786–1847) in the Chapel of St John the Evangelist, Westminster Abbey. The first two lines come from the *Benedicite* and the rest is by Tennyson (which he considered to be his best epitaph). Franklin was lost with all his crew when completing the discovery of the North-West Passage. The public reaction to the event has been compared to that surrounding the loss of Captain SCOTT over half a century later. Franklin is also commemorated by a statue in Waterloo Place, London.

FRED

~

Here lies Fred,
Who was alive and is dead:
Had it been his father,
I had much rather;
Had it been his brother,
Still better than another;
Had it been his sister
No one would have missed her;
Had it been the whole generation,
Still better for the nation:
But since 'tis only Fred,
Who was alive and is dead, –
There's no more to be said.

Epitaph on Frederick Louis, Prince of Wales (1707–1751), eldest son of George II and father of George III, quoted by Horace Walpole in an appendix to his *Memoirs of George II* (1847). Frederick quarrelled with his father and was banished from court.

Compare Frobisher (?1790), 'On a tombstone in Cornwall: Here lies honest Ned,/Because he is dead./Had it been his father . . .'

Collection (1806) has from 'a headstone in the church-yard of Storrington in the County of Sussex: Here lies the body of Edward Hide;/We laid him here because he died./We had rather it had been his father./If it had been his sister,/We should not have miss'd her./But since 'tis honest Ned/No more shall be said...' Haining (1973) has a version beginning 'Here lies HONEST NED . . .' from 'Kirkby Stephen parish church, Westmorland'.

FROHMAN

~

FOR IT IS NOT RIGHT THAT IN A HOUSE THE MUSES HAUNT MOURNING SHOULD DWELL – SUCH THINGS BEFIT US NOT.

On the *monument near the church (but outside the churchyard) of All Saints', Marlow, Buckinghamshire, to Charles Frohman (1860-1915), an influential theatrical producer in Britain and America. He it was who first presented J.M. Barrie's *Peter Pan*. He went down on the *Lusitania*. The monument shows a nude marble maiden, and the inscription runs round the base. J. Camp in *Portrait of Buckinghamshire* (1972) comments: 'His memorial is a graceful tribute to the female form, and a reminder of the pleasure his stage presentations gave to so many on both sides of the Atlantic in late Victorian and Edwardian days.' The inscription is a bit of a puzzle but does not appear to be a quotation. Frohman's body was recovered from the sea and a funeral was held for him in New York (according to a 1916 biography by I.F. Marcosson and D. Frohman). His 'last words' were reported by a survivor from the *Lusitania* as having been 'Why fear death? It is the most beautiful adventure of life' – alluding to Peter Pan's 'To die will be an awfully big adventure'.

FULLER

~

HERE LIES FULLER'S EARTH.

Epitaph suggested by himself for the grave of Thomas Fuller (1608–61), the church historian and author of *The History of the Worthies of England*. T. Webb in *A New Select Collection of Epitaphs* (1775) has it, as does Frobisher (?1790). Fuller was buried in the church of which he had been rector, at Cranford, West London, but which no longer survives. His actual epitaph was a sober Latin text.

GARFIELD

~

Life's race well run,
Life's work well done,
Life's victory won,
   Now cometh rest.

According to Benham (1907), these lines are inscribed on the tomb of President Garfield (1831–81), and come from the 'Funeral Ode on President Garfield' by Edward Hazen Parker, MD (1823–1896). Garfield was assassinated and is buried in Lakeview Cemetery, Cleveland, Ohio.

GARRICK

~

TO PAINT FAIR NATURE, BY DIVINE COMMAND,
HER MAGIC PENCIL IN HIS GLOWING HAND,
A SHAKESPEARE ROSE; THEN, TO EXPAND HIS FAME
WIDE O'ER THIS BREATHING WORLD, A GARRICK CAME:
THOUGH SUNK IN DEATH, THE FORM THE POET DREW
THE ACTOR'S GENIUS BADE THEM BREATHE ANEW;
THOUGH LIKE THE BARD HIMSELF, IN NIGHT THEY LAY,
IMMORTAL GARRICK CALL'D THEM BACK TO DAY;
AND TILL ETERNITY WITH POWER SUBLIME,
SHALL MARK THE MORTAL HOUR OF HOARY TIME,
SHAKESPEARE & GARRICK, LIKE TWIN STARS SHALL
   SHINE,
AND EARTH IRRADIATE WITH BEAMS DIVINE.

This *epitaph is to be found in Poets' Corner, Westminster Abbey, on a wall plaque separate from the grave of David Garrick (1716–79), the consummate actor of his day. The monument was erected in 1797 by his old friend Albany Wallis and the verse is signed 'S. I[?]. Pratt'.

   In 1774, before Garrick's death, Oliver Goldsmith had provided a brief epitaph in *Retaliation*:

Here lies David Garrick, describe me, who can,
An abridgement of all that was pleasant in man.

(For Garrick's reciprocal epitaph, see under GOLDSMITH). But one of the greatest epitaphs of all is that written by Garrick's friend (and one-time schoolteacher in Lichfield), Dr Samuel Johnson. In the 'Life of Edmund Smith', one of his *Lives of the English Poets* (published 1779), Johnson wrote: 'At this man's table I enjoyed many cheerful and instructive hours . . . with David Garrick, whom I hoped to have gratified with this character of our common friend; but what are the hopes of man! *I am disappointed by that stroke of death, which has eclipsed the gaiety of nations, and impoverished the public stock of harmless pleasure.*' Eva Maria, Garrick's relict (widow), had these wonderful words engraved below his *memorial bust in the South Transept of Lichfield Cathedral, in this context:

> . . . He had not only the amiable qualities of private life
> but such astonishing dramatick talents
> as too well verified the observation of his Friend
> "His death eclipsed the gaiety of nations,
> and impoverished the publick stock of harmless pleasure."

Dr Johnson's own memorial bust is a few feet away. John WILKES had his doubts about the tribute and made an 'attack' on the phrase about eclipsing the gaiety of nations. Boswell relayed this to Johnson, who replied: 'I could not have said more nor less, for 'tis truth; "eclipsed", not "extinguished", and his death did eclipse; 'twas like a storm.'

'But why *nations?*' Boswell continued. 'Did his gaiety extend farther than his own nation?' Johnson deftly tossed in the Scots ('if we allow the Scotch to be a nation, and to have gaiety') but Boswell pressed on, 'Is not *harmless pleasure* very tame?' To which Johnson replied: 'Nay, Sir, harmless pleasure is the highest praise. Pleasure is a word of dubious import; pleasure is in general dangerous, and pernicious to virtue; to be able therefore to furnish pleasure that is harmless, pleasure pure and unalloyed, is as great a power as men can possess.'

Boswell's initial account of this exchange appears in his journal for 24 April 1779 and appears substantially the same in his *Life of Johnson*.

When Charles Dickens died in 1870, Thomas Carlyle wrote, 'It is an event world-wide, a *unique* of talents suddenly extinct, and has "eclipsed" (we too may say) "the gaiety of nations".'

Garrick was no mean epitaphist himself (see GOLDSMITH, HOGARTH, QUIN, and STERNE).

GAVESTON

~

In the Hollow of this Rock
Was beheaded,
On the 17th Day of July, 1312,
By Barons lawless as himself,
PIERS GAVESTON, Earl of Cornwall;
The Minion of a hateful King:
In Life and Death,
A memorable instance of Misrule.

This inscription probably dates from 1832 when a memorial cross was erected at Leek Wootton near Warwick (according to Jo Darke, *The Monument Guide to England and Wales*, 1991). Gaveston, Earl of Cornwall, was the favourite of Edward II and was banished by parliament in 1311. Re-entering the country, he was captured by barons opposed to him. From Warwick Castle he was taken to Blacklow Hill (also called Gaversike), about a mile north of the town, and executed. His body lay in Oxford for two years and was then taken to the Dominican Friary (now ruined) at King's Langley, Hertfordshire, where it was buried (*DNB*).

GAY

~

LIFE IS A JEST, AND ALL THINGS SHOW IT;
I THOUGHT SO ONCE; AND NOW I KNOW IT.

Part of the inscription on the pedestal of the monument to the dramatist and poet John Gay (1685–1732), which used to be in the South Transept of Westminster Abbey but has now been moved to the Triforium. The lines were written by Gay himself, author of the hugely-successful *The Beggar's Opera*. On the grave of Caleb Gould (*d* 1836), a Thames lock-keeper, in Remenham churchyard, the same epitaph is written in the form: 'This world's a jest, and all things show it. I thought so once, but now I know it.'

Gay's monument in the Abbey also bears Alexander POPE's epitaph which, in its original form, read:

> Of Manners gentle, of Affections mild;
> In Wit, a Man; Simplicity, a Child:
> With native Humour temp'ring virtuous Rage;
> Form'd to delight at once and lash the age:
> Above Temptation in a low Estate,
> And uncorrupted, ev'n among the Great:
> A safe Companion and an easy Friend,
> Unblam'd thro' Life, lamented in thy End.
> These are Thy Honours! not that here thy Bust
> Is mixed with Heroes, or with Kings thy dust;
> But that the Worthy and the Good shall say,
> Striking their aching bosoms, *Here* lies GAY.

In the last line, Swift objected to the double *ing* sounds in 'striking' and 'aching', so Pope changed it to 'striking their pensive bosoms'. Sixty years later, in *The Idler*, Dr Johnson objected to almost everything about the epitaph: 'The first eight lines have no grammar, the adjectives are without any substantives, and the epithets without a subject. The thought in the last line, that Gay is buried in the bosoms of the worthy and good, who are distinguished only to lengthen the line, is so dark that few understand it; and so harsh, when it is explained to them, that still fewer approve.'

According to *Collection* (1806), Pope also penned:

> Well, then, Poor GAY lies underground!
> So there's an end of honest Jack!
> So little justice here he found,
> 'Tis ten to one he'll ne'er come back.

Under Pope's Westminster Abbey epitaph is the following eulogy by other hands:

> Here lye the ashes of Mr. JOHN GAY;
> The warmest friend;
> The most benevolent man;
> Who maintained
> Independency
> In low circumstances of fortune;
> Integrity
> In the midst of a corrupt age;
> And that equal serenity of mind

Which conscious goodness alone can give
Through the whole course of his life.

Favourite of the Muses,
He was led by them to every elegant art;
Refined in taste
And fraught with graces all his own.
In various kinds of poetry
Superior to many,
Inferior to none,
His works continue to inspire
What his example taught
Contempt of folly, however disguised
Detestation of vice, however adorned
Reverence for virtue, however disgraced.

CHARLES and CATHERINE, Duke and Duchess of
QUEENSBERRY,
Who loved this excellent Person living,
And respect him dead,
Have caused this Monument to be erected to his memory.
Died 1732.

GILBERT

~

**In loving and grateful memory
OLIVE GILBERT
1898–1981
We'll gather lilacs again.**

On the memorial *plaque in St Paul's Church, Covent Garden, London,
to the contralto who sang with Ivor NOVELLO's permanent company
from *Glamorous Night* (1936) onwards. Novello's song 'We'll Gather
Lilacs' was first sung as a duet by Miss Gilbert and Muriel Barron in Act
II of *Perchance to Dream* (1945).

GILBERT

~

In memory of Sarah the wife of Charles Gilbert,
Gent, who departed this life the 20th October 1761
in the 30th year of her age.
    She was the only daughter of and surviving child
of Mr Will Stainford: was married on 21st April and
died without issue.
    This amiable lady was truly religious virtuous and
sincere dutiful and obedient as a daughter and as a
wife the most prudent affectionate and indulging: by
her neighbours caressed and by the poor beloved.
She was of a candid open and generous disposition
and always made it her study to preserve peace
and promote Friendship. Her temper remarkably cheerful,
calm and even: and it may justly be said that all
her days were but steps to Heaven.

From West Dean churchyard, Sussex. Drawn to my attention by D.C.
Horton, Polegate, East Sussex (1982).

GILBERT

~

W.S. GILBERT
PLAYWRIGHT & POET

HIS FOE WAS FOLLY
& HIS WEAPON WIT.

On the *memorial to Sir William Schwenk Gilbert (1836–1911), writer
and librettist, on the Victoria Embankment, London (near Charing Cross
Pier, and not far from the memorial to Sir Arthur SULLIVAN in the
Embankment Gardens). Gilbert is pictured in profile, together with the
muses of tragedy and comedy. The line was provided in 1915 by
'Anthony Hope' (Sir Anthony Hope Hawkins, author of *The Prisoner of
Zenda*), who recalled: 'Whilst on the committee of the Authors' Society I
had something to do with the memorial. The words on the memorial are

mine, except that I put them first into prose – "Folly was his foe, and wit his weapon", – then somebody (I forget who) pointed out that transposed they would make a line, and this was adopted.'

Gilbert – who died of a heart attack after rescuing a girl from drowning in the pond of his home, Grimsdyke House – was cremated and his ashes buried in the churchyard of St John the Evangelist, Great Stanmore, London, under a plain white marble tomb with name and dates only.

GILL
~

**PRAY FOR ME
ERIC GILL
STONE CARVER
1882–1940
AND FOR MY
MOST DEAR WIFE
MARY ETHEL
1878–1961.**

This is the wording on the *gravestone of the celebrated sculptor and letter cutter, and his wife, in the Baptist Cemetery, Speen, Buckinghamshire. Eric Gill carved numerous gravestones and memorials for others (including those for G.K. CHESTERTON and Francis THOMPSON). He designed his own, which was cut for him by Laurie Cribb when the time came. The words about his widow were later added in the space provided.

As Fiona MacCarthy describes in her biography *Eric Gill* (1989), Gill had been preoccupied with thoughts of death for many years and earlier, in 1936, had designed himself a gravestone which was included in a London exhibition, with the wording:

REMEMBER ME
ERIC GILL
LAPIDARI . . .

HEU MIHI . . .

'Woe is me', this concludes. Perhaps *lapidarius* ('stone cutter') was intended.

GLEAVE

~

HUGH CRASWALL GLEAVE
B.LITT., M.A.OXON.
1919–1948
RECTOR OF MILTON, BERKS.
HE BEING MADE PERFECT IN A SHORT
TIME FULFILLED A LONG TIME FOR
HIS SOUL PLEASED THE LORD.

*Inscription on a grave near the south wall (exterior) of Sefton Church, Lancashire, near to that of the Revd Gleave's father (see next entry). Hugh Gleave was a cousin of my mother's and I include his epitaph because of the apt quotation from the apocryphal Wisdom of Solomon 4:13–14. It was possibly chosen by *his* mother and reflects a promising life in the church, which was suddenly cut short by poliomyelitis at the age of twenty-nine. Gleave had been married for just over a year and had only become rector of Milton, near Abingdon, a few weeks before his death.

GLEAVE

~

WILLIAM HENRY GLEAVE
DEC.8TH.1881–AUG.24TH.1943
WHEN THE MORNING WAS NOW COME
JESUS STOOD ON THE SHORE.

*Inscription on a grave by the south wall (exterior) of Sefton Church, Lancashire. Harry Gleave was secretary of a family leather tanning business in Liverpool and a keen collector of books and pictures. The text is from John 21:4. Gleave's daughter-in-law, now Barbara Wild, comments: 'He chose it himself. He didn't actually say so, but after his death he was found to have written it and left it on his bedside table. I clearly remember Hugh [see above] telling me about that.'

GOLDSMITH

~

OLIVARII GOLDSMITH, Poetae, Physici, Historici,
qui nullum fere scribendi genus non tetigit,
nullum quod tetigit non ornavit . . .

('Of Oliver Goldsmith, A Poet, Natural Philosopher, and Historian, who left no species of writing untouched by his pen, and touched none that he did not adorn . . .') Part of the *monument (1776) in Poets' Corner, Westminster Abbey, to the playwright Goldsmith (c 1730–1774). Goldsmith was buried in the Temple Church, Fleet Street, London, in an unmarked grave, and a later monument there (1837) was destroyed during an air-raid in 1941.

The Abbey's distinguished tribute was penned by Dr Samuel Johnson but not without dissent among Goldsmith's other friends and admirers. As James Boswell records in his *Life of Johnson* (16 May 1776), the 'Epitaph gave occasion to a *Remonstrance* to the MONARCH OF LITERATURE'. Various emendations were suggested to Johnson's draft and presented to him in the form of a Round Robin. Sir Joshua Reynolds took it to Johnson 'who received it with much good humour, and desired Sir Joshua to tell the gentlemen, that he would alter the Epitaph in any manner they pleased, as to the sense of it; but *he would never consent to disgrace the walls of Westminster Abbey with an English inscription.*' He argued further that, 'the language of the country of which a learned man was a native, is not the language fit for his epitaph, which should be in an ancient and permanent language. Consider, Sir; how you should feel, were you to find at Rotterdam an epitaph upon Erasmus *in Dutch*!'

And so it remained in Latin, despite the protest from Goldsmith's friends. Johnson also remarked of Goldsmith: 'Let not his frailties be remembered; he was a very great man.' While Goldsmith was alive, David GARRICK came up with the burlesque epitaph: 'Here lies Nolly Goldsmith, for shortness call'd Noll,/Who wrote like an angel, but talk'd like poor Poll.'

GORDON

~

HE SAVED AN EMPIRE BY HIS WARLIKE GENIUS, HE RULED VAST PROVINCES WITH JUSTICE, WISDOM AND POWER. AND LASTLY OBEDIENT TO HIS SOVEREIGN'S COMMAND

HE DIED IN THE HEROIC ATTEMPT TO SAVE MEN, WOMEN AND CHILDREN FROM IMMINENT AND DEADLY PERIL.

Part of the brass-plate *inscription on the monument to General Charles George Gordon (1833–85) in St Paul's Cathedral. 'Gordon of Khartoum' was killed by forces of the Mahdi besieging the Sudanese capital. His head was presented to the Mahdi; his body was never found. Tennyson wrote an epitaph for the Gordon Boys' National Memorial Home near Woking:

> Warrior of God, man's friend, and tyrant's foe,
> Now somewhere dead far in the waste Soudan,
> Thou livest in all hearts, for all men know
> This earth has never borne a nobler man.

GORDON
~

Believing that his hate for queers
Proclaimed his love for God,
He now (of all queer things, my dears)
Lies under his first sod.

Paul Dehn (1912–76) won a *New Statesman* competition in 1962 with this epitaph on John Gordon (1890–1974), editor-in-chief of the *Sunday Express*, and a columnist famous for his outspoken views.

GRAHAME
~

TO
THE BEAUTIFUL MEMORY
OF KENNETH GRAHAME
HUSBAND OF ELSPETH
AND
FATHER OF ALASTAIR
WHO PASSED THE RIVER

ON THE 6TH OF JULY 1932
LEAVING
CHILDHOOD & LITERATURE
THROUGH HIM
THE MORE BLEST
FOR ALL TIME.

AND OF HIS SON
ALASTAIR GRAHAME
COMMONER OF CHRIST CHURCH
1920.

On the *grave of the author of *The Wind in the Willows* in St Cross Churchyard, Oxford, and composed by 'Anthony Hope' (author of *The Prisoner of Zenda*), who was Grahame's cousin. The use of the phrase 'passing the river' for death is absolutely appropriate for an author who wrote so enchantingly of the river bank and 'messing about in boats'. It may also be taken to allude to the classical use of the crossing the rivers of Styx, Acheron, Lethe, and so on, as a symbol of death, but chiefly to the Christian use. In John Bunyan's *The Pilgrim's Progress*, Christian passes through the River of Death (which has no bridge) and quotes Isaiah 43:2, 'When thou passest through the waters, I will be with thee, and through the Rivers, they shall not overflow thee.'

Grahame's son, Alastair, for whom the story of *The Wind in the Willows* was originally written, met an untimely end, committing suicide while an undergraduate, on the railway line by Port Meadow, Oxford.

GRAY
~

THIS MONUMENT
IN HONOUR OF THOMAS GRAY
WAS ERECTED A.D.1799 AMONG
THE SCENES CELEBRATED BY THAT
GREAT LYRIC AND ELEGIAC POET.
HE DIED 1771 AND
LIES UNNOTICED IN THE CHURCHYARD
ADJOINING, UNDER THE TOMBSTONE ON
WHICH HE PIOUSLY AND PATHETICALLY
RECORDED THE INTERMENT OF HIS
AUNT AND LAMENTED MOTHER.

The *monument to the poet Gray (b 1716) lies about one hundred yards from the churchyard of St Giles, Stoke Poges, Buckinghamshire, which is believed to be the setting for his illustrious 'Elegy in a Country Churchyard' (completed 1750). The formidable structure, erected in 1799 by the architect James Wyatt, consists of a stone sarcophagus standing above a square pedestal on whose sides are inscribed appropriate lines from Gray's works.

As the inscription points out, Gray's actual resting place is with his mother and aunt, in a red brick-lined grave just outside the east end of the church. A *tablet on the wall nearby records:

OPPOSITE TO THIS STONE
IN THE SAME TOMB UPON WHICH HE HAS
SO FEELINGLY RECORDED HIS GRIEF
AT THE LOSS OF A BELOVED PARENT
ARE DEPOSITED THE REMAINS
OF
THOMAS GRAY
THE AUTHOR OF
"THE ELEGY WRITTEN IN A COUNTRY CHURCHYARD"
&c &c &c.
HE WAS BURIED AUGUST 6TH 1771.

The inscription by Gray, now almost illegible, runs:

In the Vault beneath are deposited,
in Hope of joyful Resurrection,
the remains of
MARY ANTROBUS.
She died unmarried, November 5, 1749
Aged 66.
In the same pious confidence,
beside her friend and sister,
here sleep the remains of
DOROTHY GRAY
Widow, the careful, tender Mother
of many children, one of whom alone
had the misfortune to survive her.
She died March 11, 1653
Aged 67.

Gray specifically requested in his will that his body be 'deposited in the vault made by my late dear mother, in the church-yard of Stoke-Pogeis, near Slough, in Buckinghamshire, by her remains in a coffin of seasoned oak, neither lined nor covered', so he was taken there from Cambridge where, at his death, he held the post of Professor of Modern History. It is not clear why his name does not appear upon the grave, except that there is no room for another name on the slab as transcribed above.

Gray's mother had moved to Stoke Poges in 1742 and the poet made many visits to her there. He is also commemorated in Poets' Corner, Westminster Abbey, on a *monument bearing this verse:

> No more the *Graecian* Muse unrival'd reigns:
>   To *Britain* let the Nations homage pay;
> She felt a HOMER's fire in MILTON's strains,
>   A PINDAR's rapture in the Lyre of *GRAY*.

In the 'Elegy', there is a part specifically labelled 'The Epitaph':

> Here rests his head upon the lap of Earth
>   A Youth, to Fortune and to Fame Unknown;
> Fair Science frown'd not on his humble birth,
>   And Melancholy mark'd him for her own.

> Large was his bounty, and his soul sincere;
>   Heaven did a recompense as largely send:
> He gave to Misery all he had, a tear,
>   He gain'd from Heaven, 'twas all he wish'd, a friend.

> No farther seeks his merits to disclose,
>   Or draw his frailties from their dread abode,
> (There they alike in trembling hope repose,)
>   The bosom of his Father and his God.

GREENWOOD

~

In memory of William Greenwood of Pecket Well, who was found dead at Bridgewellhead in Wadsworth on the 14th day of April 1820. He was forsaken by a bad wife who enforst him to serve his Majesty in the Third York Militia for 8 years. He left a girl aged 16 years to be becozened by her mother's father out of his money. His own father deposed for felony. His own brother arranged before a magistrate for his raiment which he had bequeathed to him before his

death in the presence of two witnesses.
His thread of life spun
His age near 35 years.
And in his trouble dropped down dead,
And left this vale of tears.

A tale of woe 'in Heptonstall churchyard near Hebden Bridge, W. Yorks', drawn to my attention by J.A. Wadsworth, Wareham, Dorset (1982).

GREER
~

Here lies the body of Charlotte Greer,
Whose mouth would stretch from ear to ear.
Be careful as you tread this sod
For if she gapes, you're gone, by God!

'My father maintained that in the Vale of Aylesbury about 1900 he encountered this epitaph . . . I'm afraid it was apocryphal' – E.J. Burdon, Preston, Lancs. (1982).

GREVILLE
~

FULKE GREVILL
SERVANT TO QUEENE ELIZABETH
CONCELLER TO KING JAMES
AND FRIEND TO SIR PHILIP SIDNEY
TROPHAEUM PECCATI.

Sir Fulke Greville, 1st Baron Brooke, courtier and minor poet (1554–1628), apparently wrote this epitaph for himself, and it is to be seen on his substantial monument in St Mary's Church, Warwick. His friendship with Sidney, whom he had known since their schooldays at Shrewsbury and whose superior poetry he imitated, was a principal fact of his life. Greville wrote a *Life of Sir Philip Sidney* (published 1652).

The phrase *trophaeum peccati*, meaning 'a trophy of sin', is described by Ronald A. Rebholz in *The Life of Fulke Greville* (1971) as 'the most succinct and pessimistic self-definition Greville wrote'. As John Coke wrote to Greville before his death – apparently about the proposed wording – 'the inscription condemneth the tomb, the words despise the deeds.'

The epitaph has added curiosity, given the odd circumstances of Greville's death. He was stabbed by a servant in the grounds of Warwick Castle (which he owned) – though some say this happened at his London house. The servant, who may have thought his master had made insufficient provision for him in his will, then stabbed himself, dying instantly; the 74-year-old Greville died four weeks later and was taken to Warwick to be placed in the tomb to which he had given so much thought.

GRIMALDI
~

HERE AM I.

Said by Wright (1972) to be on the *grave of Joseph Grimaldi (1779–1837), the clown, in a park on the site of the churchyard of St James, Pentonville Road, London (the church has now been converted into offices). His catchphrase was, in fact, 'Here we are again'. However, the inscription on the carefully-restored grave of 'Mr Joseph Grimaldi' does not show the words, only his name and dates.

GROBER
~

Jonathan Grober
Died dead sober.
Lord thy wonders never cease.

Quoted on *Quote . . . Unquote*, BBC Radio, 22 December 1981, but untraced.

GROVE

~

LUCY GROVE

ELDEST DAUGHTER OF EDWARD SNEYD, ESQUIRE
AND WIFE OF WILLIAM GROVE, ESQUIRE LL.D.
LATE OF COVENTRY, NOW OF LITCHFIELD CLOSE,
DIED 9TH OF DECEMBER
M.DCC.LXXXVII. IN THE
FORTIETH YEAR OF HER AGE,
AND THE TWENTIETH OF
HER MARRIAGE, LEAVING
TWO SONS AND TWO DAUGHTERS.

GRIEF, LOVE, AND GRATITUDE DEVOTE THIS STONE
　　TO HER, WHOSE VIRTUES BLEST AN HUSBAND'S LIFE.
WHEN LATE IN DUTY'S SPHERE SHE MILDLY SHONE,
　　AS FRIEND, AS SISTER, DAUGHTER, MOTHER, WIFE.

IN THE BRIGHT MORN OF BEAUTY, JOY, AND WEALTH,
　　INSIDIOUS PALSY NEAR HIS VICTIM DREW;
DASH'D FROM HER YOUTHFUL HANDS THE CUP OF HEALTH,
　　AND ROUND HER LIMBS HIS NUMBING FETTERS THREW.

YEAR AFTER YEAR HER CHRISTIAN FIRMNESS STROVE
　　TO CHECK THE RISING SIGH, THE TEAR REPRESS,
SOOTHE WITH SOFT SMILES THE FEARS OF ANXIOUS LOVE,
　　AND HEAV'N'S CORRECTING HAND IN SILENCE BLESS.

THUS TRIED HER FAITH, AND THUS PREPAR'D HER HEART,
　　THE AWFUL CALL AT LENGTH TH'ALMIGHTY GAVE:
SHE HEARD – RESIGN'D TO LINGER, OR DEPART,
　　BOW'D HER MEEK HEAD, AND SUNK INTO THE GRAVE.

From a *memorial, still to be found in the South Transept of Lichfield Cathedral – and rather more prominent, in fact, than those of GARRICK and Johnson in the same place. This text appeared in *Collection* (1806).

GWYNNE

~

Here lies the body of Mary Gwynne,
Who was so very pure within,
She cracked the shell of her earthly skin,
And hatched herself a cherubim.

In Cambridge – Fairley (1875); in St Alban's, Hertfordshire – Briscoe
(1901).

HAIG

~

HE TRUSTED IN GOD
AND TRIED TO DO THE RIGHT.

On the *grave of Douglas, 1st Earl Haig (1861–1928), in the ruins of Dryburgh Abbey, Berwickshire. Haig was Commander-in-Chief of British forces in France and Flanders for most of the First World War. The headstone, at Haig's request, is identical to those in the cemeteries of France. A notice near the grave suggests that the wording of the epitaph was that used on many graves of First World War dead of lower rank. ('For God and the right' is another form of this motto-like idea.) I do not know to what extent this derives from 'Trust in God' by the Scottish divine, Norman MacLeod DD (1812–72):

> Courage brother! do not stumble,
>   Though thy path be dark as night;
> There's a star to guide the humble;
>   Trust in God, and do the Right.

There is an equestrian statue of Haig in Whitehall. His mount was criticized on anatomical grounds when it was unveiled in 1937.

HALL

~

AND, IF GOD CHOOSE
I SHALL BUT LOVE THEE BETTER
AFTER DEATH.
UNA.

On a *tablet bearing the name and year of death (1943) of Radclyffe Hall, the writer, in Highgate Cemetery (West), London. Hall, who was born in 1883, wrote eight novels of which *The Well of Loneliness* (1928) with its frank treatment of lesbianism is the most well-known. Banned following an obscenity trial, it was eventually republished in 1949. The 'Una' is Lady Troubridge, Hall's principal lover and biographer. In *The Life and Death of Radclyffe Hall* (1961), she recalls what Hall (whom she called 'John') said the day before she died. In the throes of suffering she looked up at the nurse 'with the ghost of her jaunty smile' and exclaimed, 'What a life!' Then she added, 'But I offer it to God.'

HAMILTON-FAIRLEY

~

GORDON HAMILTON-FAIRLEY
DM FRCP
FIRST PROFESSOR OF CLINICAL ONCOLOGY
1930–1975
KILLED BY A TERRORIST BOMB

It matters not how a man dies but how he lives.

On his *memorial in the crypt of St Paul's Cathedral. The cancer specialist was killed in Campden Hill Square, London, as he passed a car containing an IRA bomb intended for his next door neighbour, Hugh Fraser, a Conservative MP. Caroline Kennedy, daughter of the late American President was staying in the Fraser house when the bomb exploded. Professor Hamilton-Fairley was head of the medical oncology unit at St Bartholomew's Hospital, London, and one of Britain's leading cancer experts.

HANDEL

~

The most excellent
Musician
Any Age has produced;
Whose compositions were a
Sentimental Language
Rather than mere Sounds;

115

And surpassed the Power of
Words in expressing
The various Passions
Of the Human Heart.

The composer, George Frederick Handel (1685–1759) is buried near
Poets' Corner in Westminster Abbey under a splendid Roubiliac statue,
bearing only his name and dates. The above anonymous epitaph
appeared in the *Universal Register* the day after Handel's funeral.

HARCOURT
~

To this Sad Shrine, who'er thou art, draw near,
If ever Friend, if ever Son was dear,
Here lies the Youth who n'er his Friend deny'd,
Or gave his Father Grief, but when he dy'd.
How vain is Reason, Eloquence how weak,
If POPE must tell what HARCOURT cannot speak.
Oh let thy once lov'd Friend inscribe thy Stone,
And with a Father's Sorrows mix his own.

Beneath a Latin inscription on the *tomb of the Hon. Simon Harcourt,
only son of Lord Chancellor Harcourt, in the Harcourt Chapel of St
Michael's Church, Stanton Harcourt, Oxfordshire. Simon Harcourt died
in Paris at the age of thirty-five in 1720. Alexander POPE's lines were
published with the second and fourth lines thus: 'Here lies the Friend
most lov'd, the Son most dear:/Who ne'er knew Joy, but Friendship
might divide . . .'

HARDY
~

HERE LIES THE HEART OF
THOMAS HARDY O.M.
SON OF THOMAS AND JEMIMA HARDY.

Not an epitaph but a curiosity of an *inscription from St Michael's churchyard, Stinsford, Dorset. When the novelist and poet died in 1928, an unseemly struggle ensued over his remains. He had wished to be buried in Dorset, but his Literary Executor and the supervisor of Poets' Corner, Westminster Abbey had other ideas. Consequently, a compromise was reached with Hardy's heart remaining in Dorset and the rest of him, or at least his ashes, going to the Abbey.

The heart is buried in the same grave as both Hardy's wives (who are each described as being relics of 'Thomas Hardy O.M.', as though the Order of Merit were part of his name.) Nearby are the graves of other relatives, including his parents.

HARTLEY &c.

~

In Memory of
the Devoted Musicians
Wallace Henry Hartley, Bandmaster
John Fredrick Preston Clark
Percy Cornelius Taylor
John Wesley Woodward
W. Theodore Brailey
John Law Hume
Georges Krins
Roger Bricoux

Who were drowned
Still playing
As the Titanic went down
April 15, 1912.

Plaque at Symphony Hall, Boston, Mass. According to Norwich (1990), the same names are recorded on a plaque in the Philharmonic Hall, Liverpool, with this inscription: 'Members of the band on board the "Titanic". They bravely continued playing to soothe the anguish of their fellow passengers until the ship sank in the deep . . . Courage and Compassion joined make the hero and the man complete.'

HAVARD

~

To the memory of John Havard Esq.,
Surgeon, who died . . . 1840.
He will be long deplored by an extensive
circle of relations and friends, and his
medical talents had rendered him
peculiarly useful in the neighbourhood.

'From a tomb in the parish churchyard of Llangeler, 15 miles north of
Carmarthen' – S.C.L. Phillips, Llandysul, Dyfed (1982).

HEMINGWAY

~

PARDON ME FOR NOT GETTING UP.

One of the playful epitaphs that celebrities were invited to suggest for
themselves, usually by American magazines in the 1920s/30s. Ernest
Hemingway (1899–1961), the writer, suggested this. He is buried at
Ketchum, Idaho, where he shot himself.

HENRY V

~

Here lies HENRY,
The Scourge of France, 1422.
Virtue surmounts all opposition.
Here also, With her Valiant Spouse, lies
The beautiful Catherine.

Keep from Sloth.

'In Westminster Abbey' according to Tegg (1876), but not visible on the tomb there of the king (who lived 1387–1422). On the whole, kings and queens are accorded minimal description on their graves and tombs.

HENRY
~

HIS FAME IS HIS BEST EPITAPH.

On the stone slab over the grave of Patrick Henry (1736–99), at Red Hill Shrine, Southern Virginia. Henry, statesman and orator, was a leading opponent of British rule at the time of the American War of Independence. In March 1775 he told assembled Virginians, in a famous speech, 'Give me liberty or give me death'.

HERBERT
~

Underneath this sable Herse
Lies the Subject of all Verse:
Sydney's Sister, Pembroke's Mother -
Death! ere thou Kill'st such another
Fair, and good, and learnd as SHEE,
Time will throw his Dart at thee.

Formerly over a grave in the floor of Salisbury Cathedral, this epitaph remembers Mary Herbert, Countess of Pembroke (1561–1621). Her brother was the poet Sir Philip Sidney and she became a patron of poets and men of letters. Aubrey (whose transcription this is) states that it was written by William Browne (d 1645), who wrote *Britannia's Pastorals*, as well as several other epitaphs.

HERRICK

~

IN MEMORY OF THE LATE DECEASED VIRGIN
MISTRIS ELIZABETH HEREICKE

SWEET VIRGIN THAT I DOE NOT SET
THY GRAVE-VERSE UP IN MOURNFULL JET
OR DAPL'D MARBLE LET THY SHADE
NOR WRATHFUL SEEME OR FRIGHT THE MAID
WHO HITHER AT HER WEEPING HOWRES
SHALL COME TO STREW THY EARTH WITH FLOWRES;
NO, I KNOW BLEST SOULE WHEN THERE'S NOT ONE
REMINDER LEFT OF BRASSE OR STONE
THY LIVING EPITAPH SHALL BE
THOUGH LOST ON THEM YET FOUND IN ME:
DEARE, IN THY BED OF ROSES THEN
TILL THIS WORLD SHALL DISSOLVE (AS MEN)
SLEEPE, WHILE WE HIDE THEE FROM THE LIGHT
DRAWING THY CURTAINS ROUND – GOOD NIGHT.

This epitaph, written by Robert Herrick for his niece (who died in 1630), was originally on a mural tablet in the middle of the North Aisle of St Margaret's Church, Westminster. In 1955, it became the somewhat odd choice to be reproduced on a *tablet on the church's south wall in memory of James Rumsey 'whom the State of West Virginia honours as the inventor of the Steamboat, which he demonstrated privately to George Washington in 1784 and publicly on the Potomac River at Shepherdstown, W. Va, 3 December 1787. Born of English parents in Cecil County, Maryland in 1743, he died while lecturing on the principles of steam navigation to English scientists in London, and was buried in St Margaret's Churchyard, 24 December 1792.'

HESTER

~

In loving memory of my beloved wife, Hester, the mother of Edward, Richard, Mary, Penelope, John, Henry, Michael, Susan, Emily, Charlotte, Amelia, George, Hugh, Hester, Christoper and Daniel. She was a great breeder of pugs, a devoted mother and a dear friend.

'I came across this many years ago in Hemel Hempstead' – N. Currer-Briggs, Riberac, France (1981).

HEWET
~

**NEAR THIS PLACE LIE THE BODIES OF
JOHN HEWET and SARAH DREW,
AN INDUSTRIOUS YOUNG MAN AND VIRTUOUS MAIDEN
OF THIS PARISH
CONTRACTED IN MARRIAGE
WHO BEING WITH MANY OTHERS AT HARVEST
WORK, WERE BOTH IN ONE INSTANT KILLED
BY LIGHTNING ON THE LAST DAY OF JULY
1718.**

*Tablet on the exterior south wall of St Michael's Church, Stanton Harcourt, Oxfordshire. In that summer of 1718, Alexander POPE and John GAY persuaded Lord Harcourt – whose house was in the village – to erect a monument with an epitaph by Pope over the grave of the 'Stanton Harcourt Lovers'. Gay's version is referred to in Goldsmith's *The Vicar of Wakefield* (1766).

Pope's epitaph (of which more than one version exists) was put on the *tablet in this form:

> Think not by rigorous judgment seiz'd,
>   A Pair so faithful could expire;
> Victims so pure, Heav'n saw well pleas'd
>   And snatch'd them in caelestial fire.

> Live well & fear no sudden fate
>   When God calls virtue to the grave
> Alike 'tis Justice, soon or late -
>   Mercy alike to kill or save.

> Virtue unmov'd can hear the Call,
> And face the Flash that melts the Ball.

Pope showed several epitaphs on the same couple to Lady Mary Wortley MONTAGU, including this other:

> Here lye two poor Lovers, who had the mishap
> Tho very chaste people, to die of a Clap.

And he told Lady Mary in a letter (dated 1 September 1718) what had happened:

I have a mind to fill the rest of this paper with an accident that happened just under my eyes, and has made a great impression on me. I have past part of this summer at an old romantic seat of my Lord Harcourt's, which he lent me. It overlooks a common field, where, under the shade of a haycock, sat two lovers, as constant as ever were found in Romance, beneath a spreading beech. The name of the one (let it sound as it will) was John Hewet, of the other Sarah Drew. John was a well-set man, about five-and-twenty; Sarah a brown [dark-complexioned, though maybe rustically suntanned] woman of eighteen. John had for several months borne the labour of the day in the same field with Sarah: when she milked, it was his morning and evening charge to bring the cows to her pail. Their love was the talk, but not the scandal, of the neighbourhood; for all they aimed at was the blameless possession of each other in marriage. It was but this very morning that he obtained her parents' consent, and it was but till the next week that they were to await to be happy. Perhaps this very day, in the intervals of their work, they were talking of their wedding-clothes; and John was now matching several kinds of poppies and field flowers to her complexion, to make her a present of knots for the day. While they were thus employed (it was on the last day of July), a terrible storm of thunder and lightning arose, that drove the labourers to what shelter the trees or hedges afforded. Sarah, frightened and out of breath, sunk down on a haycock, and John (who never separated from her) sate by her side, having raked two or three heaps together to secure her. Immediately there was heard so loud a crack as if Heaven had burst asunder. The labourers, all solicitous for each other's safety, called to one another; those who were nearest our lovers, hearing no answer, stepped to the place where they lay: they first saw a little smoke, and after, this faithful pair; – John, with one arm about his Sarah's neck, and the other held over her face, as if to screen her from the lightning. They were struck dead, and already grown stiff and cold in this tender posture. There was no mark or discolouring on their bodies, only that Sarah's eyebrow was a little singed, and a small spot appeared between her breasts. They were buried the next day in one grave, in the parish of Stanton-Harcourt, in

Oxfordshire; where my Lord Harcourt, at my request, has erected a monument over them. Of the following epitaphs which I made, the critics have chosen the godly one: I like neither, but wish you had been in England to have done this office better; I think 'twas what you could not have refused me on so moving an occasion.

> When Eastern lovers feed the fun'ral fire,
> On the same pile their faithful fair expire;
> Here pitying Heav'n that virtue mutual found,
> And blasted both, that it might neither wound.
> Hearts so sincere th'Almighty saw well pleas'd,
> Sent his own lightning, and the victims seiz'd.

[Here Pope puts the lines, as above, beginning, 'Think not, by rig'rous judgment seiz'd . . .']

Upon the whole, I can't think these people unhappy. The great happiness next to living as they would have done, was to die as they did. The greatest honour people of this low degree could have was to be remembered on a little monument; unless you will give them another, – that of being honoured with a tear from the finest eyes in the world. I know you must have it; it is the very emanation of good sense and virtue; the finest minds, like the finest metals, dissolve the easiest.

By the time Pope came to publish his letters in 1737, he had fallen out with Lady Mary and did not wish to admit that he had written to her on this subject. Hence, the letter was assigned to Gay who may not have written an epitaph at all (despite what Goldsmith believed), though it could have been written by Gay *and* Pope.

Lady Mary's original reply was dated 1 November 1718:

I have this minute received a letter of yours, sent me from Paris . . . I must applaud your good nature, in supposing that your pastoral lovers (vulgarly called haymakers) would have lived in everlasting joy and harmony, if the lightning had not interrupted their scheme of happiness. I see no reason to imagine that John Hughes [*sic* – she required a one-syllable name for her verse, see below] and Sarah Drew were either wiser or more virtuous than their neighbours. That a well-set man of twenty-five should have a fancy to marry a brown woman of eighteen, is nothing marvellous; and I cannot help thinking, that, had they married, their lives would have passed in the common track with their fellow parishioners. His endeavouring to shield her from the storm, was a natural action, and what he would have certainly done for his horse, if he had been in the same situation. Neither am I of opinion, that their sudden death was a reward of their mutual virtue.

You know the Jews were reproved for thinking a village destroyed by fire more wicked than those that had escaped the thunder. Time and chance happen to all men. Since you desire me to try my skill in an epitaph, I think the following lines perhaps more than just, though not so poetical as yours:

Here lie John Hughes and Sarah Drew;
Perhaps you'll say, what's that to you?
Believe me, friend, much may be said
On this poor couple that are dead.
On Sunday next they should have married;
But see how oddly things are carried!
On Thursday last it rain'd and lighten'd;
These tender lovers, sadly frighten'd,
Shelter'd beneath the cocking hay,
In hopes to pass the storm away;
But the bold thunder found them out
(Commission'd for that end, no doubt),
And, seizing on their trembling breath,
Consign'd them to the shades of death.
Who knows if 'twas not kindly done?
For had they seen the next year's sun,
A beaten wife and cuckold swain
Had jointly curs'd the marriage chain;
Now they are happy in their doom,
For P[ope] has wrote upon their tomb.

I confess these sentiments are not altogether so heroic as yours; but I hope you will forgive them in favour of the last two lines.

Lady Mary was not incapable of feeling (she wept over Richardson's novel *Clarissa*) and her remarks here may be more in the way of an antidote to the mawkishness she detected coming from the usually waspish Pope.

HIGLEY

~

Here lies John Higley whose father and mother were drowned in the passage from America. Had they both lived, they would have been buried here.

'Belturbet Churchyard, Ireland' – Fairley (1875).

HIND
~

Here lies the body of Richard Hind,
Who was neither ingenious, sober, nor kind.

Quoted in Hyman (1967), without source.

HOBHOUSE
~

**IN MEMORY OF
JOHN CAM HOBHOUSE, BART.
BARON BROUGHTON DE GYFFORD G.C.B.**

**. . . HE WAS EMINENT ALIKE IN POLITICAL AND
LITERARY LIFE
AND AFTER A PUBLIC CAREER OF SUCCESS AND HONOUR
FOUND UNBRIDLED HAPPINESS IN DOMESTIC REPOSE
WHICH HE ADORNED
BY HIS RARE GIFT OF SCHOLARSHIP AND ELOQUENCE.**

On the substantial *tomb of Hobhouse (1786–1869) in Kensal Green
Cemetery, London. Erected by his daughters. Hobhouse was a politician
and close friend of Lord BYRON, one of whose executors he became and
whose *Memoirs* he ensured were burnt. He coined the phrase 'His
Majesty's Opposition' in the House of Commons on 10 April 1826.

HODGES
~

**TO LIVE IN THE HEARTS
OF THOSE WE LOVE
IS NOT TO DIE.**

A familiar sentiment has been chosen for this *epitaph selected by the relatives of RAF Aircraftsman 1st Class G.C.E. Hodges, who was killed in the Second World War on 18th September 1944, age 42, and lies in Brookwood Military Cemetery, Surrey. A common variation of this theme is: 'He lives for ever in the hearts of those who loved him.'

HOGAN
~

See BLEWIT.

HOGARTH
~

**MARY SCOTT HOGARTH
DIED 7TH MAY 1837
YOUNG, BEAUTIFUL, AND GOOD,
GOD IN HIS MERCY
NUMBERED HER WITH HIS ANGELS
AT THE EARLY AGE OF
SEVENTEEN.**

The epitaph written by Charles Dickens for the sister-in-law to whom he was devoted can be found on her *grave in Kensal Green Cemetery, London. Devastated by his sister-in-law's death, Dickens for many years hoped to be buried in the same grave. However, Mary Hogarth's mother, father and brother now occupy the grave and Dickens is buried elsewhere (in Westminster Abbey).

Mary is said to have been the original for 'Little Nell', and was also very much Dickens's ideal of womanhood. He called her 'the dear girl whom I loved, after my wife, more deeply and fervently than anyone on earth'. She died in his arms. Interestingly, Dickens makes many of his heroines seventeen.

HOGARTH

~

Farewel, great Painter of Mankind!
Who reach'd the noblest point of Art
Whose *pictur'd Morals* charm the Mind,
And through the Eye correct the Heart.

If *Genius* fire thee, Reader, stay:
If *Nature* touch thee, drop a Tear;
If neither move thee, turn away,
For HOGARTH'S honour'd dust lies here.

D. Garrick

Part of the inscription on the *grave of William Hogarth (1697–1764) in the churchyard of St Nicholas, Chiswick Mall, London. The monument was erected by his friends in 1771 and the epitaph was composed by David GARRICK, the actor. Although restored in the mid-nineteenth century, the text is still difficult to read.

HOLMES

~

Now lands-men all who ever you may be,
If you want to rise to the top of the tree,
If your soul isn't fettered to an office stool,
Be careful to be guided by this golden rule,
Stick close to your desks and never to to sea,
And you all may be Rulers of the Queen's Navee.

William Holmes, Aldermen & Mayor, who was Vice-Admiral between Humber & Tyne, collector for Newburgh and borne in this cittye he dyed September 8. 1558.

Morrell (1948) draws attention to this epitaph from St Dennis, York, and its unmistakeable anticipation of the First Lord's song in *H.M.S. Pinafore* (1878) by GILBERT and SULLIVAN.

HOLST

~

IMOGEN
HOLST
1907–1984

THE
HEAVENLY
SPHERES
MAKE
MUSIC
FOR US.
ALL
THINGS
JOIN
IN THE DANCE.

On the *grave in the churchyard of St Peter and St Paul's, Aldeburgh, Suffolk. Imogen Holst was a musical educationalist, conductor, composer (especially of songs) and arranger of folk-songs. She collaborated with Benjamin Britten (d 1976) – whose grave is but a few feet in front of hers. Peter Pears, the singer (d 1986), lies next to Britten. These two share identical blue-slate gravestones, both only bearing name and dates.

Imogen Holst's father, the composer Gustav Holst (d 1934), is buried in Chichester Cathedral, without epitaph. However, he unwittingly supplied his daughter with one. It comes from a text he prepared and translated himself from the Greek of the Apocryphal Acts of St John for his *Hymn of Jesus* (1917). The passage concerns Jesus, 'before he was taken by the lawless Jews', calling on his disciples to 'sing a hymn to the Father', at which they join hands in a ring and dance. Rosamund Strode of the Holst Foundation comments: 'Since to Imogen dancing was every bit as important as music (and indeed she once hoped to be a dancer), the two lines seemed to us appropriate in every possible way.'

HOLTROP

~

"UNTIL THE DAY BREAK
AND THE SHADOWS FLEE AWAY."

On the *grave in Brookwood Military Cemetery, Surrey, of Flying Officer H.G. Holtrop, an RAF pilot who was killed on 10 June 1944, age 33. His relatives have chosen to place a very popular gravestone text which comes from the Song of Solomon 2:16 and (it is a love poem, after all) continues: 'Turn, my beloved, and be thou like a roe or a young hart upon the mountains of Bether.' Compare the use made of the text on Francis KILVERT's grave.

HOOD
∼

HE SANG THE SONG OF THE SHIRT . . .

Part of the *inscription on the red granite monument over the grave of Thomas Hood (1798-1845) in Kensal Green Cemetery, London, and an early example of what might be called the 'advertising' type of epitaph. In fact, his 'The Song of the Shirt' is a serious poem on the tragic plight of a seamstress and was, indeed, one of his most successful works, having first been published in *Punch* (1843). The monument was raised by public subscription in 1854. A bronze bust of Hood and other decorations have been stolen.

HORNE
∼

. . . In Whose Character
Depths of Learning, Brightness of Imagination,
Sanctity of Manners and Sweetness of Temper
Were United beyond the Usual Lot of Mortality . . .
His Commentary on the Psalms will continue to be
a Companion to the Closet
Till the Devotion of Earth shall end in
the Hallelujahs of Heaven.

'A plaque on the wall of the north aisle of Norwich Cathedral commemorates the Rt. Revd George Horne, D.D., President of Magdalen College, Oxford, Dean of Canterbury and Bishop of Norwich . . . Died 1792' – Norwich (1980).

HOW

∼

TO KNOW HIM WAS TO LOVE HIM.
ALWAYS IN OUR THOUGHTS.
OLIVE AND DAVID.

On the *grave in Brookwood Cemetery, Surrey, of Flight Lieutenant R.V. How, an RAF pilot who died 28th February 1944, age 30.

The line 'To know him was to love him' has an interesting history. In *The Picture of Dorian Gray* (1890), Oscar Wilde has: 'To see him is to worship him, to know him is to trust him.' Blanche Hozier wrote to Mabell, Countess of Airlie, in 1908: 'Clementine is engaged to be married to Winston Churchill. I do not know which of the two is more in love. I think that to know him is to like him.'

Thus the format existed, but as 'To Know Him Is To Love Him', it became the title of a song, written by Phil Spector in 1958. The words have a biblical ring to them, but whether Phil Spector was ever aware of the words of No. 3 in *CSSM Choruses* (3rd ed., 1928, by the Children's Special Service Mission, London) we may never know. Written by R. Hudson Pope, it goes:

> All glory be to Jesus
> The sinner's only Saviour . . .
> To know Him is to love Him,
> To trust him is to prove Him.

Robert Burns (*d* 1796) came very close to the phrase on a couple of occasions – in 'Bonnie Lesley': 'To see her is to love her/And love but her for ever', and in 'Ae Fond Kiss': 'But to see her was to love her,/ Love but her, and love for ever.' Besides, the words have often been used in an epitaph context. Fitz-Greene Halleck (1795–1867) wrote 'On the death of J.R. Drake':

> Green be the turf above thee,
> Friend of my better days;
> None knew thee but to love thee
> Nor named thee but to praise.

Samuel Rogers (1763-1855) wrote of 'Jacqueline':

Oh! she was good as she was fair.
None – none on earth above her!
As pure in thought as angels are,
To know her was to love her.

It appears that Phil Spector acquired the title of his song from the gravestone of his father, a suicide.

HOWELL
~

**TO THE MEMORY
OF EDWARD HOWELL
WHO DEPARTED THIS LIFE
NOVEMBER 9 1852
AGED 9 MONTHS**

**HERE LIES THE GRIEF
OF A FOND MOTHER
AND BLASTED EXPECTATIONS
OF AN INDULGENT FATHER.**

'From Tasmania a number of years ago' – on a *photograph sent to me by Mrs N. Ballard, Middlesbrough, Cleveland (1982).

HOWELLS
~

**Death has taken little Jerry
Son of Joseph and Serena Howells.
Seven days did he wrestle with the dysentery
Then he perished in his little bowels.**

In 'Stowe cemetery, Lincolnshire' – Haining (1973).

HUEFFER

~

His life was gentle, and the elements so mixed in him
That nature might stand up and say to all the world,
'This was a man.'

Epitaph on the fictional 'Cassius Hueffer', one of the characters who
speaks from beyond the grave in *Spoon River Anthology* (1915) by the
American poet, Edgar Lee Masters. 'Hueffer' comments on his
gravestone: 'Those who knew me smile/As they read this empty
rhetoric./. . . Now that I am dead I must submit to an epitaph/Graven
by a fool!' The quoted words are a version of Shakespeare, *Julius Caesar*
(V.v.73–5) – Mark Antony's speech on Brutus ('This was the noblest
Roman of them all').

HUNT

~

JAMES HENRY
LEIGH HUNT

"WRITE ME AS ONE
THAT LOVES HIS FELLOW MEN."

On the *grave of Hunt, poet and editor (1784–1859), in Kensal Green
Cemetery, London. The grave also contains his wife, Marianne, their
eldest son, Thornton, and his wife, Katharine. It was 'erected by
subscription' and unveiled by Lord Houghton in 1869. Hunt had a genius
for literary friendships (with BYRON, SHELLEY, KEATS, among others).
The motto is from one of his own most familiar poems – the one
beginning 'Abou Ben Adhem (may his tribe increase!)'

   Thornton Leigh Hunt (1810–73), journalist and editor, had four
children by the wife of G.H. Lewes; hence, in part, Lewes's relationship
with George ELIOT.

HUSKISSON
~

... FOR TEN YEARS THE REPRESENTATIVE OF THIS CITY
IN PARLIAMENT.
THIS STATION HE RELINQUISHED IN MDCCCXXIII,
WHEN YIELDING TO A SENSE OF PUBLICK DUTY
HE ACCEPTED THE OFFER OF BEING RETURNED FOR
LIVERPOOL ...

HIS DEATH WAS OCCASIONED BY AN ACCIDENT NEAR
THAT TOWN
ON THE XV OF SEPTEMBER MDCCCXXX
AND CHANGED A SCENE OF TRIUMPHANT REJOICING
INTO ONE OF GENERAL MOURNING.
AT THE URGENT SOLICITATION OF HIS CONSTITUENTS
HE WAS INTERRED IN THE CEMETERY THERE
AMID THE UNAFFECTED SORROW OF ALL CLASSES OF
PEOPLE ...

Part of a much longer *inscription beneath a statue of the Rt Hon.
William Huskisson (1770–1830) in Chichester Cathedral. Huskisson has
the unfortunate distinction of being one of the first people to be killed in
a railway accident. Worse, he was attending the opening of the Liverpool
to Manchester railway, the first for which high-speed locomotives were
designed, when the fatal accident occurred. Huskisson and other
dignitaries were standing about while their engine was taking on water
and he made to go and shake hands with the Duke of Wellington, who
was also present on this great occasion. Alas, a locomotive on the other
track – the Rocket, no less – came bearing down on the group.

An eye witness wrote: 'Poor Mr Huskisson, less active from the effects
of age and ill-health, bewildered, too, by the frantic cries of "Stop the
engine! Clear the track!" that resounded on all sides, completely lost his
head, looked helplessly to the right and left, and was instantaneously
prostrated by the fatal machine, which dashed down like a thunderbolt
upon him, passed over his leg, smashing and mangling it in the most
horrible way.'

JAMES

~

An upright downright honest man.

'Epitaph on John James, Ripon Cathedral, 1707' – Benham (1907).

JEFFERIES

~

**TO THE MEMORY OF
RICHARD JEFFERIES,
BORN AT COATE IN THE PARISH OF CHISELDON, AND COUNTY
OF WILTS, 6TH NOVEMBER 1848,
DIED AT GORING, IN THE COUNTY OF SUSSEX,
14TH AUGUST 1887,
WHO OBSERVING THE WORKS OF ALMIGHTY GOD,
WITH A POET'S EYE
HAS
ENRICHED THE LITERATURE OF HIS COUNTRY,
AND
WON FOR HIMSELF A PLACE AMONGST
THOSE
WHO HAVE MADE MEN HAPPIER,
AND WISER.**

Beneath the *memorial bust of the novelist and naturalist in Salisbury Cathedral. Jefferies was the author of *The Gamekeeper at Home* (1877), *Bevis* (1882) and *The Story of My Heart* (1883). According to the *DNB*, 'while in good health he was a man of splendid presence, with something of the gamekeeper and the poet combined', but he became afflicted by a wasting disease and was latterly unable even to hold his pen. Too proud to accept help from the Literary Fund, he died at Goring in Sussex and is buried in Worthing. On his death, his wife was awarded a pension and the monument was erected in Salisbury.

JEFFERSON

~

HERE WAS BURIED
THOMAS JEFFERSON
AUTHOR OF THE
DECLARATION
OF
AMERICAN INDEPENDENCE,
OF THE
STATUTE OF VIRGINIA
FOR
RELIGIOUS FREEDOM,
AND FATHER OF THE
UNIVERSITY OF VIRGINIA.

BORN APRIL 2 1743 O.S.
DIED JULY 4 1826.

Jefferson devised his own epitaph, 'Because by these, as testimonials I have lived, I wish most to be remembered.' He omitted that he had been US President for two terms. His birthdate would be April 13, following calendar revision; his draft, of course, left the date of death to be inserted. The epitaph is now to be found inscribed on an *obelisk over Jefferson's grave in the family cemetery near his house, Monticello, in Virginia, though this stone is a replacement for the original and dates only from 1883.

JENNINGS

~

SOME HAVE CHILDREN, SOME HAVE NONE:
HERE LIES THE MOTHER OF TWENTY-ONE.

'On Mrs Ann Jennings, at Wolstanton' – Stewart (1897).

JEROME
~

IN
LOVING REMEMBRANCE
OF
JEROME KLAPKA JEROME.
DIED JUNE 14TH 1927.
AGED 68 YEARS.
'FOR WE ARE LABOURERS TOGETHER WITH GOD.'
1 CORINTHIANS III.9

Inscription on the *grave which contains the ashes of the author of *Three Men in a Boat* in St Mary's churchyard, Ewelme, Oxfordshire. Jerome had lived nearby for a number of years and is buried with his wife, Ettie. The inscription is an interesting choice for a man who had written *Idle Thoughts of an Idle Fellow* and is noted for having written in his masterpiece: 'I like work: it fascinates me. I can sit and look at it for hours.'

JOHNSON
~

See FLEMING.

JOHNSON
~

ZAK
JOHNSON

Springer Spaniel
died March 12th 1986
aged 11 years

The pleasure was all ours

Dorothy
Richard
Charlotte.

On the *gravestone of a favourite dog, to be found in Rossendale Pet Cemetery, near Rawtenstall in Lancashire. Started in 1966, the cemetery now contains 1,600 graves and 800 small plots for caskets. Animals buried include a lioness, a horse, several budgies, as well as the expected cats and dogs, 'true friends', 'always in our hearts'.

JONES
~

Here lies old Jones,
Who all his life collected bones,
Till Death, that grim and sorry spectre,
That all inspecting bone collector,
Boned poor Jones, so neat and tidy
Here he lies, all bona fide.

'I remember being told about this as a schoolgirl seventy years ago and believed it to be in memory of a Professor of Archaeology at Oxford' – Mrs J. Laird, Folkestone, Kent (1982). Haining (1973) has a similar rhyme from 'St Lawrence's Church, Isle of Wight'.

JONES
~

In joyous memory of
George Jones
who was president of
the Newport Rifle Club
for twenty years.
'Always missed'.

'From America, I think' – A. Bune, Cambridge (1982).

JONES

~

Jemima Jones
passed on Jan 4 1803

This is the last long resting place
Of Aunt Jemima Jones
Her soul ascended into space
Amidst our tears and groans
She was not pleasing to the eye
Nor had she any brain
And when she talked twas through her nose
Which gave her friends much pain
But still we feel that she was worth
The money that was spent
Upon the coffin, hearse and stone
(The funeral plumes were lent).

'An epitaph from a Shropshire tombstone' – D. Richardson, Malmesbury, Wilts. (1982).

JONES

~

Here lies the body of Jessica Jones
Who died of eating cherry stones.
Her name was Smith; it was not Jones;
But Jones was put to rhyme with Stones.

This is but one form of the 'forced rhyme' epitaph. The earliest I have come across occurs in the diary of Edward Lear (entry for 20 April 1887): 'Below the high Cathedral stairs,/Lie the remains of Agnes Pears./ Her name was Wiggs; it was not Pears./ But Pears was put to rhyme with stairs.' With 'Susan Pares' replacing 'Agnes Pears', the rhyme was first published without date in *Queery Leary Nonsense* (1911), edited from mss. by Lady Constance Strachey.

I have an undated newspaper cutting (probably from the early 1900s) which states that the following version was to be found in the 'burying-ground of Evandale, Tasmania':

> Beneath these monumental stones
> Lies the body of Mary Jones.
> N.B.
> Her name was Smith, it wasn't Jones,
> But Jones was put to rhyme with Jones.

Stewart (1897) has substantially this version – with 'Lloyd', not 'Smith' – from Launceston, Tasmania. See also BUNN.

JONES
~

Here lies the body of Mary,
wife of John Jones of this parish.

Here lies the body of Martha,
wife of John Jones of this parish.

Here lies the wife of Jane,
wife of John Jones of this parish.

John Jones. At rest.

Adjacent epitaphs which used to be quoted by Lt Commander D. Gill Jones in his talk 'A quiet hour among the dead' (mid-twentieth century).

JONSON
~

O RARE
BEN JOHNSON

The poet and dramatist's original epitaph in Westminster Abbey was composed in the year he died, 1637. According to Abbey tradition (recounted in the *Official Guide*, 1988 revision), Jonson died in poverty and himself had directed that he be buried upright to save space. So he was, in the North Aisle of the Nave, with a small square stone over him. The *stone, spelt as above, was set upright in the North Aisle wall in 1821 to save the inscription from being worn away and where it may still be found. (There is also a wall *plaque 'O RARE BEN IOHNSON', erected before 1728, in Poets' Corner.)

Another tradition, according to John Aubrey, had it that the original epitaph was 'done at the charge of Jack Young, afterwards knighted, who, walking there when the grave was covering, gave the fellow eighteen pence to cut it'. The inscription has also been ascribed to the playwright D'Avenant (*d* 1668) who succeeded Jonson as unofficial Poet Laureate. His own *gravestone set in the floor of Poets' Corner reads:

O RARE

S. WILLIAM

DAVENANT

(or 'O rare Sir Will. Davenant' as Aubrey has it, 'in imitation of that on Ben Johnson'.) Either way, the spelling is not at fault – 'Jonson' is merely an alternative that has become accepted.

An attempt has been made to suggest that what the epitaphist meant to say was '*Orare Ben Jonson*' – 'pray for Ben Jonson' – but this is dubious Latin.

KAUFMAN
~

OVER MY DEAD BODY.

The suggested, jesting, epitaph of George S. Kaufman (1889–1961), the American playwright.

KEATS
~

**This Grave
contains all that was Mortal
of a
YOUNG ENGLISH POET
Who
on his Death Bed,
in the Bitterness of his Heart
at the Malicious Power of his Enemies,
Desired
these Words to be engraved on his Tomb Stone.**

**"Here lies One
Whose Name was writ in Water."**

Feb. 24th 1821

On the anonymous *grave of John Keats in the English Cemetery, Rome. The grave next to it – that of his friend, the painter Joseph SEVERN makes clear, however, who he is. A few days before he died, Keats said that on his gravestone there should be no mention of his name or country. As he lay dying, listening to the fountain outside on the Spanish Steps in Rome, it is said he kept being reminded of the lines from Beaumont and Fletcher's play *Philaster*: 'All your better deeds/Shall be in water writ.'

Joseph Severn duly worried about the gravestone. He was uncertain whether to use the bitter inscription which Keats had dictated to him and had to write to Charles Brown several times asking for advice. Two years after Keats's death the stone was at last erected at Severn's expense. His friends honoured Keats's dying wish that his grave be nameless but Brown suggested that there should be some explanation. This course was adopted, though Brown later conceded it had been a mistake. Robert Gittings in his biography of Keats (1968) comments: 'The quotations that may have suggested this phrase are many; but the gentle sound of the fountain, which had been his companion for so many nights as he lay in the narrow room above the square, may have seemed the right symbol for his end.'

Morrell (1948) has this interestingly worded memorial to the second wife of Thomas Hesketh, who died in 1653, from St Lawrence's church, York:

> Reader wouldst thou know what goodness lyeth here,
> Go to the neighbouring town and read it there,
> Though things in water writ away do glide,
> Yet these in watry characters abide
> His memory, and here writ, virtues look,
> Surer in tears than Ink, in eyes than book.

SHELLEY – whose remains were buried not far away in the same cemetery – wrote of it in his preface to *Adonais* (1821), his elegy on the death of Keats: 'The cemetery is an open space among the ruins, covered in winter with violets and daisies. It might make one in love with death, to think that one should be buried in so sweet a place.' Shelley also wrote this fragment on Keats, 'who desired that on his tomb should be inscribed':

> 'Here lieth One whose name was writ on [*sic*] water.'
> But, ere the breath that could erase it blew,
> Death, in remorse for that fell slaughter,
> Death, the immortalizing winter, flew
> Athwart the stream, – and time's printless torrent grew
> A scroll of crystal, blazoning the name
> Of Adonais!

There is a memorial plaque to Keats in Poets' Corner, Westminster Abbey. Robert Ross, one of Oscar WILDE's friends, is said to have suggested for his own tomb, towards the end of his stormy life, 'Here lies one whose name is writ in hot water'.

KENNEDY
~

See LISAGOR.

KENNEDY
~

ERECTED
by the
Parliament of Victoria
to the
Memory of
POLICE-SERGEANT
MICHAEL KENNEDY,
NATIVE OF WEST MEATH, IRELAND,
AGED 36 YEARS,
Who was
CRUELLY MURDERED BY ARMED CRIMINALS
IN THE WOMBAT RANGES NEAR MANSFIELD
ON THE 26TH OCTOBER 1878.
HE DIED IN THE SERVICE OF HIS COUNTRY
OF WHICH HE WAS AN ORNAMENT,
HIGHLY RESPECTED BY ALL GOOD CITIZENS, AND
A TERROR TO EVIL-DOERS . . .

An epitaph from among the police *graves at Mansfield, Victoria, Australia. Kennedy's widow (who lived until 1924) and son are buried with him.

KENT
~

Long as the heart beats life within her breast,
Thy child will bless thee, guardian, mother mild,
And far away thy memory will be blest,
By children of the children of thy child.

Tennyson's epitaph on the Duchess of Kent appeared in the *Court Journal* (19 March 1864), beneath the quotation, 'Her children rise up and call her blessed' after Proverbs 31:28. The Duchess – originally Victoria of Saxe-Coburg – was the mother of Queen VICTORIA. She died in 1861 and is buried in the smaller Royal Mausoleum at Frogmore, Windsor, not far from the one containing the remains of her daughter. The Duchess was a tenant of Frogmore house.

KENT
~

As I was so are
Ye, and as I am
So shall ye bee.

On William Kent, who died on 4 September 1640 and is buried at St Nicholas Church, Islip, Oxfordshire. Text from Patricia Utechin, *Epitaphs from Oxfordshire* (1980). The same rhyme has also been found at St Leonard's Church, Waterstock, Oxfordshire, and – by Bakewell (1977) – in a very old *inscription from St Eadburgha's Church, Broadway, Hereford and Worcester:

As thow
art so was
I. As I am
So shalt
Thou Bee.

KILVERT
~

In
Loving Remembrance
of the
REV. ROBERT FRANCIS KILVERT M.A.
VICAR OF THIS PARISH
DIED SEPT 23rd 1879,
AGED 38

"UNTIL THE DAY BREAK, AND THE SHADOWS FLEE AWAY"
CANTICLES ii/17
"HE BEING DEAD YET SPEAKETH"
HEB. xi.4

The Revd Francis Kilvert (1840–79) was an Anglican curate at Langley Burrell, Wiltshire, and afterwards at Clyro near the Welsh border. He was then vicar of Saint Harmon and moved to Bredwardine two years before his early death. He died a month or so after marrying. As such, he would now be completely forgotten but for the diary which he kept from 1870 to his death. Having been first pruned by his widow, selections were published in 1938–40. They are exceptionally well-written, and a classic of their kind. How appropriate therefore that the inscription on the white stone cross over Kilvert's *grave at Bredwardine should be the text from Hebrews 11:4 – chosen, presumably, by his widow, unaware how apt it was to be for a posthumously-published diarist.

For the text 'Until the day break . . .', see also HOLTROP.

KING
~

FREE AT LAST, FREE AT LAST
THANK GOD ALMIGHTY
I'M FREE AT LAST.

On the grave of the Revd Dr Martin Luther King Jr, the American civil rights leader (1929-68), in South View Cemetery, Atlanta, Georgia. This is a version of the words with which he had ended his 'I have a dream' speeches and, indeed, his last 'mountain top' speech on the night before he was assassinated.

KINGCOMBE
~

ONE OF
ENGLAND'S OLD CONTEMPTIBLES.

On the *grave of Sapper Clement R. Kingcombe, Royal Engineers, who died on 7th February 1919, in Brookwood Military Cemetery, Surrey.

The nickname 'Old Contemptibles' was gladly taken unto themselves by First World War veterans of the British Expeditionary Force who crossed the English Channel in 1914 to join the French and Belgians against the German advance. It was alleged that Kaiser Wilhelm II had described the army as 'a contemptibly little army' (referring to its size rather than its quality). The British press was then said to have mistranslated this so that it made him appear to have called them a 'contemptible little army'. The truth is that the whole episode was a propaganda ploy masterminded by the British.

KITCHEN
~

MEREDITH WE'RE IN!

This catchphrase originated as a shout of triumph in a music-hall sketch called 'The Bailiff' (or 'Moses and Son') performed by Fred Kitchen (1872–1950), leading comedian with Fred Karno's company. The sketch was first seen in about 1907. The phrase was used each time a bailiff and his assistant looked like gaining entrance to a house. Kitchen had it put on his gravestone, though the whereabouts of that is unknown.

KNELLER
~

KNELLER, by Heav'n and not a Master taught,
Whose Art was Nature, and whose Pictures Thought;
Now for two ages having snatch'd from fate
Whate'er was beauteous, or whate'er was great,
Lies crown'd with Princes honours, Poets lays,
Due to his Merit, and brave Thirst of praise.
    Living, great Nature fear'd he might outvie
Her works; and dying, fears herself may die.

The epitaph on the *monument to the German-born court painter, Sir Godfrey Kneller (?1646–1723), in the South Choir Aisle of Westminster Abbey, is signed by Alexander POPE who described it as 'the worst thing I ever wrote in my life'. Kneller is buried in St Mary's Church, Twickenham (where he was a churchwarden), having declared to Pope, on his deathbed, 'By God, I will not be buried in Westminster . . . they do bury fools there.' However, the prominent space for his monument at Twickenham was taken up by that to Alexander Pope's parents, so Kneller had to be memorialized at Westminster.

LANDSEER

~

He hath made every thing beautiful in his time.

Part of the inscription on the *monument to Sir Edwin Landseer (1802–73), the painter, in the crypt of St Paul's Cathedral. The quotation is from Ecclesiastes 3:11. It is accompanied by a reproduction of one of Landseer's most famous paintings 'The Shepherd's Mourner' (which shows a sheepdog patiently waiting by his dead master).

LAWRENCE

~

Homo sum! the adventurer.

The quotation on the *memorial to D.H. Lawrence (1885–1930), the novelist and poet, in Poets' Corner, Westminster Abbey, comes from his essay 'Climbing down Pisgah', which was published posthumously. Lawrence was buried at Vence, France, then later cremated and his ashes taken to Mexico. The Abbey memorial was unveiled during the Lawrence centenary on 16 November 1985. At a ceremony in the Abbey to mark Lawrence's birthday in September 1987, Professor James T. Boulton gave an address in which he explained his choice of this epitaph. He quoted Lawrence as saying, 'Man is nothing . . . unless he adventures. Either into the unknown of the world, of his environment. Or into the unknown of himself.' Boulton added: 'The very essence of man and human life, in Lawrence's view, is bound up with the act of knowing and the nature of knowledge . . .That commitment to adventure, in Lawrence's view, is what should motivate all human beings . . .'

LAWRENCE
~

TO THE DEAR MEMORY OF
T.E. LAWRENCE
FELLOW OF ALL SOULS COLLEGE
OXFORD
BORN 16 AUGUST 1888
DIED 19 MAY 1935

THE HOUR IS COMING & NOW IS
WHEN THE DEAD SHALL HEAR
THE VOICE OF THE
SON OF GOD
AND THEY THAT HEAR
SHALL LIVE.

On the *grave of 'Lawrence of Arabia' in the churchyard of St Nicholas, Moreton, Dorset. Lawrence lived two miles away at Clouds Hill and was killed nearby in a motor-cycle accident.

The text is from John 5:25. Also on the grave, emphasizing the Oxford connection, is a carved open book containing the university motto, 'DOMINUS ILLUMINATIO MEA'. Although there is no hint in this epitaph of his military exploits or of his Arabian connections, a recumbent effigy of Lawrence (by Eric Kennington) in full Arab costume, his head resting on a camel's saddle, is to be found not far away in St Martin's Church, Wareham, Dorset. There is also a memorial in St Paul's Cathedral, London.

LEE
~

Here lies the good old Knight Sir Harry,
Who loved well, but would not marry;
While he lived, and had his feeling,
She did lye, and he was kneeling,
Now he's dead and cannot feele
He doeth lye and shee doeth kneele.

This verse was occasioned by the death of Sir Henry Lee (1530–c 1610), a courtier of Queen Elizabeth I. Aubrey records that Lee had a monument at the foot of which his mistress's effigy was placed and that, in consequence, 'some bishop did threaten to have this monument defaced'. According to the *DNB*, 'in his later years, he carried on an amour with Anne Vavasour, daughter of Henry Vavasour of Copmanthorpe, Yorkshire; she is said in her epitaph to be buried in the same grave as Lee.'

Whatever happened, Lee's monument no longer exists, though it used to be in St Peter's Church, Quarrendon, Buckinghamshire. The inscription on it concluded thus: 'In 1611, having served five succeeding princes and kept himself right and steady in many dangerous shocks and three utter turns of state, with body bent to earth and a mind erected to heaven, aged 80, knighted 60 years, he met his long attended end.' This tablet is now preserved at Hartwell House, Buckinghamshire.

The verse above may possibly have led to the Dublin graffiti rhyme as quoted by Oliver St John Gogarty in *As I Was Going Down Sackville Street* (1937):

> Here lies the grave of Keelin,
> And on it is wife is kneeling;
> If he were alive, she would be lying,
> And he would be kneeling.

LEIGH
~

**In loving memory of
VIVIEN LEIGH
ACTRESS**

**. . . Now boast thee, death,
in thy posession lies
A lass unparallel'd . . .**

On the memorial *plaque to the actress (1913-67) in St Paul's Church, Covent Garden, London. The quotation concerns Shakespeare's Cleopatra – a role which Leigh played opposite to her then husband, Laurence OLIVIER, as Antony, in London and New York, 1951. The line was also placed by her mother on a memorial bench in private gardens in Eaton Square, opposite Vivien's old appartment.

LEWIS

~

CECIL
DAY LEWIS
1904–1972
Poet Laureate

Shall I be gone long?
For ever and a day.
To whom there belong?
Ask the stone to say.
Ask my song.

On the poet's *grave in the churchyard of St Michael, Stinsford, Dorset (near Thomas HARDY's heart), is an epitaph written for himself in 1944. 'It directs the pilgrim back to the poems where he still breathes', according to Sean Day-Lewis in the biography of his father, *C. Day-Lewis*, 1980. (The hyphenated form of his surname was only used in his pen name.)

LEWIS

~

IMMATURUS OBI: SED TU FELICIOR ANNOS
VIVE MEOS, BONA REPUBLICA! VIVE TUOS.

('I died young; but thou, O Good Republic, be more fortunate. Live out my years! Live your own.') According to Bartlett (1968), this is an 'inscription furnished by Nathaniel Cross, classics professor at the University of Nashville, on the tomb of the explorer Meriweather Lewis (1774–1809)'. Lewis was the American explorer who, with William Clark, led an overland expedition from St Louis to the Pacific Ocean (1804–6). He may have taken his own life. He was buried in Tennessee but the memorial was not raised until some considerable time after.

LIDDELL
~

THEY SHALL MOUNT UP WITH WINGS AS EAGLES
THEY SHALL RUN, AND NOT BE WEARY.

Written in gold on red granite in English and Chinese on the memorial to Eric Liddell (1902–45) in Weifang, Shandong Province, China. Liddell's refusal to race for his country on a Sunday in the 1924 Olympic Games – probably losing himself a second gold medal in the process – was celebrated in the 1981 film *Chariots of Fire*. The son of Scots missionaries, he was born in China and duly returned there after the Olympics to work for the London Missionary Society. He died of a brain tumour in the Japanese internment camp at Weifang. The memorial was not set up until June 1991. The words are from Isaiah 40:31. (Source: report by Andrew Higgins in the *Independent*, 10 June 1991.)

LINCOLN
~

**In this temple
As in the hearts of the people
For whom he saved the Union
The memory of Abraham
Lincoln
Is enshrined forever.**

Inscription above the statue of President Abraham Lincoln (1809–65) at the Lincoln Memorial, Washington DC. The words were written by Royal Cortissoz, art critic of the *New York Herald Tribune*.

LINDBERGH
~

IF I TAKE THE WINGS OF THE MORNING, AND DWELL
IN THE UTTERMOST PARTS OF THE SEA.

On the tombstone of Charles A. Lindbergh (1902–74), the US aviator, on the island of Maui, Hawaii. The text is from Psalms 139:9. Lindbergh made the first non-stop solo flight across the Atlantic in 1927.

LISAGOR
~

**PETER LISAGOR
SERGEANT
UNITED STATES ARMY
AUGUST 5, 1915
DECEMBER 10, 1976.**

This *gravestone from Arlington National Cemetery, Virginia, is typical in that it is carved on both faces. On one side of Lisagor's gravestone are carved tributes from Presidents Johnson ('AMERICANS WILL ALWAYS RESPECT THE RESPONSIBILITY WITH WHICH YOU HAVE CARRIED FORWARD THE STRATEGIC FREEDOM OF THE PRESS') and Ford ('HE WAS A JOURNALIST IN EVERY SENSE OF THE TERM, FAIR AND THOROUGH'). This is very unusual as, for the most part at Arlington, any type of epitaph is eschewed, with most gravestones just having the surname on one face and brief details on the reverse. Arlington is, after all, a military cemetery.

Pete Lisagor was bureau chief of the *Chicago Daily News* in Washington, his weekly column was syndicated to over 100 newspapers, and he was well-known as a political commentator on American television. *The Times* of London noted (13 December 1976): 'Peter Lisagor was known for directness and wit, and as a master of blunt but polite questioning at presidential press conferences.'

Elsewhere at Arlington inscriptions are more typically taken to a minimal extreme: President Kennedy's grave bears only his name and dates, though substantial quotations from his speeches are displayed on stone slabs nearby. Robert F. Kennedy's grave does not even have a stone – just a simple wooden cross bearing his name and dates (this is because he was not strictly speaking entitled to be buried at Arlington, never having served in the military). Opposite the grave site, however, extracts from his speeches are carved on stone slabs.

See also UNKNOWN SOLDIER.

LIVINGSTONE

~

BROUGHT BY FAITHFUL HANDS,
OVER LAND AND SEA,
HERE RESTS
DAVID LIVINGSTONE,
MISSIONARY,
TRAVELLER,
PHILANTHROPIST.
BORN MARCH 19, 1813,
AT BLANTYRE, LANARKSHIRE,
DIED MAY 1, 1873,
AT CHTITTAMBO'S VILLAGE, ULALA.
FOR THIRTY YEARS HIS LIFE WAS SPENT
IN AN UNWEARIED EFFORT
TO EVANGELISE THE NATIVE RACES
TO EXPLORE THE UNDISCOVERED SECRETS,
TO ABOLISH THE DESOLATING SLAVE TRADE,
OF CENTRAL AFRICA,
WHERE WITH HIS LAST WORDS HE WROTE,
"ALL I CAN ADD IN MY SOLITUDE, IS,
MAY HEAVEN'S RICH BLESSING COME DOWN
ON EVERYONE, AMERICAN, ENGLISH, OR TURK
– WHO WILL HELP HEAL
THIS OPEN SORE OF THE WORLD."

On the *tombstone of David Livingstone, the explorer and missionary (1813–73), in the floor of the nave of Westminster Abbey. His remains were interred on 18 April 1874, eleven months after his death. The quotation referring to the slave trade is taken from the last words he had addressed to the *New York Herald*.

LLOYD

~

Reader
Pause at this Humble Stone
it Records
The fall of unguarded Youth

By the allurements of vice,
and the treacherous snares
of Seduction
SARAH LLOYD
on the 23d. of April 1800,
in the 22d Year of her Age,
Suffered a Just but ignominious
Death
for admitting her abandoned seducer
into the Dwelling House of
her Mistress,
in the Night ot 3d Oct
1799,
and becoming the Instrument
in his Hands of the crimes
of Robbery and House-burning.
These were her last Words:
May my example, be a
warning to Thousands.

Andrews (1899) has this 'on a tombstone in Bury St Edmunds Cathedral'.

LOCKHART
~

HERE
AT THE FEET OF WALTER SCOTT
LIE
THE MORTAL REMAINS OF
JOHN GIBSON LOCKHART
HIS SON-IN-LAW.

Literally true. Sir Walter Scott's son-in-law and biographer (1794–1854) not only died in the room next to that in which Scott had died, but his *grave now lies at right-angles to the novelist's epitaph-free grave in the ruins of the Abbey church at Dryburgh, Berwickshire. Lockhart was a critic and editor of the *Quarterly Review*. According to one source, his substantial *Life of Scott* is 'remembered for its brilliant inaccuracies'.

In *A Writer's Diary*, Virginia Woolf describes her visit to Dryburgh in June 1938: 'We stopped at Dryburgh to see Scott's grave. It is under the broken palanquin of a ruined chapel. Just enough roof to cover it. And there he lies – Sir Walter Scott Baronet, in a caddy made of chocolate blancmange with these words cut large and plain on the lid. As Dame Charlotte who is buried beside him is covered with the same chocolate slab it must have been his taste. And there's something fitting in it. For the Abbey is impressive and the river running at the bottom of the field, and all the old Scots ruins standing round him. I picked a white syringa in memory but lost it. An airy place but Scott is much pressed together. The col. by his side, and Lockhart his son in law at his feet. Then there's HAIG's stuck about with dark red poppies.'

('Col.' would appear to be an abbreviation for 'column' = 'pillar of support' = 'wife'.)

LONGBOTTOM
~

ARS LONGA, VITA BREVIS.

A suggested epitaph (which I first came across in 1976) for the grave of a man called Longbottom.

LOWDER
~

Here lies the body of Mary Ann Lowder,
She burst while drinking a seidlitz powder.
Called from the world to her heavenly rest,
She should have waited till it effervesced.

'In Burlington Churchyard', according to Beable (1925); Diprose (1879) had earlier put 'Burlington, Mass.'

LYTTON

~

EDWARD GEORGE EARLE LYTTON BULWER LYTTON
BORN 25. MAY 1803 – DIED 18. JANUARY 1873

... LABORIOUS AND DISTINGUISHED IN ALL FIELDS OF
INTELLECTUAL ACTIVITY
INDEFATIGABLE AND ARDENT IN THE CULTIVATION
AND LOVE OF LETTERS
HIS GENIUS AS AN AUTHOR WAS DISPLAYED IN THE
MOST VARIED FORMS
WHICH HAVE CONNECTED INDISSOLUBLY
WITH EVERY DEPARTMENT OF THE LITERATURE OF HIS
TIME
THE NAME OF EDWARD BULWER LYTTON.

Part of the inscription on *the grave of the 1st Baron Lytton – Edward
Bulwer-Lytton, as he came to call himself, the prolific Victorian novelist
– who lies in the Chapel of St Edmund, Westminster Abbey. Note that
he is not to be found commemorated in Poets' Corner. Tegg recorded
the epitaph in 1876, soon after it was installed.

MACFARLANE
~

Erected to the memory of
John MacFarlane
Drowned in the Water of Leith
By a few affectionate friends.

Beable (1925) has this possibly apocryphal inscription, which refers to a river in the centre of Edinburgh.

MAGEE
~

**PILOT OFFICER
J.G. MAGEE
PILOT
ROYAL CANADIAN AIR FORCE
11TH DECEMBER 1941 AGE 19**

**"OH I HAVE SLIPPED
THE SURLY BONDS OF EARTH . . .
PUT OUT MY HAND
AND TOUCHED THE FACE OF GOD."**

On a bleak winter's day in 1991, I drove up to a service station in the tiny Lincolnshire village of Scopwick. If there had ever been any poetry in the place it might have been caught in some line of Tennyson's about the wolds, but the pump attendant sized me up instantly. 'It's Magee you've come to see?' he said, and directed me to a small burial ground (not the church graveyard) a few hundred yards away. There, amid the score or so military graves – Allied and German – from the Second World War was the *gravestone I had come to find. I wanted to see whether it bore Magee's most quoted lines. It did.

How did these lines become so famous? Because they are a classic case of a speechwriter having the appropriate quotation to hand at the right moment. On 28 January 1986, in his TV broadcast to the nation on the day of the space shuttle *Challenger* disaster, President Reagan concluded: 'We will never forget them nor the last time we saw them this morning as they prepared for their journey and waved goodbye and slipped the surly bonds of earth to touch the face of God.'

This immediately sent people the world over on fruitless journeys to their quotation books. Reagan was quoting 'High Flight', a sonnet written by John Gillespie Magee, a pilot with the Royal Canadian Air Force in the Second World War. He came to Britain, flew in a Spitfire squadron, and was killed at the age of nineteen on 11 December 1941 during a training flight from the airfield near Scopwick.

Magee had been born in Shanghai of an American father and an English mother who were missionaries. He was educated at Rugby and at a school in Connecticut. The sonnet was written on the back of a letter to his parents which stated, 'I am enclosing a verse I wrote the other day. It started at 30,000 feet, and was finished soon after I landed.' The parents were living in Washington DC at the time of his death and, according to the Library of Congress book *Respectfully Quoted*, the poem came to the attention of the Librarian of Congress, Archbald MacLeish, who acclaimed Magee as the first poet of the war.

Copies of 'High Flight' – sometimes referred to as 'the pilot's creed' – were widely distributed and plaques bearing it were sent to all R.C.A.F. airfields and training stations. It became very much the pilot's poem the world over.

Compare this, from a war *grave in Brookwood Cemetery, Surrey:

FLYING OFFICER
J.C. TODD
NAVIGATOR
ROYAL CANADIAN AIR FORCE
15TH JUNE 1945 AGE 23

I'VE TROD
THE SANCTITY OF SPACE
PUT OUT MY HAND
AND TOUCHED THE FACE OF GOD.

Magee's poem was published in 1943 in a volume called *More Poems from the Forces* (which was 'Dedicated to the USSR'). This is a transcription of the original manuscript in the Library of Congress:

Oh! I have slipped the surly bonds of Earth
And danced the skies on laughter-silvered wings;
Sunward I've climbed, and joined the tumbling mirth
Of sun-split clouds, – and done a hundred things

You have not dreamed of – wheeled and soared and swung
   High in the sunlit silence. Hov'ring there,
I've chased the shouting wind along, and flung
   My eager craft through footless halls of air . . .

Up, up the long, delirious, burning blue
   I've topped the wind-swept heights with easy grace
Where never lark, nor ever eagle flew –
   And, while with silent lifting mind I've trod
The high, untrespassed sanctity of space,
   Put out my hand and touched the face of God.

How did the poem come to be quoted by President Reagan in 1986? As it happens, he knew of the poem: 'I hadn't heard it in years, but of course I knew it from years back, the war. And I think it was written on a sort of tablet or plaque outside Patti's school that I took her to when she was a young girl.' It transpires that Reagan had also been present at a party the night fellow actor Tyrone Power returned from fighting in the Second World War – a party at which Power recited 'High Flight' from memory. (When Power died, the poem was read over his grave by Laurence Olivier.)

The sonnet was also used for years as the close-down reading of a local Washington TV station. It was generally well-known in the United States (and much more so than in Britain). One person who learned it at school was Peggy Noonan who wrote the speech for Reagan, as she decribes in her book *What I Saw at the Revolution* (1990). This is not the occasion to discuss the rights and wrongs of speechwriters 'going public' and revealing the extent to which they pull the strings. Suffice to say, it was a brilliant stroke on Noonan's part to select such an apposite quotation and one not too far-fetched in Reagan's mouth.

Two footnotes: in his lyrics for the English version of the musical *Les Misérables* (1985), Herbert Kretzmer blended Magee's words with something from Evelyn Waugh's *Brideshead Revisited* ('to know and love another human being is the root of all wisdom') to produce the line: 'To love another person is to see the face of God.' Magee's original words are curiously reminiscent of Oscar WILDE's lines prefixed to his *Poems* (Paris edition, 1903):

Surely there was a time I might have trod
The sunlit heights, and from life's dissonance
Struck one clear chord to reach the ears of God.

MAGGIE
~

In memory of
MAGGIE
Who in her time kicked
Two colonels,
Four majors,
Ten captains,
Twenty-four lieutenants,
Forty-two sergeants,
Four hundred and thirty-two other ranks
AND
One Mills Bomb.

'On the last resting place of an Army mule somewhere in France' –
J.H.A. Dick, Currie, Midlothian (1981).

MAJOR
~

BORN A DOG. DIED A GENTLEMAN.

Quoted by Naomi Lewis (1981). It seems to have been a Victorian
epitaph from an unidentified pets' cemetery.

MARCHANT
~

**NEAR THIS SPOT LIE THE REMAINS OF
NATHANIEL MARCHANT ESQ. R.A.
WHO DIED MARCH 24TH 1816, AGED 77 YEARS.**

*He was born in the County of Sussex, where his
family had long been established, and he succeeded to
the small property it possessed there, when rather*

late in life. In the mean time his skill and industry
as a Gem Engraver, had supplied the place of patronage,
by enabling him to remove to Italy to cultivate an art
to which his genius strongly inclined him. He
continued there some years, improving talents by
the close study of the remains of ancient Sculpture,
which have rendered him celebrated throughout Europe,
and do honor to his native Country. They
attracted the notice of its Government towards the
latter part of his life, and were rewarded by his
appointment to places where they could be useful.
About the same time, having become intimate
with the owner of the adjoining Manor House, and
frequently resorting to it, he was led to choose the
parish to which it belongs as the place of his
interment. He was beloved for his social qualities,
and benevolence: and esteemed for his uniform
support of a character of strict integrity.

J. FLAXMAN R.A. AS APPOINTED BY NAME IN THE WILL
OF HIS FRIEND
EXECUTED THIS MONUMENT OF HIM.

Wall *tablet in the north-west corner of Stoke Poges church. Marchant merits an entry in the *DNB* where it is stated that, among other things, 'the portrait of George III on the 3*s*. bank token was engraved by Marchant from a model taken by him from life', and that 'the Prince Regent (George IV) appointed Marchant his engraver of gems'.

MARX
~

Here lies Groucho Marx
and Lies and Lies and Lies.
PS He never kissed an ugly girl.

Suggested epitaph for Groucho Marx, the film comedian (1895–1977). It appears in his book *The Secret Word is Groucho* (1976).

MARX
~

WORKERS OF ALL LANDS
UNITE

KARL MARX

THE PHILOSOPHERS HAVE ONLY
INTERPRETED THE WORLD IN
VARIOUS WAYS. THE POINT
HOWEVER IS TO CHANGE IT.

Karl Marx (1818–83), the German-born father of Communism lived in
London from 1849 onwards. He was buried in Highgate Cemetery on 17
March 1883. His ill-kept grave remained in a far corner of the cemetery
until 1956 when the Soviet Communist Party paid for a monolithic black
marble block to be installed, with this *inscription. It is surmounted by a
massive cast iron head of Marx and bears an extract (at the top) from
his closing words to *The Communist Manifesto* (1848), written originally
in German: 'The workers have nothing to lose in this [revolution] but
their chains. They have a world to gain. Workers of the world, unite!'
The second quotation is from his *Theses on Feuerbach* (1888).

An interesting pairing is formed by the grave almost opposite and
across the path being that of Herbert Spencer (1820–1903), the
philosopher.

MARY ANNE
~

Here lies the body of Mary Anne
Safe in the arms of Abraham.
All very well for Mary Anne
But how about poor Abraham?

'In a North Devon churchyard' – D. Whitmore, Liphook, Hants. (1982);
'Mary Ann has gone to rest,/Safe at last on Abraham's breast,/Which
may be nuts for Mary Ann,/But is certainly rough on Abraham' –
Hyman (1967).

MENCKEN
∼

If after I depart this vale you ever remember me and
have thought to please my ghost, forgive some sinner
and wink your eye at some homely girl.

H.L. Mencken (1880–1956), the US newspaperman, critic and philologist,
suggested this epitaph for himself in *The Smart Set* (December 1921).
After his death, it was inscribed on a plaque in the lobby of the offices of
the Baltimore *Sun* newspapers (with which he had been associated most
of his working life).

MICHELL
∼

Christoper Michell's Sonn lyeth here, Richard Michell was his
   Name,
His father's love was so to him, he caus'd to write the same:
He was but 4 Yeares 5 Moneths old, and then was buryed here,
And of his Body the Wormes did find a Dish of dainty chere.

A seventeenth-century epitaph, quoted by Aubrey.

MILL
∼

Were there but a few hearts and intellects like hers
this earth would already become the hoped-for
heaven.

John Stuart Mill (1806–73), the English philosopher and economist,
composed this epitaph for his wife Harriet (*d* 1858/9). Her grave is in the
cemetery of St Véran, near Avignon.

MILLER

~

Here lie the remains of
Honest Joe Miller,
Who was
A tender Husband,
A sincere friend,
A facetious Companion,
And an excellent Comedian.
He departed this life the 15th day of August, 1738,
Aged 54 years . . .

In St Clement Danes burying ground, Strand, London, written by 'S. Duck'. *Collection* (1806) has two verses following. Miller (1684–1738) lent his name (posthumously and unwittingly) to a book of old jokes compiled by John Mottley and called *Joe Miller's Jest-Book*. Accordingly, a 'Joe Miller' became the term for an old joke, as though it had come from the Mottley collection. The burying ground no longer exists and the church has been re-consecrated as the Central Church of the RAF after being destroyed by enemy action in 1941.

MITFORD

~

Say not the struggle naught availeth.

The Hon. Unity Valkyrie Mitford (*b* 1914) was one of the six daughters of the 2nd Baron Redesdale. She was a member of the British Union of Fascists and a friend of Hitler. Her death in 1948 was the result of an old self-inflicted gunshot wound (she had attempted suicide on hearing that Hitler had gone to war in 1939). Her mother, Sydney, Lady Redesdale, put the quotation (from Arthur Hugh Clough's poem of that title) on Unity's *grave in the churchyard of St Mary the Virgin, Swinbrook, Oxford.

Unity's sister, Nancy (1904–73), is also buried at Swinbrook. Her gravestone simply states: 'Authoress, wife of Peter Rodd', and bears a carving of a mole.

Sacred to the memory
of
The Right Honourable
Lady MARY WORTLEY MONTAGUE,
Who happily introduc'd from Turkey,
into this Country,
The Salutary Art
Of innoculating the Small-Pox.
Convinc'd of its Efficacy
She first tried it with success
On her own Children;
And then recommended the practice of it
To her fellow-Citizens.
Thus by her Example and Advice,
We have soften'd the Virulence,
And escap'd the danger of this malignant Disease,
To perpetuate the Memory of such Benevolence;
And to express her Gratitude
For the benefit She herself has receiv'd
From this alleviating Art,
This Monument is erected
by
HENRIETTA INGE
Relict of THEODORE WILLIAM INGE ESQ.
And daughter of Sir JOHN WROTTESLEY Baronet
In the Year of Our Lord MDCCLXXXIX.

The wall *memorial by the West Door of Lichfield Cathedral, though elegantly phrased, completely ignores the chief claims to fame of Lady Mary Wortley Montagu (as we would now spell her surname) (1689–1762). These are that she was an accomplished letter writer and poet, that she mingled in literary circles (quarrelling famously with POPE), and is reputed to have uttered the wonderful dying words, 'It has all been very interesting'. She did indeed introduce the practice of innoculation against smallpox – from which she herself had suffered in 1715 – as a result of accompanying her husband to Constantinople, where he was ambassador. Her actual grave is in the vaults below the Grosvenor Chapel, South Audley Street, Mayfair, London, where there is, however, no tablet. She died in George Street, Hanover Square. There is no obvious reason why her memorial should be in Lichfield. The marble shows a female figure of Beauty, weeping over the ashes of her preserver – 'M.W.M.' – enclosed in an urn.

MOORE
~

On one who thought no other could
write such English as himself

'No mortal man beneath the shy
Can write such English as can I
They say it holds no thought my own
What then, such beauty (perfection) is not
    known.'

Heap dustbins on him:
They'll not meet
The apex of his self conceit.

'Epitaph for George Moore' – unfinished verse by Thomas HARDY, found among papers at his death and first published in the *Complete Poems* (ed. James Gibson, 1976). In fact, Moore the novelist did not die until 1933, five years after Hardy.

MORTON
~

HE FIRST DECEAS'D; SHE FOR A LITTLE TRI'D
TO LIVE WITHOUT HIM: LIK'D IT NOT, AND DI'D.

'Upon the Death of Sir Albertus Morton's Wife' by Sir Henry Wotton (1568–1639). Sir Albertus died in 1625, and was the poet's nephew. *Collection* (1806) has it as 'Sir Albertus Moreton' and 'he first departed; she for one day try'd'.

NEALE
∼

His Name, to whose Memory
This testimonial is Inscribed
Is so deeply graven on the hearts of all who knew him,
That while any of those survive
There needed not the Record of Stone or Marble
To preserve it from Oblivion,
But, because from this changeable scene
All living records swiftly pass away,
It is here Written,
As a more Durable Memorial,
That He was One
Of whom "When the ear heard, it blessed him";
Whom, "When the eye saw, it gave witness to him";
For he delivered the Poor and Fatherless
"And him who had none to help him",
And "caused the widow's heart to sing for joy".
In all the relations of life he was perfect,
(According to the measure of human imperfection).
In his daily walk with God, exemplifying the virtues of the
Christian Character,
Above all, in the largeness of his charity and in the beauty
of his humility.

Inscription on the obelisk to Admiral Sir Harry Burrard Neale (1766–
1840) at Walhampton, Hampshire. This text from Jo Darke, *The
Monument Guide to England and Wales* (1991). The *DNB* notes: 'A
handsome obelisk was erected to his memory on Mount Pleasant,
opposite the town of Lymington, of which he was lord of the manor,
and which he had represented in parliament for forty years.'

NELSON
∼

Sacred to the Memory of
HORATIO LORD NELSON,
Who, pious, brave, and fortunate,

Beloved by Men, and in peace with God,
Wanted nothing to complete the full measure
Of his glory,
But much to that of his reward;
Heaven and his country unite to discharge the debt;
Heaven by taking him to eternal happiness,
His country by devoting him to eternal remembrance.

This an epitaph from *Collection* (1806), Nelson having died at the Battle of Trafalgar the year before publication. However, it is not the text on either his grave or his memorial in St Paul's Cathedral. The latter monument, a strange concoction showing Britannia, two midshipmen, a crouching lion and sea gods, was unveiled in 1818 and bears an *inscription of which this is part:

ERECTED AT THE PUBLIC EXPENSE
TO THE MEMORY OF
VICE-ADMIRAL HORATIO, VISCOUNT NELSON, K.B.
TO RECORD HIS SPLENDID AND UNPARALLELED ACHIEVEMENTS,
DURING A LIFE SPENT IN THE SERVICE OF HIS COUNTRY,
AND TERMINATED IN THE MOMENT OF VICTORY BY A
GLORIOUS DEATH
IN THE MEMORABLE ACTION OFF CAPE TRAFALGAR ON THE XXI
OF
OCTOBER MDCCCV.

Nelson (*b* 1758) is commemorated in many other locations – not least by the column (1843) in Trafalgar Square – but he had foreseen a different burial place. At the Battle of Cape St Vincent (1797), he is reported to have said: 'Westminster Abbey or victory!'; and at the Battle of the Nile (1798):'Before this time tomorrow I shall have gained a peerage, or Westminster Abbey' (both of which echo Shakespeare, *King Henry VI, Part 3* (II.ii.174): 'And either victory, or else a grave.')

NEWCASTLE
~

Here lyes the Loyall Duke of Newcastle and his
Dutches his second wife by whom he had noe issue her
name was Margarett Lucas youngest sister to the Lord

Lucas of Colchester a noble familie for all the
Brothers were Valiant and all the Sisters virtuous.
This Dutches was a wise wittie & learned Lady, which
her many books do testifie she was a most Virtuous &
a loveing and carefull wife & was with her Lord all
the time of his banishment & miseries & when he came
home never parted from him in his solitary retirements.

On the *monument of the 1st Duke and Duchess of Newcastle in the
North Transept of Westminster Abbey. They are both buried nearby.
The monument was erected during the lifetime of William (Cavendish),
1st Duke (1592–1676), his second wife, Margaret (1623–73), having
predeceased him. A poet and playwright, he was known as the 'Loyal
Duke' for his support of Charles I during the English Civil War and
went into exile until the Restoration. His duchess was quite a figure in
her own right. She wrote plays, letters, verses, a biography of her
husband, and an autobiography. Virginia Woolf wrote of her: 'Garish in
her dress, eccentric in her habits, chaste in her conduct, coarse in her
speech, she succeeded during her lifetime in drawing upon herself the
ridicule of the great and the applause of the learned . . . But [now] . . .
she lives only in the few splendid phrases that Lamb scattered upon her
tomb . . .'

NEWTON
~

Here is deposited
Sir ISAAC NEWTON, Knight;
Who, by the Light of Mathematical Learning, and
A Force of Mind almost Divine,
First explained
The Motions and Figures of the Planets
And Planetary Orbits;
Paths of the Comets, and Tides of the Ocean;
Discover'd, what no one before ever suspected,
The Difference of the Rays of Light,
And the Distinction of Colours thence arising.
He was a diligent, penetrating, faithful interpreter
Of Nature, of Antiquity, and the Holy Scripture.

By his Philosophy, he asserted the Majesty of God,
The greatest and most glorious of all Beings;
And by his Morals expressed the Simplicity of the Gospel.
Let Mortals congratulate themselves
That there has been so Great, so Good a Man;
The Glory of the Human Race.
Born Dec.25, 1642, and died in March, 1726.

Translated from the Latin, as in Frobisher (?1790). The monument specified by Newton's heirs was finally erected in 1731 in Westminster Abbey against the choir screen in the nave. It is something of a monstrosity – with cherubs holding emblems of Newton's discoveries. His gravestone is a short distance away in the floor of the Nave.

Dr Johnson in his essay on epitaphs disapproved: 'Had only the name of Sir Isaac Newton been subjoined to the design upon his monument, instead of a long detail of his discoveries, which no philosopher can want, and which none but a philosopher can understand, those, by whose direction it was raised, had done more honour both to him and to themselves.' Johnson goes on to argue that next in dignity to a bare name would have been 'a short character, short and unadorned' and suggests: '*ISAACUS NEWTONUS, naturae legibus investigatis, his quiescit.*'

Compare Alexander POPE's lines:

Intended for Sir ISAAC NEWTON,
In Westminster-Abbey
ISAACUS NEWTONUS:
Quem Immortalem
Testantur *Tempus, Natura, Coelum:*
Mortalem
Hoc marmor fatetur.

Nature, and Nature's Laws lay hid in Night:
GOD said, *Let Newton be!* and all was Light.

Sir John Squire's later suggested response (*Poems*, 1926) was:

It did not last: the Devil howling 'Ho!
Let Einstein be!' restored the status quo.

NOVELLO

~

**Blaze of lights and music calling, Music weeping,
rising, falling, Like a rare & precious diamond
His brilliance still lives on.**

On the memorial *tablet in St Paul's Cathedral crypt to the composer
and actor, Ivor Novello (1893–1951). The lines were written by Lynn S.
Maury of the Ivor Novello Memorial Society who mounted an eight-year
campaign to have a plaque placed in the cathedral. Her monogram is
attached to the words. Novello's ashes, appropriately for the composer
of 'We'll Gather Lilacs', were placed under a lilac tree in the gardens of
Golders Green Crematorium, London. At his funeral there, Edward
Marsh produced as an epitaph his own translation of La Fontaine: 'Some
few there be, spoilt darlings of high Heaven,/To whom the magic grace
of charm is given.'

On the memorial *plaque to Novello in St Paul's Church, Covent
Garden, are these words, slightly adapted from Shakespeare, *Merchant of
Venice* (III.ii.294): 'The dearest friend, the kindest man, the best-
conditioned and unwearied spirit in doing courtesies.'

NYMAN

~

**"THERE IS NO DARKNESS
IN ALL THE WORLD
TO PUT OUT THE LIGHT
OF ONE SMALL CANDLE."**

On the *grave of Sergeant J.L. Nyman, RAF pilot, who died 8th
September 1941, age 20; in Brookwood Military Cemetery, Surrey. The
text appears to be quoting Robert Alden (*b* 1937), a US theologian:
'There is not enough darkness in all the world to put out the light of
even one small candle.'

OATES

~

Hereabouts died a very gallant gentleman, Captain
L.E.G. Oates of the Inniskilling Dragoons. In March
1912, returning from the Pole, he walked willingly
to his death in a blizzard, to try and save his
comrades, beset by hardship. This note is left by
the Relief Expedition. 1912.

On a cairn marking the spot where Captain Oates (nicknamed 'Titus') (*b*
1880) walked out to his death on Captain SCOTT's Antarctic
expedition. Suffering from scurvy, frostbitten and gangrenous feet, and
an old war wound, Oates realized he would die and did not wish to slow
his comrades down. With classic stiff-upper-lip understatement, Oates is
reported by Scott to have said, 'I am just going outside, and I may be
some time'.

The epitaph was composed by E.L. Atkinson and Apsley Cherry-
Garrard, and recorded in the latter's *The Worst Journey in the World*
(1922).

O'DAY

~

This is the grave of Mike O'Day
Who died maintaining his right of way.
His right was clear, his will was strong.
But he's just as dead as if he'd been wrong.

This is the Bartlett (1968) form of a rhyme which comes in several
versions, including: 'Here lies the body of Edmund Gray/Who died
maintaining his right of way./He was right – dead right – as he drove
along./But he's just as dead as if he'd been wrong' – quoted by Sir Huw
Wheldon (1981). There is also one to 'Timothy Jay', as in 'jay-walking'.
Presumably a suggested rather than actual epitaph.

O'HARA

~

Better than anyone else, he told the truth about his
time, the first half of the twentieth century. He
was a professional. He wrote honestly and well.

Self-composed epitaph on John O'Hara (1905–70), the US novelist and
playwright, in Princeton Cemetery. An 'astonishing claim', according to
Brendan Gill in *Here at the New Yorker* (1975), who reports it.

OLIVIER

~

1907
LAURENCE OLIVIER
O.M. ACTOR
1989

This is all that is inscribed on the diamond-shaped floor *stone unveiled
in Poets' Corner, Westminster Abbey, in September 1991 – no mention of
his knighthood or peerage. Olivier's ashes lie at the foot of the
SHAKESPEARE memorial, nearer to it than the diamond-shaped stone of
Sir Henry Irving (1838–1905), but just to one side of the grave of David
GARRICK.

O'LOONEY

~

Here lies the body of
LADY O'LOONEY
Great niece of **BURKE**
Commonly called the Sublime
She was Bland, Passionate

and deeply Religious, also
she painted in water colours
and sent several pictures
to the Exhibition
She was first Cousin to
LADY JONES
and of such is the
Kingdom of Heaven.

This most delightful of epitaphs can no longer be found. Fairley (1875) placed it in 'Pewsey churchyard'; Tegg (1876) in 'Pewsey, Bedfordshire' (which does not exist); Stewart (1897) in 'Pewsey, Wiltshire'; Briscoe (1901) in Dorsetshire; Mackae (?1910) placed it in Devon; Haining (1973) in Bridgewater Cemetery, Somerset.

Compare Reder (1969), in Bandon, Ireland: 'Sacred to the memory of Mrs Maria Boyle/Who was a good wife, a devoted Mother/And a kind and charitable neighbour./She painted in water colours,/And was the first cousin to the Earl of Cork,/And of such is the Kingdom of Heaven.'

At which point one wonders whether what Russell (1898) calls 'the best-known of all epitaphs' ever existed anywhere at all. The name O'Looney does not occur in the *DNB* or *Debrett*, though it was in the 1991 London telephone directory.

ORWELL

~

HERE LIES
ERIC ARTHUR BLAIR
BORN JUNE 25TH 1903
DIED JANUARY 21ST 1950.

This inscription from the *grave of the writer 'George Orwell' in All Saints' churchyard, Sutton Courtenay, Oxfordshire, is included because it is *not* an epitaph and pointedly refrains from mentioning the name by which the writer is better known. Though not a member of any church and (according to Tosco Fyvel) 'a complete agnostic and deeply attached to English tradition', Orwell made a will three days before he died saying that he wished to be buried according to the rites of the Church of England and for his grave to bear this headstone. His friend, David Astor, arranged it for him.

PAGE

~

HERE LYES DAME MARY PAGE
RELICT OF SIR GREGORY PAGE, BART
SHE DEPARTED THIS LIFE MARCH 4, 1728
IN THE 56 YEAR OF HER AGE.

IN 67 MONTHS SHE WAS TAPD 66 TIMES
HAD TAKEN AWAY 240 GALLONS OF WATER
WITHOUT EVER REPINING AT HER CASE
OR EVER FEARING THE OPERATION.

Collection (1806) found this in Bunhill Fields Cemetery, London, where it is still, although one or two of the letters are illegible. The two parts of the *inscription are on panels at either end of the tomb.

Compare this death notice from *The Gentleman's Magazine*, May 1732: 'The wife of Walter Newberry, merchant of Gracechurch Street, in the 33rd year of her age, of the Dropsy, for which from the Year 1728 she had been tapped 57 times, and had taken from her 240 gallons of water.' Such medical-statistical epitaphs seem to have been common about this time.

PALMER

~

Here lies John Palmer and Mary his wife
Prisoners of hope to Eternal Life
Who deceased

Hee May the 15, 1661, aged 61
Mary make room,
To thee I come
And my last home
To the day of doom
Then shall we wake rise live for ay
With Christ a never dying day
Come then my dear we'll sleep in blisse
And in the dust each other kisse

Twice sixteen years we lived together
In sunshine and in stormy weather
In wedlock bands husband and wife
In joy love peace void of all strife
And ten times changed our habitation
And here at last we find our station
When after ten years spent we have
Obtained at length a quiet grave.
Shee October the 13, 1660, aged 50
I went before
To ope death's door
I could not stay
But now give way

Palmer eram ante obitum nemo fit palmifer at nunc
Palmifer in caelis qui modo palmer eram

Palmers on earth are pilgrims such as I
My pilgrimage is done and here I ly.

From 'Nately Scures [Hampshire] and its Church' (leaflet, 1951, revised 1968): 'On the wall above the recess at the west end of the church is a brass plate of the 17th century . . . the *Gentleman's Magazine*, October 1836, mentions a 17th century brass tablet, obviously this one, as being affixed to the apse wall, so it was before the restoration of the last century that it was removed from its original position probably on the floor of the nave.'

PARKER

~

EXCUSE MY DUST.

Suggested epitaph for herself by the American writer and wit, Dorothy Parker (1893-1967). She also suggested, for her tombstone, 'This is on me', and, 'If you can read this, you are standing too close'. These epitaphs are recorded by John Keats in his biography of Parker, *You Might As Well Live* (1970).

PARSLEY

~

Here lies the Man whose Name in Spight of Death
Renowned lives by Blast of Golden Fame;
Whose Harmony survives his vital Breath,
Whose Skill no Pride did spot, whose Life no Blame;
Whose low Estate was blest with quiet Mind
As our sweet Cords with Discords mixed be:
Whose life in *Seventy* and *Four* Years entwind
As falleth mellow Apples from the Tree.
Whose Deeds were Rules, whose Words were Verity;
Who here a Singing-Man did spend his Days.
Full *Fifty* Years in our Church Melody
His Memory shines bright whom thus we praise.

Plaque in Norwich Cathedral to an old chorister, Osbert Parsley, who died in 1585. Transcription from Norwich (1980). Parsley is in the *DNB* as a composer.

PARTRIDGE

~

**WHAT! KILL A PARTRIDGE IN THE MONTH OF MAY!
WAS THAT DONE LIKE A SPORTSMAN? EH, DEATH, EH?**

Described as a 'Norfolk Epitaph, 1861' in *The Week-End Book* (1955).

PEARS

~

See HOLST.

PEGG

~

Here lies the body of Dame Margaret Pegg
Who never had issue except in her leg
So great was her art, so deep was her cunning,
While one leg kept still the other kept running.

'On an old lady who had suffered from an ulcerated leg' – quoted by Lt
Commander D. Gill Jones in his talk 'A quiet hour among the dead'
(mid-twentieth century).

PENNEFATHER

~

"WITH CHRIST, WHICH IS FAR BETTER."

This text to be found on a *gravestone in the main avenue of Brompton
Cemetery, London – though quite a common epitaph – I first saw in
1978 and considered a little ungenerous even then. It is attached to the
memorial for Margaret, widow of General John Lysaght Pennefather
GCB. He died in 1872 and she followed in 1880. 'Better than what?' one
is tempted to ask. The allusion is to St Paul's Epistle to the Philippians
(1:23) where Paul compares the folly of living with the wisdom of dying:
'For I am in a strait betwixt the two, having a desire to depart, and to
be with Christ; which is far better.'

PEPYS

~

HERE LIES
ELIZABETH PEPYS
TO WHOM
Somerset gave her cradle, Octob: 23, 1640 . . .

Wife of Samuel Pepys (who serves the Royal Navy).
She was educated first in a convent, and then in a seminary of
France.
She was distinguished by the excellence of both at once,
Gifted with beauty, accomplishments, tongues,
She bore no offspring, for she could not have borne her like.
At length when she had bidden this world a gentle farewell,
(After a journey completed through, we may say, the lovelier
sights of Europe) –
A returning pilgrim, she took her departure to wander through
a grander world.

She died on the 10th of November,
In the 29th year of her age,
In the 15th of her marriage,
In the year of Our Lord 1669.

Translation (from Marjorie Astin, *Mrs Pepys Her Book*, 1929) of part of
the *memorial in St Olave's Church, Hart Street, City of London. Samuel
Pepys erected the bust to his wife at her death in 1669 (which was after
he had given up writing his first main diary). The epitaph records in
elaborate Latin that she bore no children because she could bear none
worthy of herself ('*Prolem enixa, quia parem non potuit, nullam*'). This
is a nice conceit, especially as her childlessness may have been caused by
Pepys's own sterility. They are buried together elsewhere in the church.
He has a later memorial (1884) which bears no epitaph.

PHILBY
~

THE GREATEST EXPLORER OF THEM ALL.

From the inscription on the grave of Harry St John Bridger Philby (1885–
1960), the British-born Arabist, in the Muslim cemetery in the Basta
quarter of Beirut. His son, Kim, wrote this epitaph for the tomb, three
years before he defected to the Soviet Union (according to *Philby: The
Spy Who Betrayed a Generation*, 1968). James Morris, *Farewell the
Trumpets* (1978), has it rather as 'Greatest of Arabian explorers'. St John
Philby's last words on his deathbed were, 'God, I'm bored'.

PHILIPS

~

Near this place
lies
CHARLES CLAUDIUS PHILIPS
Whose absolute contempt of Riches,
And inimitable performance on the Violin
Made him the admiration of all who knew him.
He was born in Wales,
Made the tour of Europe,
And, after the experience of both kinds of fortune,
Died in 1732.

Exalted soul! thy various sounds could please
The love-sick virgin, and the gouty ease;
Could jarring crowds like old AMPHION move
To beauteous order, and harmonious love;
Here rest in peace, till angels bid thee rise,
To join thy Saviour's concert in the skies.

Mackae (?1910) says this comes from the porch of Wolverhampton church and that it is quoted by James Boswell in his *Life of Johnson*. In fact, only the verse is quoted by Boswell and differs in some respects from what is printed above.

Collection (1806) conveys Boswell's anecdote thus: 'Garrick repeating this epitaph (which is by a Dr Wilkes) to Dr Johnson, the latter shook his head, and said, "I think, Davy, I can make a better." Then stirring about his tea, for a little while, in a state of meditation, he almost extempore produced the following lines – which are so exquisitely beautiful, that Lord Kames, strangely prejudiced as he was against Dr Johnson, was compelled to allow them very high praise':

PHILIPS, whose touch harmonious could remove
The pangs of guilty power or helpless love;
Rest here! distress'd by poverty no more,
Here find that calm, thou gav'st so oft before.
Sleep, undisturb'd, within this peaceful shrine,
'Till angels wake thee with a note like thine!

PIMM

~

A sudden change dear friends upon me fell
I had not time to bid you all farewell.
Think nothing strange, death happens unto all,
My lot to day to morrow yours may fall.

On the *gravestone in Stanton Harcourt churchyard of Susanah Pimm,
who died in 1864, aged 55 years.

PITMAN

~

In memori ov
MERI PITMAN
Weif ov Mr Eizak Pitman
Fonetik Printer, ov this Siti.
Died 19 August 1857, edjed 64.
"Preper tu mit thei God."
– *Emos* 4–12.

Epitaph on the wife of Isaac Pitman (knighted 1894, died 1897), the
inventor of a shorthand system, and written to demonstrate his interest
in spelling reform. This text is from Haining (1973) who says it is in
Lansdown Cemetery, Bath.

PITT

~

ERECTED BY
THE KING AND PARLIAMENT
AS A TESTIMONY TO
THE VIRTUES AND ABILITY
OF
WILLIAM PITT, EARL OF CHATHAM
DURING WHOSE ADMINISTRATION,

IN THE REIGNS OF GEORGE THE SECOND AND
GEORGE THE THIRD,
DIVINE PROVIDENCE
EXALTED GREAT BRITAIN
TO AN HEIGHT OF PROSPERITY AND GLORY
UNKNOWN TO ANY FORMER AGE.

Part of the inscription on the *memorial and grave of William Pitt, the
Elder (1708–78), in the North Transept of Westminster Abbey. His son
(1759–1806) is buried in the same tomb, though his memorial is over the
door at the west end ofthe nave. It was for the *son* that Byron composed
his 'Epitaph for William Pitt' (in January 1820): 'With death doom'd to
grapple,/Beneath this cold slab, he/Who lied in the Chapel/Now lies in
the Abbey.'

POPE
~

ALEXANDRO POPE
M.H.
GULIELMUS EPISCOPUS GLOCETRIENSIS
AMICITIAE CAUSA, FAC. CUR.
MDCCLXI

POETA LOQUITUR

For one who would not be buried in Westminster Abbey

Heroes and Kings! your distance keep:
In peace let one poor Poet sleep,
Who never flatter'd Folks like you:
Let Horace blush, and Virgil too!

This is the wording on the medallion portrait *monument to Alexander
Pope (1688–1744) on the north wall of the gallery in St Mary's church,
Twickenham. As the Latin records, the monument was not raised until
seventeen years after Pope's death – by which time his friend, editor and

literary executor, William Warburton, was able to mention himself as Bishop of Gloucester. The English words were written by Pope, though they were almost certainly not intended for any monument. His will stipulated that he should be buried near the prominent monument to his parents (on the east wall) and he only wanted mention of his death to be added to his parents' memorial. His actual resting place is in the middle aisle of the church, just before the chancel steps, under a stone bearing simply the letter P, though a brass plate given in the 1960s by some American scholars now provides more detail.

Robert Carruthers in his *Life of Alexander Pope* (1858) fires off this dart in Bishop Warburton's direction: 'The bad taste evinced in parading these careless and petulant lines on the walls of a church, near the poet's grave, is too glaring to require comment. Any such inscription was a direct violation of the wishes and feelings of Pope as expressed in his will.'

At least, Pope is not commemorated at all in Westminster Abbey, not even in Poets' Corner, though his epitaphs on others (James CRAGGS, Sir Godfrey KNELLER, etc.) *are* displayed.

PORT
~

TO THE MEMORY OF
THOMAS PORT,
SON OF JOHN PORT, OF BURTON-UPON-TRENT,
IN THE COUNTY OF STAFFORD, HAT MANUFACTURER,
WHO NEAR THIS TOWN HAD BOTH HIS LEGS
SEVERED FROM HIS BODY BY THE *RAILWAY TRAIN*.
WITH THE GREATEST FORTITUDE HE BORE A
SECOND AMPUTATION BY THE SURGEONS, AND
DIED FROM LOSS OF BLOOD.

Bright rose the morn and vigorous rose poor *Port*,
Gay on the *TRAIN* he used his wonted sport.
Ere noon arrived, his mangled form they bore,
With pain distorted and o'rewhelmed with gore;
When evening came to close the fatal day,
A mutilated corpse the sufferer lay.

'In the churchyard of Harrow-on-the-Hill' – Russell (1898).

POUND

~

In Memory of William Pound,
many years one of the Porters of this College,
who, by an exemplary Life and Behaviour,
and an honest attention
to the Duties of his Station,
deserved and obtained
the approbation and esteem
of the whole Society.
1787

Wall *plaque in the cloister below the Cathedral, Christ Church, Oxford. Dacre Balsdon in *Oxford Life* (1957) comments: 'Reflect, as you read it, that when a memorial can be erected to a Dean of Christ Church praising him for the honest attention which he paid to the Duties of his Station, the social revolution in England will have been accomplished.'

PRUDEN

~

Sleep on, dear Howard, in your foreign grave,
Your life to your country you nobly gave,
Though we did not see you to say goodbye,
Now in God's keeping you safely lie.

On a memorial tablet in Mapleton, Manitoba, Canada, to Private Howard Pruden, killed in France during the First World War. Recorded in James Morris, *Farewell the Trumpets*, (1978).

PURCELL

~

Here Lyes
HENRY PURCELL Esq.
Who left this Life
And is gone to that Blessed Place

Where only his Harmony
can be exceeded . . .

Part of the inscription on the *commemorative shield in the North Choir Aisle of the nave, Westminster Abbey. Henry Purcell (*c* 1658–95), the composer (and Abbey organist), is also commemorated by a Latin inscription on his gravestone nearby. Mackae (?1910) tells the story of the widow of a fireworks manufacturer who was so impressed by this epitaph that she caused to be placed on her husband's grave the words: 'He has gone to the only place/Where his own works are excelled.'

QUIN

~

That tongue which set the table in a roar,
And charm'd the public ear, is heard no more;
Closed are those eyes, the harbingers of wit,
Which spoke, before the tongue, which Shakespeare writ;
Cold are those hands, which living, were stretch'd forth,
At friendship's call to succour modest worth.
Here is James Quin! Deign, reader, to be taught,
Whate'er thy strength of body, force of thought,
In Nature's happiest mould however cast,
'To this complexion thou must come at last.'

On James Quin (1693–1766), the actor, in Bath Abbey. Written by David GARRICK. Quin turned down the part of Captain Macheath in Gay's *The Beggar's Opera*. The epitaph is to be found in *Collection* (1806); the above transcription is from Briscoe (1901).

RALEIGH

~

WITHIN THE CHANCEL OF THIS CHURCH WAS INTERRED
THE BODY OF THE
GREAT SR. WALTER RALEIGH KT
ON THE DAY HE WAS BEHEADED
IN OLD PALACE YARD, WESTMINSTER
OCT 29TH ANO DOM 1618

READER – Should you reflect on his errors
Remember his many virtues
And that he was a mortal.

On a brass *tablet by the east door of St Margaret's Church, Westminster. Raleigh (*b* 1552), the explorer, writer and courtier of Elizabeth I, fell further out of favour with James I and was executed on his return from a dismal expedition to the Orinoco. It is said that his decapitated body lies before the altar here and his head at West Horsley, Surrey.

RHODES

~

CECIL JOHN
RHODES
1853–1902
YOUR HINTERLAND
IS THERE.

An epitaph-like inscription on a gesturing *statue of Rhodes in a Cape Town park, South Africa. Rhodes was buried at a site of his own choosing in the Matopo Hills near Bulawayo, Southern Rhodesia, in what is now called Zimbabwe. The granite gravestone bears only the words he himself chose: 'HERE LIE THE REMAINS OF CECIL JOHN RHODES'.

He is commemorated by a number of other monuments in southern Africa, especially by a huge one in Cape Town, and also by a simple plaque in the South Aisle of the Henry VII Chapel, Westminster Abbey, London.

RICHARDSON
~

He bowled his best but was himself bowled by the best on July 2nd 1912.

On Tom Richardson, a Surrey and England cricketer, buried in Richmond Cemetery, Grove Road, Richmond, Surrey. Quoted in Meller (1981).

ROGERS
~

I NEVER MET A MAN I DIDN'T LIKE.

Epitaph suggested for himself by Will Rogers (1879–1935), the folksy American 'cowboy comedian' of the 1920/30s. It is a little more believable in context: 'When I die, my epitaph or whatever you call those signs on gravestones is going to read: "I joked about every prominent man of my time, but I never met one I dident [*sic*] like." I am so proud of that I can hardly wait to die so it can be carved. And when you come to my grave you will find me sitting there, proudly reading it.'

According to Paula McSpadden Love, *The Will Rogers Book* (1972), the utterance was first printed in the *Boston Globe*, 16 June 1930. However, the *Saturday Evening Post* (6 November 1926) has: 'I bet you if I had met him [Trotsky] and had a chat with him, I would have found him a very interesting and human fellow, for I never yet met a man that I didn't like.'

As to the uses it has been put to, the *Independent* (15 May 1987) cited a car sticker in New York which stated: 'Will Rogers never met Marvin Hamlisch.'

ROOSEVELT

~

FRANKLIN DELANO ROOSEVELT
1882–1945

ANNA ELEANOR ROOSEVELT
1884–1962

This gravestone *inscription is included because it is totally epitaph-free ... Curiously, for one of America's most noted presidents (who served three and a half terms, dying in office), Roosevelt has no national memorial. He is buried with his wife in a rose garden ('Roosevelt' is Dutch for 'rosefield') at Hyde Park, the family home where he was born and lived, in New York State. The words are carved on a large white oblong stone – the proportions of which FDR had decreed, as also the simple inscription. In a memorandum dated 26 December 1937, FDR stipulated that 'the monument contain no device or inscription except the following [as above]'.

ROSE

~

DIED APRIL 20TH 1913
FROM THE EFFECTS OF AN AEROPLANE FLIGHT.

Part of the memorial to Sir Charles Rose in St Margaret's Church, Mapledurham, quoted by Christopher Matthew (1981).

ROSEVEAR

~

Time was we's stood where thou do't now
And view the dead as thou dost we.
E're long thou'st lay as low as we
And others stand to look on thee.

'On the headstone of William Rosevear, by the wall of the cottage garden on the west boundary, the second grave from the end near the tower' – guidebook to St Ewe church, Cornwall (1982). 'Here once I stood,/As thou dost now,/And viewed the grave/As thou do'st me,/Er'e long you'll lie/As low as I,/And others stand/And look at thee!' – 'from an old tombstone in St Miniver, Cornwall' – G. Burchell, Gloucester (1981).

ROUTLEIGH
~

Here lies, in horizontal position,
the outside case of
GEORGE ROUTLEIGH, Watchmaker;
Whose abilities in that line
Were an honour to his profession.
Integrity was the Mainspring, and prudence the Regulator
Of all the actions of his life.
Humane, generous and liberal,
his Hand never stopped
till he had relieved Distress.
So nicely regulated were all his motions,
that he never went wrong,
except when set a-going
by people
who did not know his Key;
Even then he was easily
set right again.
He had the art of disposing his time so well,
that his hours glided away
in one continual round
of pleasure and delight,
until an unlucky minute put a period
to his existence.
He departed this life,
Nov. 14, 1802,
aged 57:
wound up,
in hopes of being taken in hand
by his Maker;
and of being thoroughly cleaned, repaired,
and set a-going
in the world to come.

In Lydford church, Devon. Wright (1972) has this extended version as well as the information that the inscription is on the upper surface of a chest-tomb. Benham (1948) has an extract, but puts the name as 'George Roughfield'.

RUDD
~

IN LOVING MEMORY OF HANNAH, WIFE OF
HENRY WILLIAM RUDD
OF THIS PARISH
WHO DEPARTED THIS LIFE
24TH APRIL 1884

REJOICING IN HOPE.

SHE WAS A WOMAN AND BY SO MUCH
NEARER TO GOD AS THAT MAKES ONE.

Inscription on *gravestone in the churchyard of St Andrew, East Hagbourne, Berkshire. The first text is from Romans 12:12; the second has not been identified.

RUMBOLD
~

He liv'd one hundred and five
Sanguine and Strong
An hundred to five
You do not live so long.

On the *gravestone of Stephen Rumbold, born February 1582, died 4 March 1687, aged 105. The stone is now to be found under a mat in the porch of the church of St Bartholomew, Brightwell Baldwin, Oxfordshire. It looks as if it has been recut. The deceased's name continues to be remembered locally in 'Rumbold's Lane' and 'Rumbold's Copse' (possibly on the site of his house). *Collection* (1806) has it.

RUMSEY

~

See HERRICK.

RUSSELL

~

**In memory
of . . .
THOMAS RUSSELL,
Blacksmith of this Town . . .
who Died 24th May 1838
Aged 46 Years.**

*My Sledge and Hammer lie reclined,
My Bellows too have lost their wind.
My Fires extinct, my Forge decayed
And in the dust my Vice is laid.
My Coal is spent, my Iron gone,
My Nails are drove, my work is done;
My Fire-dried Corpse lies here at rest,
And, Smoke-like, soars up to be bless'd.*

This example of a popular epitaph for blacksmiths can be found on a *grave on the south side of St Michael and All Angels, Ledbury. It appears on an upright slab bearing at the top the name of Russell's wife Marriot who predeceased him in 1823. The final couplet is no longer legible, as the stone has crumbled, but may be supplied from Andrews (1883).

The rhyme has been attributed to a poet called Hayley and the example, said to date from 1746 in the churchyard of St Bartholomew, Nettlebed, Oxfordshire, is one of the earliest. On the other hand, if the poet was *William* Hayley (see also under William COLLINS), he was only born in 1745. Benham (1948) cites a version 'in Awre churchyard, Gloucestershire, in memory of John Shaw, blacksmith, of Blakeney, d. Dec 24, 1743.'

Of the three versions of the rhyme from Midlands churches quoted in the *Oxford Book of Local Verses*, each has only six lines. *Collection*

(1806) has an eight line version, to William Braithwaite (*d* 1757), from St Albans, Hertfordshire.

As recently as 1926, Jabez White, a blacksmith buried in Charlton Cemetery, London SE7, was commemorated with this short version:

> My anvil's worn my forge decayed
> My body in the dust is laid
> My coal is burnt my iron's run
> My last nail is in my work is done.

RUSSELL
~

The first and greatest of war correspondents.

Part of the inscription on the *monument to Sir William Howard Russell (1820–1907) in St Paul's Cathedral crypt. He reported on the Crimean War for *The Times*, coining the phrase 'thin red line' for the supposed invincibility of British infantry tactics. A bronze bust shows him with notebook and pencil in hand.

SCOTT

~

TO STRIVE, TO SEEK, TO FIND, AND NOT TO YIELD . . .

This line from Tennyson's 'Ulysses' appears on a memorial to Captain Scott, Captain OATES and others, at the South Pole. It was chosen by Apsley Cherry-Garrard, author of *The Worst Journey in the World* (1922), who in that book describes an earlier 'note' (dated 12 November 1912) left at the cairn over the bodies:

> This Cross and Cairn are erected over the bodies of Capt. Scott, C.V.O., R.N.; Dr. E.A. Wilson, M.B., B.A. Cantab.; Lt. H.R. Bowers, Royal Indian Marines. A slight token to perpetuate their gallant and successful attempt to reach the Pole. This they did on the 17th January 1912 after the Norwegian expedition had already done so. Inclement weather and lack of fuel was the cause of their death.
>
> Also to commemorate their two gallant comrades, Capt. L.E.G. Oates of the Inniskilling Dragoons, who walked to his death in a blizzard to save his comrades, about 18 miles south of this position; also of Seaman Edgar Evans, who died at the foot of the Beardmore Glacier.
>
> The Lord gave and the Lord taketh away. Blessed be the name of the Lord.
>
> Relief Expedition
(Signed by all members of the party.)

On the 1915 *memorial to Captain Scott and his companions in Waterloo Place, London (a statue of Scott in polar wear, sculpted by his widow), is inscribed this passage from the 'Message to the Public' in Scott's diary, 22/23 March 1912:

> . . . HAD WE LIVED, I SHOULD HAVE HAD A TALE TO TELL OF THE HARDIHOOD, ENDURANCE, AND COURAGE OF MY COMPANIONS WHICH WOULD HAVE STIRRED THE HEART OF EVERY ENGLISHMAN. THESE ROUGH NOTES AND OUR DEAD BODIES MUST TELL THE TALE.

SELBACH

~

R.I.P.

HE DIED
AS HE LIVED
A CYCLIST.
In Loving Memory of
MY DEAR HUSBAND
MAURICE C. SELBACH
WHO WAS KILLED WHILST CYCLING
SEPTEMBER 26. 1935, AGED 46.
"UNTIL WE MEET AGAIN."

Selbach's *tombstone in Streatham Park Cemetery, Rowan Road, London SW16, not only incorporates a small portrait of him but also a carving of a bicycle (with drop handlebars) and a signpost.

The phrase 'Until we meet again' is, of course, a staple thought of the bereaved. One can't help wondering, however, whether its popularity, particularly on war graves, has anything to do with the enormous success of Vera Lynn's song 'We'll meet again, don't know where,/Don't know when,/But I know we'll meet again some sunny day' (1939), written by Ross Parker and Hugh Charles. However, in 1918, there had been a song with the title 'Till We Meet Again' which was a great success for its writers Richard Whiting and Ray Egar.

From the *grave in Brookwood Military Cemetery, Surrey, of Sergeant D.J. Ansell, 'wireless operator/air gunner, Royal Air Force' who died on 23rd September 1944, aged 34 years:

HE IS ALWAYS IN OUR HEARTS
UNTIL WE MEET AGAIN.

'Always In My Heart' was, incidentally, the title of a song (1942) by Kim Gannon and Ernesto Lecuona, popularized by Deanna Durbin.

SELBY

~

She was DORCAS
Whose curious Needle wound th'abused Stage
Of this lewd World into the golden Age

Whose Pen of steel and silked lock enroll'd
The Acts of Jonah in records of Gold.
Whose Arte disclosed that Plot, which, had it taken,
Rome had triumphed and Britain's walls had shaken.

She was
In heart a Lydia, and in tongue a Hanna,
In Zeale a Ruth, in wedlock a Susanna,
Prudently simple, providently Wary,
To the world a Martha, and to heaven a Mary.

Who put on   )   in the year of)   Pilgrimage 69
IMMORTALITY)   her   )   REDEEMER 1641

Epitaph on the *monument to Dame Dorothy Selby (d 1641), in Ightham
Church, Sevenoaks, Kent. (Similar epitaphs to that in the second 'verse'
are found elsewhere.) But the 'plot' reference in the first verse is to the
Gunpowder Plot, of which Dame Dorothy was traditionally the
discoverer.

SEVERN
~

To the Memory of
JOSEPH SEVERN,
Devoted Friend and Deathbed Companion
of
JOHN KEATS,
whom he lived to see numbered among
the Immortal Poets of England.

An Artist eminent for his Representations
of Italian Life and Nature.
British Consul at Rome from 1861 to 1872:
And Officer of the Crown of Italy,
In recognition of his services to
Freedom and Humanity.

Died 3 Aug 1879 aged 85.

Severn was not at first buried in what is known as the English or Old Protestant Cemetery in Rome, near his friend KEATS, but was moved there in 1881, two years after his death. His *stone is a yard away from that of Keats and has an artist's palate and brushes motif, whereas that of Keats has a lyre. SHELLEY is also buried nearby. The final text was by Richard Monckton Milnes, Lord Houghton. (Details from *Life and Letters of Joseph Severn*, William Sharp, 1892.)

In a note dated 1 November 1881, Tennyson had suggested a different epitaph, thus: 'To the Memory of Joseph Severn, the Devoted Friend of John Keats, by whose deathbed he watched and whose name he lived to see inscribed among those of the Immortal Poets of England' – the rest as Houghton's. To another suggestion from Walter Severn, his son, that the text should be, 'In their death they were not divided', the argument was advanced that it 'must seem highly inappropriate to anyone who recollects the original application of the phrase' – Saul and Jonathan who died on the same battlefield – 'as more than sixty years elapsed between Keats's death and your father's.'

SEWARD

~

AMID THESE AISLES, WHERE ONCE HIS PRECEPTS
    SHEW'D
THE HEAVENWARD PATH-WAY WHICH IN LIFE HE TROD,
THIS SIMPLE TABLET MARKS A FATHER'S BIER,
AND THOSE HE LOV'D IN LIFE, IN DEATH ARE NEAR.
FOR HIM, FOR THEM, A DAUGHTER BADE IT RISE,
MEMORIAL OF DOMESTIC CHARITIES.
STILL, WOULD YOU KNOW WHY O'ER THE MARBLE
    SPREAD,
IN FEMALE GRACE THE WILLOW DROOPS HER HEAD?
WHY ON HER BRANCHES SILENT AND UNSTRUNG
THE MINSTREL HARP IS EMBLEMATIC HUNG?
WHAT POET'S VOICE LIES SMOTHER'D HERE IN DUST
TILL WAK'D TO JOIN THE CHORUS OF THE JUST?
LO, ONE BRIEF LINE AN ANSWER SAD SUPPLIES,
HONOUR'D, BELOV'D, AND MOURN'D, HERE SEWARD
    LIES.
HER WORTH, HER WARMTH OF HEART OUR SORROWS
    SAY
GO SEEK HER GENIUS IN HER LIVING LAY.

This verse on the *memorial to various Sewards by the West Door of Lichfield Cathedral seems not to know quite whom it is memorializing. The monument, though headed by the name of Ann Seward (1747–1809), the minor poet and so-called 'Swan of Lichfield', is 'by her order' erected to Thomas Seward, her father and a canon residentiary of the cathedral (d 1790). The names of her mother and sister are also appended. Could it be that the verse was written by her?

SHAKESPEARE
~

**GOOD FREND FOR IESUS SAKE FORBEARE,
TO DIGG THE DUST ENCLOASED HEARE:
BLESTE BE YE MAN [THA]T SPARES THES STONES,
AND CURST BE HE [THA]T MOVES MY BONES.**

On the *grave of William Shakespeare (1564–1616) on the north side of the chancel in Holy Trinity church, Stratford-upon-Avon. The playwright was buried in this privileged position as he had become a 'lay rector' in 1605. Although he is buried with other members of his family, his grave, rather curiously, does not actually bear his name.

According to S. Schoenbaum, *William Shakespeare: A Documentary Life* (1975), several seventeenth century sources suggest that Shakespeare wrote his own epitaph. However, perhaps the point is rather that he may have *chosen* it rather than *composed* it. In the mid-eighteenth century the gravestone was so worn that it was replaced. In the nineteenth century, Halliwell Phillips was curtly dismissing this 'wretched doggerel', but James Walter in *Shakespeare's True Life* (1890) was asking, 'Who dares question the words being those of the great dramatist himself?' Walter seemed to accept that because the words were 'there chiselled when the great one was laid in his grave', they must, therefore, have been written by him. Hesketh Pearson in his biography argues that Shakespeare chose to phrase his wish simply and clearly, and not in the words of a King Lear, because of a very real fear that his remains would be removed. As Bailey notes: 'The charnel-house at Stratford, demolished in 1799, was reached from inside the church by a door in the north wall of the chancel, [near Shakespeare's tomb. Hence] . . . a plea that his bones should not be thrown in the charnel-house when subsequent burials uncovered them, as was the custom; but the curse prevented his widow being buried in the same grave, as she had wished, because no one dared disturb it.'

An additional monument incorporating a bust of Shakespeare and another inscription were placed on the wall a few feet above the grave by 1623 – in the lifetime of his widow and many of his friends. Also in that year, Leonard Digges alluded to the monument in a dedicatory poem that appears in the First Folio. The *inscription (author unknown) reads:

JUDICIO PYLIUM, GENIO SOCRATEM, ARTE MARONEM:
TERRA TEGIT, POPULAS MAERET, OLYMPUS HABET.

STAY PASSENGER, WHY GOEST THOU BY SO FAST?
READ IF THOU CANST, WHOM ENVIOUS DEATH HATH PLAST,
WITH IN THIS MONUMENT SHAKESPEARE: WITH WHOME,
QUICK NATURE DIDE: WHOSE NAME DOTH DECK YS TOMBE,
FAR MORE THAN COST: [SITH] ALL, YT HE HATH WRITT,
LEAVES LIVING ART, BUT PAGE, TO SERVE HIS WITT.
　　　　OBIIT AÑO DOi 1616
　　　　AETATIS . 53 DIE 23 APR.

In Poets' Corner, Westminster Abbey, Shakespeare is commemorated by the Kent/Scheemakers *statue (erected in about 1740) on which the playwright is pointing with his left hand at a short manuscript bearing lines adapted from *The Tempest* (IV.i.152):

　　　　The Cloud cupt Tow'rs,
　　　　The Gorgeous Palaces,
　　　　The Solemn Temples,
　　　　The Great Globe itself,
　　　　Yea, all which it Inherit,
　　　　Shall Dissolve,
　　　　And like the baseless Fabrick of a Vision
　　　　Leave not a wreck behind.

Oddly, there are a number of mistakes in this quotation and 'baseless fabric of a vision' (Shakespeare wrote '*this* vision') has been inserted in place of the usual 'this insubstantial pageant faded'. 'Cloud-capt' rather than '-cupt' would make more sense in the first line; there is no justification for 'Shall Dissolve' having a line to itself, nor capitals to each word; 'fabric' is actually written as 'fnbric'; 'wreck' should be 'wrack'. Baconians believe that the inscription is a cipher using a word square which yields the statement 'FRANCIS BACON AUTHOR'.

Above Shakespeare's head is a Latin inscription, noting, somewhat reproachfully, that it was 'erected by public love [i.e. subscription] 124 years after his death'.

SHEE

~

NEAR THIS SPOT
ARE DEPOSITED THE MORTAL REMAINS OF
JANE, THE WIFE OF SIR GEORGE SHEE, BART.
OF MUDIFORD HOUSE.
IN THE MERIDIAN OF HER DAYS
AND IN THE FULL ENJOYMENT OF EXISTENCE
SHE WAS SUMMONED
UNWARNED BUT IT IS HUMBLY HOPED
NOT UNPREPARED
TO THE PRESENCE OF HER MAKER
LEAVING
A HUSBAND TO MOURN A FAITHFUL WIFE
DEPENDANTS TO LAMENT A KIND MISTRESS
FRIENDS TO REGRET AN AMIABLE COMPANION
THE POOR TO MISS A CHARITABLE BENEFACTRESS.
"IN THE MIDST OF LIFE WE ARE IN DEATH",
BUT
SALVATION COMETH THROUGH JESUS CHRIST.
OB A.D. 1832, AET 43.

Wall *memorial in Priory Church, Christchurch, Hampshire. 'In the midst. . .' comes from the Burial of the Dead in the Book of Common Prayer and Benham (1948) adds: 'These words are a translation of the ancient antiphon beginning *"media vita morte sumus"*, said to have been composed about AD 911 by St Notker Balbulus (840?-912?), a Swiss monk, of the monastery of St Gall (Switzerland).'

SHELLEY

~

PERCY BYSSHE SHELLEY

COR CORDIUM

NATUS IV AUG. MDCCXCII
OBIIT VIII JUL. MDCCCXXII

"Nothing of him that doth fade
But doth suffer a sea-change
Into something rich and strange."

This is the *inscription on the tomb containing the ashes of the poet Percy Bysshe Shelley (1792–1822) in the Protestant Cemetery at Rome. Shelley was drowned while sailing near Spezzia and cremated on the beach at Viareggio. The Latin phrase (chosen by Leigh HUNT) means 'heart of hearts'. The quotation from Shakespeare, *The Tempest* (I.ii.402), was chosen by E.J. Trelawny who had been present at the cremation and who was himself buried (1881) in an adjoining tomb.

There are also Shelley memorials in Westminster Abbey (delayed until 1954 because of his avowed atheism), at University College, Oxford, and in the Priory Church, Christchurch, Hampshire. Shelley's heart (or liver), snatched from the flames by Trelawny, is buried with Mary, his second wife, in St Peter's churchyard, Bournemouth, although no mention is made of the fact on the tomb. Shelley's father-in-law, William Godwin ('AUTHOR OF "POLITICAL JUSTICE"'), and mother-in-law, Mary Wollstonecraft ('AUTHOR OF "A VINDICATION OF THE RIGHTS OF WOMAN"'), also lie in this impressive white *tomb. The reason for the gathering of memorials on the south coast is simply because Sir Percy Florence Shelley, the poet's son, lived at Boscombe, near Bournemouth.

SHIRLEY
~

In the yeare 1653
when all thinges Sacred were throughout the nation
Either demollisht or profaned
Sir Robert Shirley, Barronet
Founded this Church
whose singular praise it is
to have done the best thinges in the worst times
And
hoped them in the most callamitous.
The righteous shall be had in everlasting remembrance.

This is an *epitaph, really. It is to be found over the West Door, on the outside of Staunton Harold church, Leicestershire. Sir Robert Shirley (*b* 1629) incensed Oliver Cromwell by building such a magnificent church – Cromwell said that a man who could afford to build it could pay for a regiment. Shirley, a Royalist, declined and was sent to the Tower where he died at the age of twenty-seven. He is buried beneath the chancel of the church.

SIMON

~

This stone with not unpardonable pride,
Proves by its record what the world denied:
Simon could do a natural thing – he died.

Suggested epitaph for Sir John, later Viscount, Simon (1873–1954), lawyer and Liberal politician. 'Lord Simon has died . . . John Sparrow wrote this epitaph many years ago . . . But then John Simon helped John Sparrow to become Warden of All Souls, and the latter came to regret his epigram' – *Harold Nicolson's Diaries and Letters 1945–1962* (entry for 11 January 1954). In Sparrow's *Grave Epigrams and Other Verses* (1981), 'Simon' is replaced with '*Nemo*'.

It was of Simon that David Lloyd George said: 'He has sat so long upon the fence that the iron has entered into his soul.'

SIMS

~

As blossoms in the early Spring
Do wither and decay:
So God cutt off her youthful days
And took her life away.

Verse on the *grave of Ann Sims who died 16th August 1794, aged 15, and is buried outside the West Door of the church of St Michael on Greenhill, Lichfield. I take it that this simple verse was not original and is probably to be found on the graves of many who died young.

SITWELL

~

**THE PAST AND PRESENT
ARE AS ONE –
ACCORDANT AND DISCORDANT
YOUTH AND AGE
AND DEATH AND BIRTH –
FOR OUT OF ONE CAME ALL
FROM ALL COMES ONE.**

Dame Edith Sitwell (1887–1964), the poet and writer, is buried in St Mary's churchyard extension, Weedon Lois, Northamptonshire, under a *headstone designed by Henry Moore. It bears Sitwell's version of words from Heraclitus which she quotes in the concluding lines of her poem 'The Wind of Early Spring'.

SKUGG

~

**Here Skugg
Lies snug
As a bug
In a rug.**

Benjamin Franklin in a letter to Georgiana Shipley on the death of her pet squirrel 26 September 1772. 'Skug' was an American dialect word for squirrel.

SMITH

~

**CAPT. OF R.M.S. TITANIC
COMMANDER
EDWARD JOHN SMITH R.D. R.N.R.**

BORN JANUARY 27 1850 DIED APRIL 15 1912
BEQUEATHING TO HIS COUNTRYMEN
THE MEMORY & EXAMPLE OF A GREAT HEART
A BRAVE LIFE AND A HEROIC DEATH.
BE BRITISH.

In the city of Lichfield, not far from the Cathedral and near what used to be the Library, is a small public park. Standing in it, somewhat forlornly, is a statue to – of all people – the captain of the *Titanic*. As I understand it, Commander Smith had nothing to do with Lichfield at all. He was born some miles away in Hanley, Staffordshire, and the statue was wished upon this unlikely spot when his native town rejected it. However, when quite recently Stafford tried to get the statue back, Lichfield apparently refused.

Under the figure, bearded and in naval uniform, now a very green bronze, is the *tablet bearing the above words. The statue was unveiled by Smith's daughter on 29 July 1914 in the presence of the usual 'distinguished dignitaries' and Lady Scott – not only the statue's sculptor but the widow of Capt. SCOTT, who perished in that other great British disaster of 1912, the fatal (for him) expedition to the South Pole.

As for 'Be British': Smith reputedly said, 'Be British, boys, be British' to his crew some time in the hours between the *Titanic* hitting its iceberg and his going down with the ship. Michael Davie in his book on the disaster describes the evidence for this as 'flimsy', but obviously the legend was well established by 1914 when the statue was erected.

SMITH

~

**In memory of Jane Emily Smith
Died 10 Apr. 1804, aged 74
'Believing, we rejoice to see the curse removed'.**

'In South Ealing cemetery', according to a correspondent, but untraced.

SMITH

~

TO PERPETUATE
WHILE LANGUAGE AND MARBLE SHALL REMAIN
THE NAME AND CHARACTER OF
THE REVD. SYDNEY SMITH,
ONE OF THE BEST OF MEN.
HIS TALENTS, THOUGH ADMITTED BY HIS
CONTEMPORARIES TO BE GREAT,
WERE SURPASSED BY HIS UNOSTENTATIOUS
BENEVOLENCE,
HIS FEARLESS LOVE OF TRUTH, AND HIS ENDEAVOUR
TO PROMOTE THE HAPPINESS OF MANKIND
BY RELIGIOUS TOLERATION AND BY RATIONAL
FREEDOM.
HE WAS BORN THE 3RD OF JUNE, 1771;
HE BECAME CANON RESIDENTIARY OF ST PAUL'S
CATHEDRAL, 1831;
HE DIED FEBRUARY THE 22ND, 1845.

Epitaph on the *grave of the Revd Sydney Smith in Kensal Green Cemetery, London. Only the first five lines are now legible on the side of the low stone chest. The rest of the above text is taken from the 1855 *Memoir* written by his daughter Saba, Lady Holland, who was subsequently buried with him. It is possible that an illegible inscription on the top of the chest refers to her.

Presumably, Lady Holland wrote the epitaph – though regrettably, unlike her *Memoir*, it does not begin to convey the character of one of the wittiest and likeable men of the nineteenth century. It was Smith who said, 'My idea of heaven is eating *pâté de foie gras* to the sound of trumpets.'

SMITH

~

HERE LIES WILL SMITH – AND, WHAT'S SOMETHING RARISH,
HE WAS BORN, BRED, AND HANGED, ALL IN THE SAME PARISH.

Quoted in Hyman (1965). Klinger (1979) has it from 'Penryn'.

SOUTH

~

HER TIME WAS SHORT.

On the tombstone of Mary Ann South in Ayot St Lawrence churchyard, Hertfordshire. She had lived in the village for seventy years, from 1825–95. Bernard Shaw, when asked why he had chosen to live in the same village, would explain that if the biblical span of three score years and ten was considered short there, it had to be a good place to live. He himself managed to live to the age of 94. His observation is recorded in Michael Holroyd, *Bernard Shaw Vol.II: The Pursuit of Power* (1989).

SOUTHEY

~

Ye vales and hills, whose beauty hither drew
The poet's steps, and fixed him here, on you
His eyes have closed! And ye, lov'd books, no more
Shall Southey feed upon your precious lore,
To works that ne'er shall forfeit their renown,
Adding immortal labours of his own –
Whether he traced historic truth, with zeal
For the State's guidance, or the Church's weal,
Or Fancy, disciplined by studious art,
Inform'd his pen, or wisdom of the heart,
Or judgements sanctioned in the Patriot's mind
By reverence for the rights of all mankind.
Wide were his aims, yet in no human breast
Could private feelings meet for holier rest.
His joys, his griefs, have vanished like a cloud
From Skiddaw's top; but he to heaven was vowed
Through his industrious life, and Christian faith
Calmed in his soul the fear of change and death.

The poet Robert Southey (1774–1843) is buried in St Kentigern's churchyard, Crosthwaite, Keswick, Cumbria. His monument inside the church bears words written by William Wordsworth as a last tribute to his friend. Wordsworth attended the funeral, though he had not been invited, and succeeded Southey as Poet Laureate. In Poets' Corner, Westminster Abbey, there is another monument bearing only Southey's name and dates.

SPENSER

~

HEARE LYES (EXPECTING THE SECOND COMMINGE OF OUR SAVIOUR CHRIST JESUS) THE BODY OF EDMOND SPENCER, THE PRINCE OF POETS IN HIS TYME WHOSE DIVINE SPIRRIT NEEDS NOE OTHIR WITNESSE THEN THE WORKS WHICH HE LEFT BEHINDE HIM. HE WAS BORNE IN LONDON, IN THE YEARE 1553, AND DYED IN THE YEARE 1598.

On the *grave of Edmund Spenser (dates now usually given as *c* 1552–99) in Poets' Corner, Westminster Abbey. This monument is said to be an exact 1778 copy of the 1620 original. However, the dates have been 'improved'. Originally – as transcribed, for example, by Aubrey in the mid-seventeenth century – they were forty-two years out on his birth and three on his death, so making the poet eighty-six at death instead of forty-seven.

STAMP

~

MISS EMILY STAMP, POSTMISTRESS. RETURNED OPENED.

'On a comic post card [of a gravestone] at Blackpool' – Bryan Glover on *Quote . . . Unquote*, BBC Radio, 9 February 1982.

STANDING

~

FAITHFUL UNTO DEATH.

On the *grave in Brookwood Military Cemetery, Surrey, of Private J.W. Standing of the Tank Corps, who died on 23rd January 1919, age 32.

The phrase occurs in Revelation 2:10: 'Be thou faithful unto death and I will give thee a crown of life.' Compare its use on the statue of Edith CAVELL.

'Faithful Unto Death' was also the title of a painting by Sir Edward John Poynter PRA which shows a centurion staying at his sentry post during the eruption of Vesuvius which destroyed Pompeii in AD 79. In the background, citizens are panicking as molten lava falls upon them. The picture was inspired by the discovery of the skeleton of a soldier in full armour excavated at Pompeii in the late eighteenth or early nineteenth century. Many such remains were found of people 'frozen' in the positions they had held as they died. Bulwer-Lytton described what might have happened to the soldier in his *Last Days of Pompeii* (1834). Poynter painted the scene in 1865; it now hangs in the Walker Art Gallery, Liverpool.

STANIER

~

IN LOVING MEMORY
OF
FRANK STANIER
OF
STAFFORDSHIRE
WHO LEFT US IN PEACE
FEB. 2ND. 1910

*Epitaph in the English cemetery on the island of San Michele, Venice, which was first drawn to my attention by Margaret R. Jackson, Chipping Camden (1982), though it had already been transcribed (differently) in James Morris, *Venice* (1960/1974).

STANLEY

~

HENRY MORTON
STANLEY
BULA MATARI
1841–1904
AFRICA

On the *grave of Sir Henry Morton Stanley in St Michael and All
Angels' churchyard, Pirbright, Surrey. A huge chunk of granite, ten feet
tall and totally strange in an English country churchyard, bears the
explorer and journalist's Congolese name (meaning 'Breaker of Rocks')
and, as an epitaph, the one word 'Africa', appropriate for one who
'found' Dr Livingstone in Africa and wrote such works as *Through the
Dark Continent* (1878) and *Through Darkest Africa* (1890). An American
citizen for a while, Stanley regained his British citizenship, became an
MP, and was knighted in 1899 for 'services to Africa'.

His wife Dorothy – who tried without success to have him buried in
Westminster Abbey (with LIVINGSTONE) – lies with him and is also
mentioned on the stone.

STERNE

~

Shall Pride a heap of sculptur'd marble raise
Some worthless, unmourn'd, titled fool to praise;
And shall we not one poor grave stone learn,
Where Genius, Wit, and Humour, sleep with Sterne.

According to Morrell (1948), this epitaph on Laurence Sterne (1713–68),
the clergyman and author of *Tristram Shandy*, was written by David
GARRICK. Sterne was originally buried in St George's Burial Ground,
Uxbridge Road, London, but when that was built over in 1969, his
remains were removed to St Michael's, Coxwold, North Yorkshire,
where he had been vicar. Here they lie under the original tombstone.

STEVENSON
~

Under the wide and starry sky
Dig the grave and let me lie.
Glad did I live and gladly die,
And I laid me down with a will.

This be the verse you grave for me:
Here he lies where he longed to be;
Home is the sailor, home from the sea
And the hunter home from the hill.

Part of Robert Louis Stevenson's *gravestone on Mount Vaea, Somoa. It wrongly transcribes his poem 'Requiem' (1887), as above. The penultimate line should read 'Home is the sailor, home from sea', without the definite article – but this is a common error of quotation. The inscription is headed '1850 ROBERT LOUIS STEVENSON 1894'. The poem is also inscribed on Stevenson's memorial in St Giles's Cathedral, Edinburgh.

In *Across the Plains* (1892), Stevenson had composed an epitaph of which any man 'need not be ashamed': '*Here lies one who meant well, tried a little, failed much.*'

STRANGE
~

HERE LIES AN HONEST LAWYER, —
THAT IS STRANGE.

On the 'eminent barrister, Sir John Strange' – Fairley (1875); 'on Mr Strange, a lawyer' – Tegg (1876). The only notable lawyer of this name mentioned in the *DNB* is Sir John Strange (1696–1754), who was Master of the Rolls.

Compare what Aubrey earlier recorded: 'Ben JO(H)NSON, riding through Surrey, found the Women weeping and wailing, lamenting the Death of a Lawyer, who lived there: He enquired why so great Grief for the Losse of a Lawyer? Oh, said they, we have the greatest Loss imaginable; he kept us all in Peace and Quietness, and was a most charitable good Man: Whereupon Ben made this Distich: "God works Wonders now and then,/Behold a Miracle, deny't who can,/Here lies a *Lawyer* and an *honest* man." 'Tis Pity that good Man's Name should not be remember'd.'

STRATFORD DE REDCLIFFE
~

IN MEMORY OF
A GREAT ENGLISHMAN . . .

**THOU THIRD GREAT CANNING, STAND AMONG OUR BEST
AND NOBLEST, NOW THY LONG DAY'S WORK HATH CEASED,
HERE SILENT IN OUR MINSTER OF THE WEST
WHO WERT THE VOICE OF ENGLAND IN THE EAST.**

Tennyson's epitaph on Stratford Canning, 1st Viscount Stratford de Redcliffe (1786–1880), diplomatist, 'for fifty years the honoured representative of his sovereign in Turkey and other foreign countries'. The words are inscribed on a *plaque beneath a statue in the North Transept of Westminster Abbey. Stratford de Redcliffe is buried at Frant, Sussex.

STRATHMORE
~

Neath this sod another lies,
An aristocrat of Scots assize,
Long dead but not forgotten.
When writhe and maggots eat his eyes,
They'll cause his lordship no surprise,
For while he lived, the man was rotten.

'On the 14th Earl of Strathmore and Kinghorne (*d* 1944), maternal grandfather of the present Queen, by a Scottish poet called Clarke (who also wrote 'The Skull'), quoted by a friend of mine in 1947' – L. Morris, Catchgate, Co. Durham (1982).

SULLIVAN
~

IS LIFE A BOON?
IF SO, IT WILL BEFAL
THAT DEATH, WHENE'ER HE CALL,
MUST CALL TOO SOON.

The *memorial to Sir Arthur Sullivan, the composer (1842–1900), in Victoria Embankment Gardens, London (quite close to the Savoy Theatre where his operettas were performed) bears this signed verse by W.S. GILBERT from *The Yeomen of the Guard* (1888). Given their uneasy relationship, it is slightly ironic that Gilbert's verse (and name) should appear so prominently on the Sullivan memorial. It is also remarkable for the erotic, semi-naked woman in black stone weeping beneath the solemn bust of the composer of 'Onward Christian Soldiers' and 'The Lost Chord'.

Sullivan is buried in St Paul's Cathedral crypt, and there is a further memorial in the floor of the North Transept.

SUMNER
~

SUMNER IS A-GOING OUT
LOUD SING BOO-HOO.

Attributed remark by Sir Maurice BOWRA at the funeral of Humphrey Sumner (1893–1951), the Oxford historian and Warden of All Souls, alluding to the thirteenth-century rhyme, 'Sumer is icumen in,/Lhude sing cuccu!' Quoted by Alan Bennett on *Quote . . . Unquote*, BBC Radio, 26 January 1982.

SWIFT
~

HIC DEPOSITUM EST CORPUS
JONATHAN SWIFT, S.T.P.
HUIUS ECCLESIAE CATHEDRALIS DECANI,
UBI SAEVA INDIGNATIO
ULTERIUS COR LACERARE NEQUIT.
ABI, VIATOR,
ET IMITARE, SI POTERIS,
STRENUUM PRO VIRILI LIBERTATIS VINDICEM.
OBIIT ANNO MDCCXLV
MENSIS OCTOBRIS DIE 19
AETATIS ANNO LXXVIII.

('Here lies the body of Jonathan Swift, Professor of Holy Theology, Dean of this cathedral church, where savage indignation can tear his heart no more. Go, traveller, and if you can imitate one who with his utmost strength protected liberty. He died in the year 1745, on the 19th of October, aged seventy-eight.') This is the epitaph Swift wrote for himself and may be found on a *tablet in St Patrick's Cathedral, Dublin, where he lies buried. W.B. YEATS said: 'Swift sleeps under the greatest epitaph in history.'

SYMPSON
~

Tony Sympson
Actor
1906–83
Inspired player of small parts.

Amidst the scores of memorial plaques to the great names of theatre in St Paul's Church, Covent Garden, London, it is good to encounter this one. Sympson, of whom I had never heard until I saw this *plaque, was accorded an obituary in *The Times* which suggested, 'His motto could have been: "The readiness is all".' He began his theatrical career as a speciality dancer and ended up in such roles as 'Saucepan Man' in *Noddy in Toyland.*

214

SZAMUELY

~

IN LOVING MEMORY OF
TIBOR SZAMUELY
1925–1972

Who devoted his life to the pursuit of truth
and the defence of freedom and who lies here
in the country he loved and made his home.

AND OF

NINA SZAMUELY
1923–1974

The brave and devoted wife of Tibor, whom she
supported through many trials, whose happiness
was her happiness and with whom, her work of
scholarship unfinished, she lies here.

On their joint *grave in Kensal Green Cemetery, London. Tibor Szamuely was born in Moscow of Hungarian-Jewish stock. He became mixed up in various activities in both the Soviet Union and Hungary – possibly including spying – and was imprisoned for a period by the Russians. He came to England in 1964 and became, in the words of the *DNB*, 'a brilliant critic of the Soviet regime' and a man who was 'always ready to recall his tragic experiences' to those who were interested. I remember him advising me on the eve of my visiting Moscow for the first time in 1968 (a visit which, as it happened, was cancelled because of the Soviet invasion of Czechoslovakia) to try at all costs to speak to ordinary Russians in the street.

His wife, Dr Nina Szamuely, taught Russian at St Paul's Girls' School, London, and contributed to the *Concise Oxford English-Russian Dictionary*.

I came upon these epitaphs by chance in Kensal Green – they are right on the main drive – and was pleased to find that the art of writing pleasing tributes has not completely died out in modern times.

TENNANT

~

"When things were at their worst
he would go up and down in the
trenches cheering the men, when
danger was greatest his smile was
loveliest."

In proud and unfading memory of
EDWARD:WYNDHAM:TENNANT
4th Batt. Grenadier Guards, eldest son of Lord and Lady
Glenconner, who passed to the fuller life in the battle of
the Somme 22nd September 1916. Aged 19 years.

He gave his earthly life to such matter as he set great
store by: the honour of his country and his home.

On the *memorial in Salisbury Cathedral. Tennant was also a poet,
though not one usually included among the War Poets. In a letter to his
mother, Lady Glenconner, dated just before going into action (and
printed in *The Times*, 27 September 1916), he had said: 'This is written
in case anything happens to me, for I should like you to have just a little
message from my own hand. Your love for me and my love for you have
made my whole life one of the happiest there has ever been. This is a
great day for me. "High heart, high speech, high deeds, 'mid honouring
eyes." God bless you, and give you peace.' (For the quotation, see
CUST.)

THEODORE

~

NEAR THIS PLACE IS INTERRED
THEODORE, KING OF CORSICA;
WHO DIED IN THIS PARISH, DEC.11, 1756
IMMEDIATELY AFTER LEAVING
THE KING'S BENCH PRISON,
BY THE BENEFIT OF THE ACT OF INSOLVENCY,
IN CONSEQUENCE OF WHICH

HE REGISTERED THE KINGDOM OF CORSICA
FOR THE USE OF HIS CREDITORS.

THE GRAVE, GREAT TEACHER, TO A LEVEL BRINGS
HEROES AND BEGGARS, GALLEY-SLAVES AND KINGS.
BUT THEODORE THIS MORAL LESSON LEARN'D, ERE DEAD;
FATE POUR'D ITS LESSONS ON HIS LIVING HEAD,
BESTOW'D A KINGDOM, AND DENIED HIM BREAD.

Collection (1806) has this in St Anne's churchyard, Soho, where, indeed, it still can be seen displayed on the exterior of the tower (all that remains of the church), though it has obviously been recut quite recently. It was composed by Horace Walpole who had earlier organized a benefit performance for the King which rather pointedly consisted of David Garrick in *King Lear* ('that classic portrayal of royalty in distress' – R.W. Ketton-Cremer), and, unfortunately, only raised fifty pounds in subscriptions. Theodore, though taking the money, complained of the liberty taken with his name. Walpole referred to this 'dirty knavery' and said, 'I have done with countenancing kings!'

THETCHER
~

**In Memory Of
THOMAS THETCHER
a Grenadier in the North Reg.
of Hants Milita, who died of a
violent Fever contracted by drinking
Small Beer when hot the 12th of May
1764, Aged 26 Years.**

In grateful remembrance of whose universal
good will towards his Comrades, this Stone
is placed here at their expence as a small
testimony of their regard and concern.
Here sleeps in peace a Hampshire Grenadier
Who caught his death by drinking cold small Beer.
Soldiers be wise from his untimely fall
And when ye're hot drink Strong or none at all.

This memorial being decay'd was restor'd
by the Officers of the Garrison A.D. 1781.

An honest Soldier never is forgot
Whether he died by Musket or by Pot.

The Stone was replaced by the North Hants
Militia when disembodied at Winchester
on 26th April 1802, in consequence of
the original Stone being destroyed.

This *grave is easily located near one of the paths leading to the West Door of Winchester Cathedral, and was recorded in *Collection* (1806). The stone was 'again replaced by the Royal Hampshire Regiment 1966' and this is duly recorded on it.

Bill Wilson, the American co-founder of Alcoholics Anonymous, recalled seeing the inscription when in Europe as a soldier on his way to the First World War and called it an 'ominous warning – which I failed to heed'.

THOMAS
~

Time held me green and dying
Though I sang in my chains like the sea . . .

Part of the inscription on the *memorial to the poet Dylan Thomas (1914–53) in Poets' Corner, Westminster Abbey. The quotation is from his poem 'Fern Hill' and the memorial was unveiled on St David's Day 1982. The second line is also quoted on the statue of him and on a stone monument, both in Swansea. On Thomas's modest grave in the Welsh town of Laugharne there is but a wooden cross, bearing his name, dates and 'RIP'.

THOMPSON
~

LOOK FOR ME IN THE NURSERIES OF HEAVEN. . .

On the grave of the poet Francis Thompson (1859–1907), on his tomb in the Roman Catholic annexe to Kensal Green Cemetery, London. The quotation was carved by Eric Gill and is from Thompson's poem 'To My Godchild'.

THOMSON
~

He gave a new direction to the British newspaper
industry. A strange and adventurous man from nowhere,
ennobled by the great virtues of courage and integrity
and faithfulness.

On the *memorial to Lord Thomson of Fleet (1894–1976) in St Paul's Cathedral crypt. Canadian-born Roy Thomson acquired extensive newspaper interests in Britain (Times Newspapers, in particular), and described commercial television as a 'licence to print money'. It is surely odd to call any man 'strange' on his memorial.

THORNDIKE
~

DAME SYBIL THORNDIKE CH
wife of
SIR LEWIS CASSON

Saint Joan or Hecuba, great actress of your age,
All womanhood your part, the world your stage.
To each good cause you lent your vigorous tongue,
Swept through the years the champion of the young.
And now the scripts lie fading on the shelf,
We celebrate your finest role – yourself;
The calls, the lights grow dim, but not this part,
The Christian spirit, the great generous heart.

On the *gravestone in the South Choir Aisle, Westminster Abbey of Dame Sybil Thorndike (1882–1976), the actress. The lines, according to the *Official Guide*, are based on some which J.B. Priestley composed in honour of Dame Sybil's eightieth birthday. 'Specially adapted for her epitaph,' the *Guide* notes, 'these appear to be the first verses so written and placed on an Abbey grave since Tennyson's lines on Lord STRATFORD DE REDCLIFFE.'

Dame Sybil is also remembered on a plaque in St Paul's Church, Covent Garden, London.

TIPPER
~

To the Memory of
THOMAS TIPPER, who
departed this life May ye 14,
1785, Aged 54 Years.

READER, with kind regard this GRAVE survey,
Nor heedless pass where TIPPER'S ashes lay.
Honest he was, ingenuous, blunt, and kind;
And dared do, what few dare do, speak his mind.
PHILOSOPHY and HISTORY well he knew,
Was versed in PHYSICK and in SURGERY too.

The best old STINGO he both brewed and sold
Nor did one knavish act to get his Gold.
He played through Life a varied comic part
And knew immortal HUDIBRAS by heart.
READER, in real truth, such was the Man:
Be better, wiser, laugh more if you can.

On a *gravestone at Newhaven, Sussex, remembering the man who brewed George IV's favourite ale.

TOKE
~

He married five wives
Whom he survived.
At the age of 93 he walked to London
to seek a sixth but died before he found her.

Quoted by Klinger (1979), who names the subject as 'Nicholas Toke' of Great Chart, Kent.

TRADDLESTON
~

Both soul and body coming here to try
The things below, she found but vanity.
She stayed a while and, liking not the same,
She thought it best to go whence she came.
And, shaking hands, they parted all in love.
The body's here, the better part's above.

'Grace, the daughter of Christopher Traddleston, in St Gennys churchyard, [near Bude,] Cornwall' – quoted by Edward Blishen (1982).

TREEO
~

Poorly lived,
And poorly died,
Poorly buried,
And no one cried.

On the gravestone of John Treeo(?), who died aged 74 in 1810, in Bebington churchyard, Cheshire – at least, according to Nathaniel Hawthorne in *Our Old Home* (1863). Hawthorne was recalling a visit to the churchyard during his days as American Consul in Liverpool. He comments: 'It would be hard to compress the story of a cold and luckless life, death, and burial, into fewer words, or more impressive ones; at least, we found them impressive, perhaps because we had to re-create the inscription by scraping away the lichens from the faintly traced letters ... It is questionable whether anybody will ever be at the trouble of decyphering it again.'

TROLLOPE
~

**IN MEMORY OF
ANTHONY TROLLOPE
BORN 24TH APRIL 1815   DIED 6TH DECEMBER 1882
HE WAS A LOVING HUSBAND, A LOVING FATHER,
AND A TRUE FRIEND**

"INTO THY HANDS I COMMIT MY SPIRIT."

Inscription on the *tomb of the novelist (1815–82) in Kensal Green
Cemetery, London. In 1991, it was reported that the authorities of
Westminster Abbey had regretfully turned down an application from the
Trollope Society for a memorial in Poets' Corner because of lack of
space.

TWYNNOY
~

**IN MEMORY OF
HANNAH TWYNNOY
Who died October 23rd 1703
Aged 33 Years.**

**In bloom of Life
She's snatchd from hence,
She had not room
To make defence;
For Tyger fierce
Took Life away.
And here she lies
In a bed of Clay,
Until the Resurrection Day.**

On a *gravestone (restored) at Malmesbury, Wiltshire – an unlikely
location, it might seem, for the event described, but the tiger had escaped
from a circus.

TURNER
~

Beneath this stone are deposited the remains of RICHARD TURNER, author of the word *Teetotal* as applied to abstinence from all intoxicating liquors, who departed this life on the 27th day of October, 1846, aged 56 years.

Andrews (1899) has it that Turner was a fish-hawker and is buried in Preston. His coinage of the word is said to have taken place at a meeting in the Preston Cock-pit in September 1833. 'Dicky' Turner evidently had a way of emphasizing words and, when it came to the need for 'entire' abstinence, he declared that 'nothing but the te-te-total will do'. 'That shall be the name!' declared a colleague, and so it was.

UNKNOWN – 1

~

Affliction sore
Long time I bore,
Physicians were in vain
Till Heaven did please
My woes to ease
With water on the brain.

'In a little village churchyard somewhere on the Brighton road – I think it was Horley' – E.U.C. Pearson, Woodbridge, Suffolk (1981).

UNKNOWN – 2

~

**ALWAYS TIDY, NEAT AND CLEAN.
LOST HIS LIFE IN A SUBMARINE.**

From memorial notice in a Scottish newspaper – told to me by Alan Nixon (1982).

UNKNOWN – 3

~

The angel's trumpet sounded,
St Peter called out 'Come',
The pearly gates swung open,
And in walked Mum.

'This must have appeared at least 30 years ago . . . I remember a correspondence about it in the Live Letters column of the *Daily Mirror*, where some readers condemned its tastelessness, and others praised its simple sentiment' – Margaret Holt, Manchester (1981). Morrell (1948) notes that it has had 'wide publicity' and offers another example where 'sentiment or the poetry' are not quite well-enough expressed:

> We often sit and think of you,
> We often speak your name;
> There is nothing left to answer
> But your photo in the frame.

UNKNOWN – 4
~

AT REST WITH JESUS.

ASLEEP WITH MARY.

'On the adjacent tombstones of a husband and wife, Myrtle Beach, South Carolina' – The Revd Jonathan Meyrick, Barbados (1982).

UNKNOWN – 5
~

Beneath this stone in hopes of Zion,
Doth lie the landlord of the Lion,
His son keeps on the business still,
Resigned upon the heavenly will.

Said to be in the churchyard of Upton-upon-Severn, Worcestershire, and also displayed by a monumental mason in Great Bedwyn, Wiltshire – according to Wright (1972). *Fairley's Epitaphiana* (1875) also has a version. Yet another has the deceased's name as 'McGill'.

Klinger (1979) has this from Bideford, Devon:

Here lies the Landlord of 'The Lion'
His hopes removed to lands of Sion.
His wife resigned to Heaven's will,
Will carry on the business still.

(*Two years later*)

Here lies the Landlord's loving wife,
Her soul removed from lands of strife.
She's gone aloft her spouse to tell
The Inn he left her turned out well.

UNKNOWN – 6
~

Beneath this stone our baby lies.
It neither cries nor hollers.
It lived but one and twenty days
And cost us ninety dollars.

'An aunt of mine came across this near Seattle, Washington' – A.D.G.
Oates, London SE25.

UNKNOWN – 7
~

BE THOU WHAT YOU THINK I OUGHT TO HAVE BEEN.

Cited as 'very epigrammatic and ironical' in *Armstrong's Norfolk Diary*,
an account of a parish priest's life in East Dereham. On 6 July 1853,
Armstrong commented gratefully that, in his own, there was 'a paucity
of those singular and joking epitaphs which disgrace many English
churchyards'.

UNKNOWN – 8
~

**BY AND BY
GOD CAUGHT HIS EYE.**

An epitaph on a waiter, credited to the poet David McCord (1897–), from *Bay Window Ballads* (1935).

UNKNOWN – 9
~

**By my i i i i
Here he lies
In a sad pickle
Kill'd by icicle
1776.**

'On a small stone inset in the tower of the parish church at Bampton, Devon. . .There is no name attached' – J. Eyles, London NW3 (1982).

UNKNOWN – 10
~

**Came in,
Walked about,
Didn't like it,
Walked out.**

'Suffolk churchyard, on child who died at eighteen months' – Reder (1969).

UNKNOWN – 11
~

CHEERIO, SEE YOU SOON.

'On English gravestone' – quoted by A. Andrews in *Quotations for Speakers and Writers* (1970).

UNKNOWN – 12
~

Don't weep for me now
Don't weep for me ever
I'm going to do nothing
For ever and ever.

'In a small churchyard on the Great Orme, Llandudno' – Dorothy Dunn, North Gosforth (1982). Compare UNKNOWN – 22.

UNKNOWN – 13

Down the lanes of memory
The lights are never dim
Until the stars forget to shine
We shall remember her.

Quoted by Alan Bennett from 'a Lancashire newspaper' on *Quote . . . Unquote*, BBC Radio, 26 January 1982. In their Classified Ads offices, many provincial newspapers keep a volume of standard tributes for the bereaved to consult. Presumably it was one such stock verse that gave rise to this interesting rhyme.

Dry up your tears, and weep no more,
I am not dead, but gone before,
Remember me, and bear in mind
You have not long to stay behind.

'On a woman's gravestone in Canada some years ago' – C.A. Wanostrocht, Sandwich, Kent (1982). According to Benham (1907), 'Not lost but gone before' was the title of a song published in Smith's *Edinburgh Harmony*, 1829, and it is one of the standard epitaphs now imprinted on countless graves. It may have been popularized by its use as the title of a poem by Caroline Norton (1808-77), which goes:

For death and life in ceaseless strife,
Beat wild on this world's shore,
And all our calm is in that balm–
Not lost but gone before.

The variant form occurs in *Human Life* (1819) by Samuel Rogers:

Those whom he loved so long and sees no more,
Loved, and still loves – not dead – but gone before.

However, according to *H.L. Mencken's Dictionary of Quotations* (1942), the phrase occurs in one of Alexander POPE's epitaphs for 'Elijah Fenton, Easthampstead England' (*c* 1731) – though this is one is not included in *Pope's Poetical Works*:

'Weep not,' ye mourners, for the dead,
But in this hope your spirits soar,
That ye can say of those ye mourn,
They are not lost but gone before.

And to Philip Henry (1631-96) is ascribed the couplet:

They are not *amissi*, but *praemissi*;
Not lost but gone before.

Seneca wrote: '*Non amittuntur sed praemittuntur*' ('They are not lost but sent before'). So the concept is, indeed, a very old one. The simple phrase 'gone before' meaning 'dead' was well established in English by the early sixteenth century.

In *Heaven's Command* (1973), James Morris quotes the epitaph on Lt Christopher Hyland of the 62nd Regt., who died in Bermuda in 1837:

> Alas, he is not lost,
> But is gone before.

Compare this, from Morrell (1948), on George Bellerby, late inspector of the York Police Force, who died in 1853:

> Fret not for me, my wife and children dear
> I am not dead but sleeping here,
> My debt is paid, my bed you see,
> Prepare yourselves to follow me.

'Not dead but sleeping' was also a familiar refrain of nineteenth century epitaphs.

UNKNOWN – 15
~

Dulce et decorum est pro patria mori.

('It is sweet and honourable to die for one's country.') From Horace *Odes*, III.ii.13. Frequently put in the shortened form *'pro patria mori'* on the graves of those killed on active service. Also a family motto. Wilfred Owen treated the saying with savage irony in his 1917 poem 'Dulce et Decorum est':

> If you could hear, at every jolt, the blood
> Come gargling from the froth-corrupted lungs,
> Obscene as cancer, bitter as the cud
> Of vile, incurable sores on innocent tongues, –
> My friend, you would not tell with such high zest
> To children ardent for some desperate glory,
> The old Lie: Dulce et decorum est
> Pro patria mori.

Et in Arcadia ego.

These are words associated with tombs, skulls and Arcadian shepherds in classical paintings, but not before the seventeenth century. Most notably the phrase occurs in two paintings by the French artist Nicolas Poussin, both of which depict shepherds reading the words carved on a tomb. One painted 1626–28 hangs in Chatsworth House, Derbyshire; the other, 'The Shepherds of Arcady', 1630-35, in the Louvre.

Just before this, however, and no later than 1623, the Italian artist Guercino had painted a work known as '*Et in Arcadia ego*' which hangs in the Galleria Corsino, Rome. Is the inscription meant to suggest that, in death, the speaker is in Arcadia – the Greek name for a place of rural peace and calm, taken from that of an actual area in the Peloponnese? Or is he saying he was formerly there? '*Et in Arcadia ego vixi*' ('I lived') or '*Et in Arcadia fui pastor*' ('I was a shepherd') are variants. Or is it Death speaking – 'Even in Arcadia, I, Death, cannot be avoided'?

As L.A. Moritz of University College, Cardiff, pointed out in a letter to *The Times* (27 January 1982), 'The Latin cannot mean what Goethe and many others . . . took it to mean: "I too was in Arcadia." Its only possible meaning is, "Even in Arcadia am I" . . . this association of the pastoral Arcadia with death goes back to Virgil's tenth *Eclogue*, which first placed idyllic shepherds in an Arcadian landscape.'

Erwin Panofsky had claimed in *Philosophy and History, Essays presented to E. Cassirer* (1936) that since the eighteenth century the English had had an instinct not shared by Continentals for making a special kind of sense out of the classical tag. '"Even in Arcadia I, Death, hold sway" . . . while long forgotten on the Continent remained familiar [in England, and ultimately] became part of what may be termed a specifically English or "insular" tradition – a tradition which tended to retain the idea of a *memento mori*. Skulls juxtaposed with roses could be conventionally employed as an emblem of the omnipotence of Death, whose power is not finally to be excluded even from the sequestered "safe" world of pastoral.'

In German literature, the phrase first appeared in *Winterreise* (1769) by Johann Georg Jacobi: 'Whenever, in a beautiful landscape, I encounter a tomb with the inscription: "I too was in Arcadia", I point it out to my friends, we stop a moment, press each other's hands, and proceed.' In the same year in England, Sir Joshua Reynolds painted a picture on which a tomb inscribed with the words can be seen. The phrase was later used by Goethe as the motto of his *Travels in Italy* (1816).

In Evelyn Waugh's *Brideshead Revisited* (1945), the narrator, while an undergraduate at Oxford, adorns his rooms with a 'human skull lately purchased from the School of Medicine which, resting in a bowl of roses, formed, at the moment, the chief decoration of my table. It bore the motto "*Et in Arcadia ego*" inscribed on its forehead.' (Book One of the novel is entitled '*Et in Arcadia Ego*'.) On the other hand, Marie Belloc-Lowndes was clearly eschewing any connotation of death when she entitled a volume of memoirs *I Too Have Lived In Arcadia* (1941).

UNKNOWN – 17
~

FATHER FARE THEE WELL . . .

'On a child aged seven' – quoted on *Quote . . . Unquote*, BBC Radio, 9 February 1982.

UNKNOWN – 18
~

For the Lord Jesus Christ's sake,
Do all the good you can,
To all the people you can,
In all the ways you can,
As long as ever you can.

Said by Benham (1948) to be from a tombstone at Shrewsbury and quoted by D.L. Moody, the American evangelist.

UNKNOWN – 19
~

God Took Our Norman,
It Was His Will.
Forget Him, No,
We Never Will.

On an Anzac grave in Gallipoli. James Morris in *Farewell the Trumpets* (1978) records that this was placed by the boy's parents in 'one of the lonely cemeteries' in which the Anzacs were buried where they died.

UNKNOWN – 20
~

Here lie I and my three daughters,
All from drinking the Cheltenham waters.
While if we had kept to the Epsom salts,
We should not now be in these here vaults.

This well-known rhyming epitaph appeared in Booth (1868). Russell (1898) commented sniffily, 'With professedly comic epitaphs – the *crambe repetita* of "Cheltenham Waters" . . . I do not purpose to insult the intelligence of my readers.' Mackae (1910?) said it came from Droitwich, dated 1701. Haining (1973) has it in St Giles's Church, Cheltenham.

UNKNOWN – 21
~

Here lie I by the churchyard door.
Here lie I because I'm poor.
The farther in, the more you pay,
But here lie I as warm as they.

Booth (1868) has 'Here I lie at the chancel door. . .'; Tegg (1876) has it in Dawlish Churchyard and at Kingsbridge Church, Devon; Beable (1925) has it as being 'outside the Priest's Door, Kingsbridge Church, Devon . . . in memory of Robert Phillip, commonly called Bone (due to he being the chief parish gravedigger) died 1795'.

UNKNOWN – 22

~

Here lies a poor woman who always was tired,
For she lived in a place where help wasn't hired,
Her last words on earth were, 'Dear friends, I am
   going,
Where washing ain't done nor cooking nor sewing,
And everything there is exact to my wishes,
For there they don't eat, there's no washing of dishes,
I'll be where loud anthems will always be ringing
(But having no voice, I'll be out of the singing).
Don't mourn for me now, don't grieve for me never,
For I'm going to do nothing for ever and ever'.

Sometimes referred to as 'The Maid-of-all-Works' Epitaph' or 'The Tired Woman's Epitaph', this has two possible sources. As 'an epitaph for Catherine Alsopp, a Sheffield washerwoman, who hanged herself, 7 August 1905', it was composed by herself and included in E. Jameson, *1000 Curiosities of Britain* (1937). But a letter in the *Spectator* (2 December 1922) from a correspondent at the British Museum states that the inscription was once to be found in Bushey churchyard. A copy of the text was made before 1860, but the actual stone had been destroyed by 1916. Stewart (1897) has it as 'quoted by James Payn in the *Cornhill Magazine*'. It was also discussed in *Notes and Queries* for March 1889 and *Longman's Magazine* for January 1884. Benham (1907) states that it had been quoted 'before 1850'.

Compare UNKNOWN – 12.

UNKNOWN – 23

~

HERE LIES
HENRY WILLIAM, TWENTY-SECOND LORD ————,
IN JOYFUL EXPECTATION OF THE LAST TRUMP.

'Suggested by the famous Lord Alvanley for a noble friend of his who had been expelled from society for cheating at whist' – Russell (1898).

UNKNOWN – 24
~

Here lies my wife,
Here lies she;
Hallelujah!
Hallelujee!

'At Leeds' – Hyman (1967).

UNKNOWN – 25
~

Here lies W ——— S ————
Died 14th May 1843.
'All his life he loved sailors'.

Epitaph said to be on a grave at Sonning, Berkshire, quoted on *Quote*
. . . *Unquote*, BBC Radio, 26 January 1982.

UNKNOWN – 26
~

Here lie the remains of His Grace the Bishop of Sierra Leone who
for the last twenty years of his life was a martyr to gonorrhoea.

'Freetown cemetery, West Africa' – F. Walter, London W6 (1982).

UNKNOWN – 27
~

HE WAS LITERALLY A FATHER TO ALL THE CHILDREN OF
THE PARISH.

'The obituary for a much-loved vicar which is supposed to have appeared in the *Church Times*' – B.W.H. Taylor, Chalfont St Giles, Bucks. (1979).

UNKNOWN – 28
~

His end was all most sudden
As though the mandate came
    express from Heaven
His foot it slipt and he did fall
'Help, help' he cried and that was all.

'Seen in a churchyard on Helston Riverside' – Mrs E. Brown, Thorpe Bay, Essex (1982).

UNKNOWN – 29
~

His last words were unspoken
He never said 'Good-bye'
He was gone before he knew it
And only God knows why.

'Appeared some time ago in a local paper' – E. Taylor, Reigate, Surrey (1983).

UNKNOWN – 30
~

His strength much resembled the strength of an oak
And his beauty the verdure of May.
But death cut him down in his bloom at a stroke
To admonish the healthy and gay.

'Seen on a tombstone in a Cornish churchyard – name of which I forget' – Miss E. Weston, Pett, East Sussex (1982).

If you think, have a kindly thought,
If you speak, speak generously
Of those who as heroes fought
And died to keep you free.

On a stone *tablet above the entrance to the Memorial Chamber in the
War Memorial Clock Tower in the town of Dudley, Worcestershire. As
William W. Morgan describes in *The Thomas Hardy Journal* (January
1985), these words were written by Thomas Hardy during September
1925 in response to a request from the Mayor of Dudley, James Smellie.
Smellie had in fact submitted the lines to Hardy in draft form and Hardy
improved them metrically.

UNKNOWN – 32
~

'I HOPE TO SEE MY PILOT FACE TO FACE
WHEN I HAVE CROST THE BAR'.

'On the grave of the local publican. "Yes," said my grandfather, a
monumental mason, "and all who come to visit the grave will surely
reflect, Well, he often did – with a pint of beer in both hands"' – O.C.
Spencer, Burnham, Bucks. (1982). The quotation is from Tennyson,
'Crossing the Bar' (1899).

UNKNOWN – 33
~

In loving memory of our dear brother Richard, who
went to the War in the cause of Peace and died
fighting, without hate, that love might live.

James Crockett in *The English Spirit* (1940) calls this: '. . . An English epitaph published somewhere years ago . . . an epitaph which Britain's children, and the children of America, should remember, so that its spirit may prevail to help humanity . . . In all God's acres of this war-torn world, where other than in England shall one look for such an epitaph, inscribed, as this was, in the stress of total war?'

UNKNOWN – 34
~

In Memory of the Brave Sons of Smith's Parish who Risked their Lives in Defence of the Empire against the unscrupulous German Foe.

Memorial slab (referring to the First World War) in the church of St Mark's, Bermuda. Recorded by James Morris, *Farewell the Trumpets* (1978).

UNKNOWN – 35
~

**In this grave here do lie
Back to back my wife and I
When the last trump the air shall fill
If she gets up, I'll just lie still.**

Remembered by Dr A.J. Nimmo, London SE22 (1982).

UNKNOWN – 36
~

**IT IS SO SOON THAT I AM DONE FOR,
I WONDER WHAT I WAS BEGUN FOR.**

'For a child aged three weeks, Cheltenham Churchyard' (seventeenth century) – Bartlett (1968).

UNKNOWN – 37

~

I TOLD YOU I WAS SICK.

Epitaph on a hypochondriac – from the southern US – remembered on *Quote . . . Unquote*, BBC Radio, 22 December 1981.

UNKNOWN – 38

~

LEG OF AN ITALIAN SAILOR, 1898.

Grave inscription from Jeddah, Saudi Arabia, quoted by Robert Lacey (1981).

UNKNOWN – 39

~

LEST WE FORGET.

A famous phrase from Rudyard Kipling's poem 'Recessional' (1897), written as a Jubilee Day warning that while empires pass away, God lives on. Kipling himself, however, may have agreed to the adoption of 'Lest we forget' as a standard military epitaph at the time of his work for the Imperial War Graves Commission after the First World War.

Lest We Forget was also the title of the Fritz Lang film *Hangmen Also Die* (US, 1943) when it was re-issued.

UNKNOWN – 40

~

THE LORD HATH NEED OF HIM.
MARK XI.3.

'On a gravestone in Weston-super-Mare . . . of course the joke only becomes clear when you realize that the words were originally spoken about an ass' – letter from the Revd S.G.N. Brindley, Sheffield (1981). Joke or not, it is quite a common text on gravestones.

UNKNOWN – 41
~

LORD SHE IS THIN.

It is said that this epitaph appears at the bottom of a Tasmanian tombstone. The 'e' is on the back, the stonemason not having left himself enough room to carve it on the front. Is there a source for this much-told joke?

UNKNOWN – 42
~

NOW HE'S GONE TOO.

'From Kew, if I remember rightly, which might be about 1850 . . . About half the tombstone is covered with a long panegyric on his dead wife by a bereaved husband. At the bottom of the stone is a later inscription which reads "Now he's gone too" . . . Since the decay of the belief in personal immortality, death has never seemed funny, and it will be a long time before it does so again. Hence the disappearance of the facetious epitaph, once a common feature of country churchyards' – George Orwell in *Tribune*, 14 February 1947.

UNKNOWN – 43
~

On Thursday she was born,
On Thursday made a bride,
On Thursday her leg was broke,
And on Thursday she died.

'On a gravestone at the Parish Church of Church Stretton, Salop' – J. Turner, Canterbury (1982).

UNKNOWN – 44

~

Reader, pass on nor waste thy time
On bad biography or bitter rhyme
For what I am my humble dust enclose
And what I was is no affair of yours.

'From Kersey, Suffolk' – Mrs B.M. Moss, Bourne, Lincs. (1982).
    Klinger (1979) has a similar verse from 'West Down, Devonshire, 1797' as well as from Guildford, Surrey.

UNKNOWN – 45

~

**REST IN PEACE
UNTIL WE MEET AGAIN.**

'Put by a loving wife in memory of her husband, Hindhead, Surrey' – Patricia Spencer, Edgware (1981). See also SELBACH.

UNKNOWN – 46

~

**SAFE IN THE ARMS OF JESUS.
(INSERTED BY HER LOVING HUSBAND).**

'An In Memoriam notice from the Calcutta *Statesman* in the 1930s' – K.W. Bevan (1982). 'Safe in the Arms of Jesus' is the title of a Moody and Sankey type chorus, words by F.J. Crosby. Morrell (1948) cites a newspaper 'In Memoriam' notice which 'might have been expressed better':

> In loving memory of our grandson Peter
> Safe in the arms of Jesus
> From Grandma, Aunties and Uncles.

UNKNOWN – 47
~

SEEING I WAS HERE FOR SUCH A TIME, IT WAS HARDLY WORTH COMING AT ALL.

Epitaph on a baby who was born at 12 and died at two minutes past. Quoted in Atkins & Newman, *Beecham Stories* (1978).

UNKNOWN – 48
~

SHE AS WAS, IS GONE FROM WE. US AS IS, MUST GO TO SHE.

ı 'In a Cornish churchyard' – Doris Edwards, Axminster, Devon.

UNKNOWN – 49
~

SHE SLEEPS ALONE AT LAST.

Epitaph for an unnamed movie queen, suggested by Robert Benchley (1889–1945).

UNKNOWN – 50
~

She was a Mother without knowing it,
And a Wife, without letting her Husband know it,
Except by her kind indulgences to him.

'From the famous tombstone of Plymouth, Tobago, dating from 1783. Copied from a leaflet issued by the Trinidad and Tobago Tourist Board, "which inscription baffles interpretation"' – C. Millett, Baltimore, Maryland (1982).

UNKNOWN – 51
~

SIR WILLIAM ———, OF 170 QUEENS GATE, S.W.7

'Walking in Brompton Cemetery during the war, I noticed this memorial . . . It seemed odd, to put one's address on one's tombstone! But I think it was a beautiful house' – Miss B.K. Jones, East Worthing, Sussex (1982). Some of the graves in Kensal Green Cemetery also bear the former earthly addresses of the occupants (see CRUIKSHANK, for example).

UNKNOWN – 52
~

Sleep here Awhile
Thou dearest part of me
In Little Time
I'll come and Sleep with Thee.

On the outer wall of the south porch of St Buryan Church, Cornwall. Set up by the widow of a man who died in 1795. This transcription from Norwich (1990).

UNKNOWN – 53
~

A SOLDIER OF THE GREAT WAR KNOWN UNTO GOD.

This was the standard epitaph over the graves of the unidentified dead from the First World War. It was chosen by Rudyard Kipling, literary adviser to the Imperial War Graves Commission. In the majority of cases, the phrase was abbreviated – as on this *gravestone in the churchyard of St Peter and St Paul's, Aldeburgh:

A SEAMAN
OF THE GREAT WAR
ROYAL NAVY
7TH NOVEMBER 1914

KNOWN UNTO GOD.

UNKNOWN – 54
~

Stop stranger as you pass by
As you are now so once was I
As I am now so will you be
So be prepared to follow me.

'On a gravestone at Anworth, Gatehouse of Fleet, and below someone had added, "To follow you I'd be content/If I only knew which way you went"' – letter from Mrs A.R. Harding, Penpont, Dumfriesshire (1981). 'This same inscription appears on the grave of my convict ancestor at

Wiseman's Ferry, New South Wales, Australia (transported 1791)' – L. Craft, Killara, NSW, Australia (1984). Mackae (1910) recorded an inscription for Joseph Dain, who died 26 May 1751, and is buried in a 'churchyard near Hastings':

> Good peppell all, as you pass by,
> I pray you on me cast an eye;
> For as you am so wounce was I,
> And as I am so must you be.
> Therefore prepare to follow me.

Reder (1969) and Brown (1973) both have a version from 'Painswick, Glos.' and Haining (1973) has one from 'Great Burstead Church, Essex' – all noting the scribbled addition. The earliest noting of the inscription and addition comes from 'Marnhull Churchyard', in Fairley (1875). In 'Remarks at the Eighty-fourth Annual Dinner of the Irish American Historical Society', New York City, 6 November 1981, President Ronald Reagan none too helpfully claimed that the rhyme and the addition were to be found in a cemetery near Rock of Cashel, Co. Tipperary, Ireland. Compare also William KENT.

The form of epitaph writing that begins or includes, 'Stop, stranger/passer-by' is of ancient origin. See also BROWN and CASTLEREAGH. James Morris in *Farewell the Trumpets* (1978) records that a Turkish poet, Mehmet Akif Ersoy, is quoted on a memorial above Kilid Bahr at Gallipoli (recalling the debacle of 1915): 'Stop, passer-by! The earth you have just unknowingly trodden is the spot where an era ended and where the heart of a nation beats.'

UNKNOWN – 55
~

**Stranger, pass by and waste no time
On bad biography and careless rhyme.
For what I am, this humble dust discloses;
And what I was is no affair of yourses.**

Described as a 'Suffolk epitaph, 1870' in *The Week-End Book* (1955).

UNKNOWN – 56

~

TELL ENGLAND, YE WHO PASS THIS MONUMENT, WE DIED FOR HER, AND HERE WE REST CONTENT.

From the novel *Tell England* (1922) by Ernest Raymond: 'We had walked right on to the grave of our friend. His name stood on a cross with those of six other officers, and beneath was written in pencil the famous epitaph . . . The perfect words went straight to Doe's heart. "Roop," he said, "if I'm killed you can put those lines over me".' (Bk II, Ch. XII). The book (and film, UK 1931) is about a group of English public school boys who all end up at Gallipoli.

Quite where the epitaph originated is hard to say. In *Farewell the Trumpets* (1978), James Morris finds it on a memorial from the Boer War at Wagon Hill, Ladysmith, in the form:

> Tell England, ye who pass this monument,
> We, who died serving her, rest here content.

Presumably, this memorial was erected *before* the First World War and *before* Raymond's book popularized the couplet. Whatever the case, the words clearly echo the epitaph by the ancient Greek poet Simonides on the Spartans who died at Thermopylae (delaying the vastly greater Persian army at the cost of their own lives): 'Tell the Spartans, stranger, that here we lie, obeying their orders'. Indeed, Diana Raymond, the novelist's widow, commented (1992): 'I (and all the family) always understood from Ernest that he had taken the lines from the epitaph for the Spartans who died at Thermopylae, substituting "England" for "Sparta" and making his own translation. This leaves the problem of the Boer War memorial at Ladysmith. Either two people had the same idea; or else Ernest had somewhere at the back of his mind without realizing it a memory of this. I rather think the first answer is the right one; he was very accurate in his references. . .

'There is a reference to the title in Ernest's first volume of his autobiography, *The Story of My Days*. When *Tell England*, after twelve rejections, was accepted by Newman Flower of Cassell, he said that Ernest had found a "selling title" – which indeed it proved to be.

'Ernest came to regret much of the sentiment in *Tell England*. But the book stayed in print for over fifty years, so it must have had some something!'

UNKNOWN – 57

~

THEIR NAME LIVETH FOR EVERMORE.

The standard epitaph on the Great War Stone which stands in every cemetery of First World War dead in the care of the Imperial War Graves Commission. It was chosen by Rudyard Kipling, the Commission's literary adviser and is based on the apocryphal Ecclesiasticus 44:14: 'Their bodies are buried in peace; but their name liveth for evermore.'

The Revd Francis KILVERT, the diarist, wrote on 31 January 1875: 'So Charles Kingsley is dead. "His body is buried in peace, but his name liveth for evermore." We could ill spare him.'

UNKNOWN – 58

~

They tasted of life's bitter cup,
Refused to drink the(ir) potion up,
But turned their little heads aside
Disgusted with the taste – and died.

'Written across the many graves of the children of an eighteenth century vicar . . . in Nevern churchyard near St Davids, Wales' – Mrs K. Jessel, Guildford (1982). Mrs M.H. Gaukroger, Hove, adds (1992) that the graves are dated '1783' and the names of the children are Anna, Letitia and George.

UNKNOWN – 59

~

TO THE WORLD HE WAS A SOLDIER
TO ME HE WAS THE WORLD.

Said to be on a Second World War grave in the Western Desert. On the *grave in Brookwood Military Cemetery, Surrey, of Wing Commander H.J. Fish, RAF, who died on the 19th October 1945, age 30, we find:

TO THE WORLD
HE WAS JUST A PART
TO ME HE WAS THE WORLD.

UNKNOWN – 60
~

We miss him in the morning
We miss him at evening, too.
But we miss him most on Sundays
Because we have less to do.

'In the *Gloucestershire Citizen* many years ago' – E. Harris, Stroud (1981).

UNKNOWN – 61
~

Went the day well?
We died and never knew.
But, well or ill,
Freedom, we died for you.

This anonymous epigraph appears on screen at the start of the 1942 British film *Went the Day Well?* (script by Angus McPhail, John Dighton and Diana Morgan). At the time the film was released a classics teacher suggested that this was a version of a Greek epitaph – perhaps that by Simonides, as at UNKNOWN – 56. In the US, the film was re-titled *48 Hours*. It was based on a story by Graham Greene entitled *The Lieutenant Died Last* and tells of a typical English village repelling Nazi invaders in its midst. The epigraph presumably refers to the villagers who died defending 'Bramley End'.

The question, 'Went the day well?' sounds as if it ought to come from Shakespeare's *Henry V*, though it does not. However, in the battle in *King John*, the King has the understandable query, 'How goes the day with us?' (V.iii.1).

Penelope Houston in her British Film Institute monograph about the film (1992) describes the epigraph and title as a quotation from an anonymous poem that appeared in an anthology of tributes to people already killed in the war – and also called *Went the Day Well?* – which was published in the summer of 1942. The poem was included in a memoir of the director Pen Tennyson contributed by Michael Balcon, head of Ealing Studios.

But it is not an anonymous poem. *The Times* for 6 February 1918 printed this:

FOUR EPITAPHS.

For a General Grave on Vimy Ridge.

> You come from England; is she England still?
> Yes, thanks to you that died upon this hill.

On Some who died early in the Day of Battle.

> Went the day well? we died and never knew;
> But well or ill, England we died for you.

On those who died at the Battle of Jutland.

> Proud we went down, and there content we lie
> 'Neath English sea if not 'neath English sky.

For a Village War Memorial.

> Ye that live on 'mid English pastures green,
> Remember us, and think what might have been.

J.M. EDMONDS

This is the same J.M. Edmonds as the one who composed UNKNOWN – 63, below.

UNKNOWN – 62

~

When the Archangel's trump shall blow
And souls to bodies join,
Thousands will wish their life below
Had been as brief as mine.

'Bodley Coxe – the Bodleian Librarian at Oxford . . . instantly wrote
[down] an epitaph [for Dean Burgon] which he had read on an infant's
grave in Eglingham churchyard, Northumberland' – Russell (1898).

UNKNOWN – 63

~

When you go home
Tell them of us and say
For your tomorrow
We gave our today.

This is the text placed on the 2nd British Division's Memorial at Kohima
War Cemetery, Assam (now Nagaland), India, which was in place by
1944. It is widely believed to have been inspired by Simonides's 'Tell the
Spartans' (see UNKNOWN – 56), but this is not the case. The words
were written by John Maxwell Edmonds (1875-1958) during the *First*
World War:

> When you go home, tell them of us, and say
> "For your to-morrow these gave their to-day."

This first appeared in the letters column of the *Times Literary
Supplement* on 4 July 1918 and had been written by Edmonds in a series
of suggested epitaphs, this one 'for a British graveyard in France', which
were reprinted the following year in *Inscriptions Suggested for War
Memorials*.

By the Second World War, and in publications like *Poems from India*,
it was frequently stated that 'the words are a translation from the

Greek'. The BBC possesses a somewhat crusty letter from Edmonds (by this time a Fellow of Jesus College, Cambridge), dated 23 July 1953, in which he says, 'I thought the Greek origin of my epitaph used – and altered – at Kohima had been denied in print often enough; but here it is again. It is no translation, nor is it true to say it was suggested by one of the beautiful couplets which you will find in *Lyrica Graeca* (Loeb Classical Library), though I *was* at work on that book in 1917 when my Twelve War Epitaphs were first printed in *The Times* and its *Literary Supplement* . . . The epitaph, of course, should be used only abroad. Used in England its "home" may be just round the corner – which makes the whole thing laughable.'

An amended plaque was evidently ⸱rected at Kohima in 1963. An example of a further editing of the text can be found in Brookwood Cemetery, Surrey, on the *grave of Captain G.F. Slater, of the Parachute Regiment, Army Air Corps, who died 20th March 1945, age 32:

> FOR YOUR TOMORROW
> HE GAVE HIS TODAY.

UNKNOWN – 64
~

Wherever you be
Let your wind go free.
For it was keeping it in
That was the death of me.

'Traditional, from Ireland', quoted on *Quote . . . Unquote*, BBC Radio, 2 March 1982.

UNKNOWN WARRIOR
~

BENEATH THIS STONE RESTS THE BODY
OF A BRITISH WARRIOR
UNKNOWN BY NAME OR RANK

BROUGHT FROM FRANCE TO LIE AMONG
THE MOST ILLUSTRIOUS OF THE LAND
AND BURIED HERE ON ARMISTICE DAY
11 NOV: 1920, IN THE PRESENCE OF
HIS MAJESTY KING GEORGE V
HIS MINISTERS OF STATE
THE CHIEFS OF HIS FORCES
AND A VAST CONCOURSE OF THE NATION.

THUS ARE COMMEMORATED THE MANY
MULTITUDES WHO DURING THE GREAT
WAR OF 1914–1918 GAVE THE MOST THAT
MAN CAN GIVE LIFE ITSELF
FOR GOD
FOR KING AND COUNTRY
FOR LOVED ONES HOME AND EMPIRE
FOR THE SACRED CAUSE OF JUSTICE AND
THE FREEDOM OF THE WORLD.

THEY BURIED HIM AMONG THE KINGS BECAUSE HE
HAD DONE GOOD TOWARD GOD AND TOWARD
HIS HOUSE.

Part of the epitaph on the 'Unknown Warrior' buried in Westminster Abbey on Armistice Day 1920. On the *tombstone, set into the floor of the nave, is an inscription, written by Dean Ryle, concluding with the words, 'They buried him among the kings because he had done good toward God and toward his house.'

This is based on 2 Chronicles 24:16 (concerning Jehoida, a 130-year-old man): 'And they buried him in the city of David among the kings, because he had done good in Israel, both toward God, and toward his house.' The line had earlier been used in the Abbey on the tomb of John de Waltham, Bishop of Salisbury, in 1395. He was buried in the Chapel of the Kings at Richard II's behest and to general indignation.

The idea of such a warrior's burial first came to a chaplain at the Front in 1916 after he had seen a grave in a back garden in Armentières, at the head of which was a rough wooden cross and the pencilled words, 'An unknown British Soldier'.

The American 'Unknown Soldier' was buried on 11 November 1921 at Arlington National Cemetery, Virginia, and lies under the inscription:

HERE RESTS IN
HONORED GLORY
AN AMERICAN
SOLDIER
KNOWN BUT TO GOD.

This form was also used on the graves of other unidentified soldiers in other American military cemeteries (as in the one at Brookwood, Surrey). Subsequently, the Unknown at Arlington has been joined by three others whose graves are marked only by the dates of the wars in which they fell – '1941–1945' (The Second World War), '1950–1953' (Korea) and '1958–1975' (Vietnam). Collectively, the site is known as 'The Tomb of the Unknowns'.

VANBRUGH
~

Under this stone, Reader, survey
Dead Sir John Vanbrugh's house of clay.
Lie heavy on him, Earth! for he
Laid many heavy loads on thee!

This epitaph on Vanbrugh (1664–1726), the dramatist and architect, was written by Dr Abel Evans (1679–1737) thinking of Blenheim Palace, though it has also been ascribed to the architect, Nicholas Hawksmoor. The above version is the one in Booth (1868). *Collection* (1806) has: 'Lie *light* upon him earth! tho' he/Laid many a heavy load on thee.' (Compare, on Pelham: 'Lie heavy on him, land, for he/Laid many a heavy tax on thee'.)

Vanbrugh is buried in the North Aisle of St Stephen's Church, Walbrook, City of London. His wife was later buried within this family vault but no sign of the epitaph is apparent. One doubts if it was ever put on the grave.

Benham (1907) compares the Latin, *'Sit tibi terra gravis!'* ('May the earth be heavy upon thee'), which contrasts with *'Sit tibi terra levis!'* ('Let the earth lie light upon you',sometimes abbreviated to 'S.T.T.L.').

VICTORIA
~

Depositum Serenissimae Potentissimae et Excellentissimae Principis Victoriae Dei Gratia Britanniarum Reginae Fidei Defensoris Indiae Imperatricis Obiit XXII, Die Januarii Anno Domini MDCCCCI. Aetatis Suae LXXXII. Regnique Sui LXIV.

Inscription on the coffin and its lead case of Queen Victoria in the Royal Mausoleum, Frogmore, Windsor, Berkshire: 'Here lies the body of the most serene, powerful and excellent Prince, Victoria, by the Grace of God, of the British Dominions, Queen, Defender of the Faith, Empress of India, who died on 22 January 1901 in the eighty-second year of her life and the sixty-fourth of her reign.' For a royal 'epitaph', this is a shade more forthcoming than the usual bare name and dates.

Victoria lies alongside her beloved consort, Prince Albert, for whom she had originally erected the mausoleum, putting an *inscription over the door: *'VALE DESIDERATISSIME! HIC DOMUM CONQUIESCAM TECUM; TECUM IN CHRISTO CONSURGAM'* ('Farewell, most beloved! Here at last I will rest with thee; with thee in Christ I shall rise again').

WALDECK-PYRMONT &c.

~

**IN MEMORY OF THE MEN OF THIS COLLEGE WHO
COMING FROM A FOREIGN LAND ENTERED INTO THE
INHERITANCE OF THIS PLACE & RETURNING FOUGHT &
DIED FOR THEIR COUNTRY IN THE WAR 1914–1919
  PRINZ WOLRAD-FRIEDRICH ZU WALDECK-PYRMONT
FREIHERR WILHELM VON SELL
ERWIN BEIT VON SPEYER**

*Plaque on the east wall of the Chapel of New College, Oxford, commemorating those members of the college who had fought on the German side in the First World War. The names of other members of the college who lost their lives are commemorated on the south wall.

WALL

~

To the Memory of
DAVID WALL
whose superior performance on the
bassoon endeared him to an
extensive musical acquaintance.
His social life closed on the
4th Dec., 1796, in his 57th year.

Tablet in the church of Ashover, Derbyshire – Andrews (1899).

WALLIS

~

. . . That Learning and Good Sense,
Which render'd HIM fit for any Publick Station
Induc'd Him to Choose
A Private Life.

An interesting explanation on a wall *tablet close to the grave of John Wallis (*d* 1717, aged 66) in St Bartholomew's Church, Nettlebed, Oxfordshire. That he inherited land may have helped him make his choice, I suppose.

WARBURTON
~

Here lies the body of George Warburton
late of Guildford, England,
who died 23 October 1850
by the explosion of his own pistol.
It was one of the modern sort
but an old-fashioned breech-loader
with the barrel bound in brass wire.
And of such is the kingdom of Heaven.

On a tombstone in the Presidio area of San Francisco. Discovered on a postcard by Sir David Hunt during the Second World War.

WARNEFORD
~

COURAGE
INITIATIVE INTEGRITY

FLIGHT SUB. LIEUT REGINALD
ALEXANDER JOHN WARNEFORD
VC RNAS BORN 15 OCT. 1891
ACCIDENTALLY KILLED 17 JUNE 1915

ERECTED BY READERS OF THE DAILY
EXPRESS TO COMMEMORATE THE HEROIC
EXPLOIT IN DESTROYING A ZEPPELIN
AIRSHIP NEAR GHENT JUNE 7 1915.

Inscription on a striking *grave near the main avenue of Brompton Cemetery, London. Not only is there a portrait on it of Warneford himself but a dramatic representation of his plane attacking the Zeppelin. This heroic deed, for which he was awarded the VC, occurred a mere ten days before his own death. *The Times* of 19 June recalled: 'It was on the morning of June 7, at 3 a.m., that he attacked a Zeppelin, which he had chased from the coast of Flanders to Ghent, at a height of 6,000 ft., by dropping six bombs upon it. The airship exploded, fell to the ground, and burnt for some time, while the force of the explosion caused the Morano monoplane to turn upside down. The pilot righted his machine, but was forced to land in the enemy's country. He restarted the engine within 15 minutes, however, and so reached the aerodrome safely. Next day it was announced that King George had . . . conferred upon him the Victoria Cross.'

Warneford died when the biplane he was piloting to Dunkirk in the company of an American journalist suddenly developed engine trouble and crashed. A few days later, *The Times* carried this epitaph from the *Iliad* (xvi.676–683), translated by 'B.N.':

> Whom the gods loved, they gave in youth's first flower
> One infinite hour of glory. That same hour,
> Before a leaf droops from the laurel, come
> Winged Death and Sleep to bear Sarpedon home.

WASHINGTON
~

**To the memory of the Man, first in war, first in
peace, and first in the hearts of his countrymen.**

The best-remembered epitaph on George Washington comes from a Resolution presented to the US House of Representatives on his death in December 1799. It was composed by Henry ('Light-Horse Harry') Lee. The Washington Monunument – a gigantic pointed pillar in Washington DC, 'the tallest masonry structure in the world' – does not contain epitaphs or memorials or quotations from his works (as do the major monuments to Presidents LINCOLN and JEFFERSON, and even the gravesite of President Kennedy).

Washington was buried, at his insistence, near his home, Mount

Vernon, in Virginia. There, his body was originally placed in a family vault, looking rather like a coal bunker. In 1830, it was transferred to a white marble *tomb bearing the name 'WASHINGTON' solely, next to one containing the remains of his wife, 'MARTHA WASHINGTON', who died three years after him. A tablet set in the wall contains the text from John 11:25, 'I am the resurrection and the life, saith the Lord . . . whosoever liveth and believeth in me shall never die.'

WELSTED
~

Beneath this Marble is Buried
Tho. Welsted
Who was Struck Down by the Throwing of a Stone.
He was First in this School
And we Hope is not Last in Heaven
Whither he went
Instead of to Oxford.
January 13, 1676
Aged 18.

Translation of a Latin inscription to be found in the Old Cloisters at Winchester College.

WESLEY
~

To the Memory of
THE VENERABLE JOHN WESLEY, A.M.
Late Fellow of Lincoln College, OXFORD.

This GREAT LIGHT arose
(By the singular Providence of GOD)
To enlighten THESE NATIONS,
And to *revive, enforce, and defend*
The Pure Apostolical DOCTRINES and PRACTICES of

THE PRIMITIVE CHURCH:
Which he continued to do, both by his WRITINGS and his
LABOURS
For more than HALF A CENTURY:
And to his inexpressible Joy,
Not only beheld their INFLUENCE extending,
And their efficacy witness'd,
In the Hearts and Lives of MANY THOUSANDS,
As well in THE WESTERN WORLD as in THESE KINGDOMS:
But also far above all human Power of Expectation,
Liv'd to see PROVISION made by the singular Grace of GOD
For their CONTINUANCE and ESTABLISHMENT,
TO THE JOY OF FUTURE GENERATIONS.

READER, if thou art constrain'd to bless the INSTRUMENT,
GIVE GOD THE GLORY.

After having languished a few Days, He at length finished his
COURSE
and his LIFE together, Gloriously triumphing over DEATH March
2nd
An Dom 1791, in the Eighty eighth Year of his Age.

The epitaph on the *monument to John Wesley (1703–1791), founder of
Methodism, located to the rear of the John Wesley Chapel, in the City
Road, London, and not far from the actual grave. *Collection* (1806) has
it.

John Wesley, together with his hymn-writing brother Charles (1708–
88), is also commemorated by a wall plaque (erected 1876) in
Westminster Abbey. This bears three sayings associated with John
Wesley:

"THE BEST OF ALL IS, GOD IS WITH US."

"I LOOK UPON ALL THE WORLD AS MY PARISH."

"GOD BURIES HIS WORKMEN, BUT CARRIES ON HIS WORK."

The first is what John Wesley 'said emphatically' the day before he died.
The second comes from a letter of 1739, answering charges that he had
invaded the parishes of other clergymen.

WHELDON
~

He never used a sentence
where a paragraph would do.

Sir Huw Wheldon, the broadcaster (1916–86) suggested this epitaph for himself in response to a newspaper's request (*Daily Mail*, 9 June 1976). The headstone of his grave in St Peris churchyard, Nant Peris, Snowdonia, calls him 'Soldier, Broadcaster, Administrator'.

WHITE
~

Here lies the body of Emily White,
She signalled left, and then turned right.

– Mrs E.M. Hollingworth, Huddersfield (1981).

WHITTY
~

MAY   **BEN**
WHITTY   **WEBSTER**

They were lovely and pleasant in their lives
and in their death they were not divided.

On the memorial *plaque to the British-born husband-and-wife actors, Dame May Whitty (1865–1948) and Ben Webster (1864–1947) in St Paul's Church, Covent Garden, London. She had considerable success as a character actress in Hollywood from the mid-1930s onwards; he was an English character actor 'of the old school'.

The use of the quotation from 2 Samuel 1:23, though charming, is open to question, though for a different reason than that advanced regarding KEATS and SEVERN. Here it must be pointed out that the original couple, Jonathan and Saul, were of the same sex and died on the battlefield. However, in *The Mill on the Floss* (1860), George ELIOT had put this epitaph on the tomb of Tom and Maggie Tulliver, who were brother and sister.

WILDE
~

**And alien tears will fill for him
Pity's long broken urn,
For his mourners will be outcast men,
And outcasts always mourn.**

On the tomb of Oscar Wilde (1854–1900) in Père Lachaise Cemetery, Paris, and taken from his *The Ballad of Reading Gaol*. Wilde's remains were moved from their initial resting place at Bagneux when the famous monument by Epstein was placed in Père Lachaise in 1909.

WILKES
~

**NEAR THIS PLACE ARE DEPOSITED
THE REMAINS
OF JOHN WILKES
A FRIEND OF LIBERTY**

A wall *plaque in the balcony of the Grosvenor Chapel, South Audley Street, London, referring to remains that lie in a vault below. This is the inevitable epitaph for the radical politician (1727–97), who became a swashbuckling campaigner for free speech, and it is believed he composed the epitaph himself. 'Wilkes and Liberty!' was the cry of the London mob in 1764 when Wilkes was repeatedly elected to Parliament despite ministerial attempts to exclude him because of his scurrilous attacks on the government. He was a popular champion of parliamentary reform and of the cause of the colonies in the War of American Independence.

WILLIAMS
~

See BILL.

WILLIAMS
~

BRANSBY WILLIAMS
AUGUST 1870 – DECEMBER 1961

For him in vain the envious seasons roll
Who bears eternal summer in his soul.

On the memorial *plaque to a character actor of the old school, in St
Paul's Church, Covent Garden, London. He began his career in music
hall, doing imitations of actors like Irving and Tree, and was noted for
his impressions of characters from Dickens – Micawber, Uriah Heep,
Little Nell's grandfather, and so on. He was the first person to recite
'The Green Eye of the Little Yellow God'. His obituary in *The Times*
(12 December 1961) described him as 'a very competent actor in an
extremely old-fashioned way, speaking resonantly and clearly, and
making great play of stage business.'

The text, appropriately, is from 'The Old Player' by Oliver Wendell
Holmes.

WILLIE
~

Alas Poor Willie is dead,
His friends know him no more,
For what he thought was H_2O
Proved H_2SO_4.

'Of the lab. boy in a chemo physics lab.' – J. Greatorex, Calpe, Spain
(1982).

WOLFIT

~

"Is't not the King? Ay, every inch a King"   KING LEAR
"Well roared, Lion!"   MIDSUMMER NIGHT'S DREAM

Two well-chosen Shakespeare quotations on the memorial *plaque to Sir
Donald Wolfit (1902–68), last of the actor-managers, in St Paul's Church,
Covent Garden, London.

WOLSEY

~

And though, from his own store, Wolsey might have
A Palace or a Colledge for his Grave,
Yet here he lies interr'd, as if that all
Of him to be remembred were his Fall.
If thou art thus neglected, what shall wee
Hope after Death that are but Shreds of thee?

Aubrey quotes this fragment when remarking that Cardinal Thomas
Wolsey (1475–1530) was buried at Leicester but without a monument.
Wolsey had died at Leicester on his way to the Tower of London under
arrest for high treason and is buried in the Lady Chapel of Leicester
Abbey with the simple inscription:

Cardinal Wolsey, Obit A.D. 1530
"Give him a little earth for charity."

WOODCROFT

~

IN MEMORY OF
BENNET WOODCROFT F.R.S.
LATE PROFESSOR OF MACHINERY AT UNIVERSITY COLLEGE

AND CHIEF OF HER MAJESTY'S PATENT OFFICE.
BORN 29TH DEC. 1803, DIED 7TH FEB.1878.
HE WAS THE INVENTOR OF THE INCREASING AND VARYING
PITCH SCREW PROPELLERS
ALSO OF THE IMPROVED [?] OR LOOMS.
THE AUTHOR OF SEVERAL WORKS AND FOUNDER
OF THE PATENT OFFICE LIBRARY AND MUSEUM . . .

On Woodcroft's *grave by the main avenue of Brompton Cemetery, London. Erected by his widow, who is now buried with him.

WOODFORDE
~

SACRED
to the Memory of the
Revd JAS WOODFORDE
29 Years Rector of this Parish
who died January 1, 1803
Aged 63 Years.
His Parishioners held him in the
highest esteem and veneration and
as a tribute to his memory
followed him to the Grave.

The poor feel a severe loss as they were
the constant objects
of his bounty.

This tablet is erected
by his nephew
WILLIAM & ANNA MARIA WOODFORDE
his neice
as a token of their sincere
regard for his many
VIRTUES.

The *memorial to the Revd James Woodforde (1740–1803) – 'Parson Woodforde', the diarist – in his church at Weston Longville, Norfolk. He is buried in the Chancel. ('Neice' is one of the old spellings of 'niece'.)

WORDSWORTH
~

TO THE MEMORY OF
WILLIAM WORDSWORTH
A TRUE PROPHET AND POET
WHO, BY THE SPECIAL GIFT AND CALLING OF
ALMIGHTY GOD,
WHETHER HE DISCOURSED ON MAN OR NATURE,
FAILED NOT TO LIFT UP THE HEART
TO HOLY THINGS,
TIRED NOT OF MAINTAINING THE CAUSE
OF THE POOR AND SIMPLE;
AND SO, IN PERILOUS TIMES WAS RAISED UP
TO BE A CHIEF MINISTER,
NOT ONLY OF NOBLEST POESY,
BUT OF HIGH AND SACRED TRUTH.

THIS MEMORIAL
IS PLACED HERE BY HIS FRIENDS AND NEIGHBOURS
IN TESTIMONY OF
RESPECT, AFFECTION AND GRATITUDE,
ANNO MDCCCLI.

Memorial *tablet (with medallion portrait) to the poet Wordsworth (1770-1850) in the Nave of St Oswald's Church, Grasmere. The inscription is a translation of the Latin dedication to Wordsworth of John Keble's 'Oxford Lectures on Poetry' (delivered 1831-41). Wordsworth is buried in the same grave as his wife in the churchyard, under the stark inscription:

WILLIAM WORDSWORTH
1850.
MARY WORDSWORTH
1859.

He is also commemorated by a seated statue in Poets' Corner, Westminster Abbey. This bears the words from his 'Personal Talk':

Blessings be with them – and eternal praise,
Who gave us nobler loves and nobler cares –
The poets who on earth have made us heirs
Of truth and pure delight by heavenly lays!

WOTTON

~

Hic jacet hujus sententiae primus author
disputandi pruritus, ecclesiarium scabies.
Nomen alias quaere.

Sir Henry Wotton (1567–1639), the diplomat and poet, left instructions that his epitaph was to state: 'Here lies the first author of the sentence: The Itch of Disputation will prove the Scab [or Leprosy] of the Churches. Inquire his name elsewhere.' The sentence occurs in his 'Panegyric to King Charles'. A.W. Ward in his book *Sir Henry Wotton* (1898) comments: 'What I take it he meant to imply by his farewell aphorism was the principle that in the controversies about the non-essentials is to be found the bane of the religious life which it is the one Divine purpose of the Churches to advance.'

Accordingly, the epitaph (in Latin, as above) is on his grave, now to be found on one of the stones leading into the Chɔir of Eton College Chapel. Wotton was Provost of Eton at his death. He is also the man who said an ambassador was 'an honest man sent to lie abroad for his countrymen'.

WRAXALL

~

Men, measures, scenes, and facts all
Misquoting, misstating,
Misplacing, misdating,
Here *lies* Sir Nathaniel Wraxall.

Suggested epitaph for Sir Nathaniel Wraxall (1751–1831) who was attacked for the innaccuracies in his historical memoirs. The epigram comes in various forms, but may have been written by George Colman, the Younger (d 1836). Wraxall is buried in St James's Church, Dover.

WREN
~

SUBTUS CONDITOR
HUIUS ECCLESIAE ET URBIS CONDITOR
CHRISTOPHER WREN
QUI VIXIT ANNOS ULTRA NONAGINA,
NON SIBI SED BONO PUBLICO.
LECTOR, SI MONUMENTUM REQUIRIS,
CIRCUMSPICE . . .

On the white marble *tablet in the wall by the burial place of Sir
Christopher Wren (1632–1723) in the crypt of St Paul's Cathedral which
he designed. The last two lines translate as, 'Reader, if you seek his
monument, look around'. His gravestone has a factual description. This
famous epitaph was reputedly composed by his son. 'Would be equally
applicable to a physician buried in a churchyard' – Horace Smith (1779–
1849).

WYATT
~

WYAT RESTETH HERE, THAT QUICK COULD NEVER REST.

Henry Howard, Earl of Surrey wrote this epitaph on Sir Thomas Wyatt
(1503–1542), the statesman and poet. He is buried in the North Transept
of Sherborne Abbey Church, Dorset; the precise spot not being known.

WYATT
~

At rest beneath the churchyard stone
Lies stingy Jemmy Wyatt.
He died one morning just at ten
And saved a dinner by it.

'On a tombstone – Studley parish church, Wilts.' – Doris Edwards, Axminster, Devon (1981).

WYNTON
~

Alone, unarm'd, a tyger he oppress'd,
And crush'd to death the monster of a beast;
Twice twenty mounted Moors he overthrew
Singly on foot; some wounded, some he slew,
Dispers'd the rest. What more could Samson do?

On the tomb of Sir Edward Wynton (d 1636) in St Mary's Church, Battersea – quoted in J. Timbs, *Curiosities of London* (1855).

YAPP

~

**SACRED
TO THE MEMORY OF
JOSEPH YAPP YOON CHIN
WHO DEPARTED THIS LIFE ON THE
4TH SEPTEMBER 1917
AGED 70 YEARS**

A Bitter Grieve, a shock severe,
To part from one we love so dear.
Our loss is great we won't complain
But hope to Christ will meet again.

ERECTED BY A YAPP.

'I have a snapshot of the tombstone concerned, taken in Borneo' – J.
Chippendale, Portugal (1982).

YEAST

~

**HERE LIES JOHN YEAST.
PARDON ME FOR NOT RISING.**

Epitaph 'from Mexico' – quoted in Reder (1969).

YEATS

~

Cast a cold Eye
On Life, on Death.
Horseman, pass by!
W.B. YEATS

June 13th 1865
January 28th 1939.

The epitaph on the *grave of the poet in Drumcliff churchyard, Co. Sligo, Ireland, was written by Yeats himself. The wording, and the place of burial, are described in 'Under Ben Bulben', written on 4 September 1938 – a few months before his death:

> Under bare Ben Bulben's head
> In Drumcliff churchyard Yeats is laid . . .
> On limestone quarried near the spot
> By his command these words are cut:
>
> *Cast a cold eye* &c.

(Ben Bulben is the mountain above Drumcliff.) In fact, Yeats died in France and because of the Second World War his remains were not brought back for burial at the designated spot until 1948.

YOUNG
~

**UNDERNEATH THIS SOD LIES ARABELLA YOUNG,
WHO ON THE 5TH OF MAY BEGAN TO HOLD HER TONGUE.**

This text is from Fairley (1875). Tegg (1876) has 'On Miss Arabella Young, a logquacious lady: Here rests in silent clay/Miss Arabella Young,/Who on the 21st of May/Began to hold her tongue'.

YOUNG
~

**Here Lyeth John Young
Who to ye King did belong
He liv'd to be old
And yet Dyed Young.**

On John Young, who died 19 November 1688, aged 100. The inscription (re-cut) is to be found in the churchyard of St Andrew, Headington, Oxfordshire. Text from Patricia Utechin, *Epitaphs from Oxfordshire* (1980).

INDEX

~

'Must the book end, as you would end it,
With testamentary appendices
And graveyard indices?'

Robert Graves, 'Leaving the Rest Unsaid'

Vanbrugh, Sir John 254
Victoria, Queen 37, 75,
143–4, 254–5
virgin(ity) 50, 52, 74, 208

waiter 227
Waldeck-Pyrmont, Prinz
zu 256
Wall, David 256
Wallis, John 257–8
Walpole, Horace 59, 217
Warburton, George 257
Warburton, Bishop
William 184
Warneford, A.J. 257–8
Washington, George 258–9
watchmaker 191
water(s) 176, 224, 233
Wavell viii
way, right of 173
Webster, Ben 261–2
'Well done thou good and
faithful servant' 29
Wellington, 1st Duke of
viii, 24, 64, 133

Welstead, Thomas 259
'Went the day well?' 248
Wesley, John & Charles
259–60
Westminster Abbey (see
also Poets' Corner) 21,
45, 48, 52, 56, 63, 66,
75, 91–2, 95, 99–100,
119, 147, 154, 169, 170,
183–4, 186, 188, 202,
210, 212, 219, 252, 260
Wheldon, Sir Huw 261
whist 234
White, Emily 261
White, Jabez 194
Whitty, Dame May 261–2
Wiggs, Agnes 138
Wild, G. 80
Wilde, Oscar 130, 142,
160, 262
Wilkes, John 98, 262
Williams, Bransby 263
Williams, Jack 27
Willie 263
Wolfit, Sir Donald 264

Wollstonecraft, Mary 202
Wolsey, Cardinal Thomas
264
Wood, John 39
Woodcroft, Bennet 264–5
Woodforde, Revd James
265
Woolf, Virginia 84, 156,
Wordsworth, William x,
65, 208, 266
Wotton, Sir Henry 167,
267
Wraxall, Sir Nathaniel
267
Wren, Sir Christopher 268
Wyatt, Jemmy 268–9
Wynton, Sir Edward 269

Yapp, Joseph 270
Yeast, John 270
Yeats, W.B. 22, 214,
270–71
Young, Arabella 271
Young, John 271